MW00387228

RIVER

WINTER
QUARTERS ⊙ ⊙ *** ⊙ MT. PISGAH
KANESVILLE   ⊙ **** ⊙ NAUVOO
            GARDEN
            GROVE

RIVER

FT. LEAVENWORTH ⊙
        ⊙
    ⊙ INDEPENDENCE

ARKANSAS

RIVER

MISSISSIPPI RIVER

NAUVOO TO THE MISSOURI ****
MORMON TRAIL ●●●●●●●●●●●
OREGON TRAIL ooooooooooo
MORMON BATTALION ▬ ▬ ▬ ▬
CALIFORNIA TRAIL ▰▰▰▰▰▰▰▰
MORMON CORRIDOR ◁◁◁◁◁◁◁◁
HASTINGS CUTOFF ◆◆◆◆◆◆◆◆

THIS
IS THE
PLACE

THIS
IS THE
PLACE

Brigham Young
and the New Zion

ERNEST H. TAVES

Prometheus Books
Buffalo, New York

95 94 93 92 91   5 4 3 2 1

Library of Congress Cataloging-in-Publication Data

Taves, Ernest H. (Ernest Henry), 1916–
    This is the Place : Brigham Young and the New Zion / Ernest H. Taves.
        p.   cm.
    Includes bibliographical reference and index.
    ISBN 0-87975-628-4
    1. Young, Brigham, 1801-1877. 2. Church of Jesus Christ of Latter-day Saints—History—19th century. 3. Mormon Church—United States—History—19th century. 4. Utah—Church history. I. Title.
BX8695, Y7T38   1990
289.3'32—dc20   90-43590
                                                                                  CIP

Printed in the United States of America on acid-free paper.

To
Melanie
and
Tiffany

Welcome, friends.
Have great lives.

With love,
Grandpa

"This is the place."

 —Attributed to Brigham Young, upon
 first seeing the Great Salt Lake valley.

Contents

Acknowledgments

I am grateful for the help of the staffs of numerous libraries and archives, and I am particularly indebted to the following: the staffs of the Widener and Houghton libraries of Harvard University, Peter Blodgett and Thomas V. Lange of the Huntington Library, Ann Buttars of the Merrill Library of Utah State University, Walter R. Jones of the Marriott Library of the University of Utah, and Susan Whetstone of the Utah State Historical Society.

I am indebted to Howard E. Hardy for making available to me the journal of Madison Daniel Hambleton, and to Richard F. Kieffer for bringing to my attention an account of a recent happening relative to the Mountain Meadows Massacre.

Again I am deeply appreciative of the help of Andrew Q. Morton, my mentor in stylometry.

I wish also to thank Cynthia Dwyer for copyediting, and I am, again, most grateful for the skillful editorial expertise of Doris Doyle.

Author's Note

The Great Basin, named by explorer John Charles Frémont, is what it sounds like—a large depression. It is variously defined, but in a general way it is bounded on the west by the Sierra Nevada and on the east by the Rocky Mountains. It extends southward to the Colorado Plateau and the Sonoran Desert, northward to the Snake River Plain in Idaho. The northern part of the basin is the one of interest here; it includes approximately the western third of Utah, thus comprising the center, more or less, of what is thought of by many as Mormon Country. This is an uncommon terrain and one of great geologic interest, remarkable in that its lowest outlet is about 600 feet above the present level of Great Salt Lake.

In the latter part of the Pleistocene Epoch, 25,000 to 50,000 years ago, this part of the basin contained Lake Bonneville, named long after it was gone for the explorer and trapper, Benjamin Louis Eulalie de Bonneville. Its high shoreline terraces are a prominent feature of the landscape just north of Salt Lake City, where various levels of this great freshwater lake were etched into the slopes of the Wasatch Mountains. These remnants bemused me when, as a child, I traveled the road at the foot of these mountains. This had all been *visibly* under water a long time ago, and it gave me an eerie feeling and a sense of wonder as I tried to understand that we were traversing the floor of what had once been a mighty lake.

Today U.S. Highway 91 follows the floor of Lake Bonneville's ancient outlet, descending northward from Red Rock Pass toward Pocatello, Idaho, southward toward Ogden and Salt Lake City in Utah. From this point, midway between the towns of Swan Lake and Downey in Idaho, the waters of Lake Bonneville then flowed northward into the Snake River Plain, thence into the Columbia River and the Pacific Ocean.

Much later, the principal gateway opening *into* this place, as the west was being opened by immigrants and trappers laying down the

Oregon and other trails, was South Pass—a broad and surprisingly level plain flowing right over the Rockies in southwestern Wyoming.

Brigham Young traveled through this pass for the first time in 1847. He was at the time a sick man, recovering from a severe attack of "mountain fever." As he progressed southwestward from South Pass, over rough terrain, winding through steep-sided canyons, suddenly the plain of the Great Salt Lake lay spread before him, far below. They had been a long time getting there, and the sight must have been breathtaking The ill leader said, "Go ahead, this is the right place," and thus established the site of the center of the Mormon empire.

This is the part of our land in which I grew up, and it has continued to tug at me as I have lived in other places in later years. Here I spent my formative years, surrounded by a large family, half Mormon, half Mennonite. I was surrounded also, or within easy reach of, some of the most appealing parts of our national heritage. Reality seems to me— and I can't account for this—more sharply defined out there where the sky is high and big. I first gave public expression to my interest in the history of this region in *Trouble Enough,* in which I wrote of Joseph Smith and the beginnings of the Mormon Church. Though the scope of that book did not extend to the Great Basin, it was headed that way, and here I am again, picking up the thread where the lynch mob left it on bloody ground outside the jail in Carthage, Illinois. Joseph Smith has been murdered, and his following, his church, mourns in grief and shock. The work will go forward, however. The work was picked up, with vigor and purpose, by his devoted friend and disciple, Brigham Young.

My intent here is not to present another biography of Brigham Young. These are readily available, particularly Leonard J. Arrington's comprehensive *American Moses* (1985). Nor is this work intended to be a comprehensive history of the Church of Jesus Christ of Latter-day Saints from the assassination of Joseph Smith to the completion of the transcontinental railroad. Detailed coverage of the period would, and has, required many volumes.

This narrative is intended, rather, to relate some interesting aspects of Mormon history in this period, as I saw them. The book concludes with a new, and preliminary, stylometric analysis of some parts of the Mormon canon, raising again the always lively question of authorship.

Part One

1

Palmyra to Nauvoo

Never, perhaps, has a mighty empire begun from such a small, homely, domestic, and cheerful beginning.

Joseph Smith, founder and prophet of the Church of Jesus Christ of Latter-day Saints—usually referred to as the Mormon Church—was murdered by a mob on 27 June 1844, while being held in jail in Carthage, Illinois. The charge upon which he was being held was the destruction of an opposition press in Nauvoo, also in Illinois, where most of the Mormons lived and where the church had its headquarters. With Joseph in jail was his brother, Hyrum, who was killed at the same time. In this book I shall follow the history of the church after Joseph's assassination. The early history of the founding and the rise of the Mormon Church may be found in many sources, including my *Trouble Enough,* and that history will not be covered in this narrative, although a brief summary is in order to set the stage for later events.

Joseph Jr., a farm boy living with his family between Manchester and Palmyra, in the Finger Lakes region of New York State, was allegedly visited when he was 17 by the angel Moroni, who informed him that God had a work for him, Joseph, to perform. Moroni described a book written upon gold plates, whose content was an account of the former inhabitants of this continent. This was, the angel is supposed to have said, a sacred record, containing within it the fullness of the everlasting Gospel as it had been given by the Savior to these early people. (This would be published by Joseph, in 1830, as the Book of Mormon. Mormon was Moroni's father, the last great leader of the Nephites, one of the two major tribes of Israel that had supposedly inhabited the New World in ancient days.) Deposited with the plates were two stones set in silver bows—the Urim and Thummim; these were fastened to a breastplate, such as were worn by priests in ancient times. The stones were for the purpose of translating the book, for it was written in strange hieroglyphs. As Moroni spoke, Joseph had a vision of where they were to be found—on a small hill near Palmyra. Until permission might be given, Joseph was forbidden to show these artifacts to anyone. The interview ended as a shaft of light appeared, ascending aloft, within which the angel rose and disappeared.

The night had not yet finished for Joseph, for the angel appeared two more times before morning, each time bringing the same message. The next day a fatigued Joseph went out to work in the fields with his father, Joseph Sr., who thought his son looked so pale that he sent him home. As Joseph climbed a fence on the way, he fell to the ground, unconscious. Moroni appeared yet again, and told Joseph to tell his father what had happened. Joseph did so and his father said he must do as the angel commanded.

So Joseph went to the small hill, known since as the Hill Cumorah, there to discover a stone box, almost buried, with only the lid showing. Joseph pried off the lid, and there were the contents as Moroni had described. Joseph tried to remove them but was told by the angel that he was not to have them until four years had passed.

(Be it noted that this account is, essentially, a sketchy statement of the "official" version subscribed to by the church today. There were other, and different, contemporary accounts of the events leading to the publication of the Book of Mormon. The reader is alerted that the church was founded amid controversy, and that this continued. It should also be noted that prior to the discovery of the Golden Book, Joseph had a wide reputation as the user of a peep stone, or seer stone, with which he attempted to locate buried treasure.)

Four years passed and, as the church account has it, Joseph got the golden plates and the Urim and Thummim and took them home. This was in 1827. Word of the discovery quickly spread through the small town, and Joseph was subjected to harassment and disbelief. Before the work of translation could begin, it was necessary to find a better working environment. Accordingly, Joseph and his wife, Emma, traveled to Harmony, Pennsylvania, where they moved into an attic room in the house of Emma's father, Isaac Hale. The young couple must have made this trip with some trepidation; Isaac had taken a dim view of Joseph's activities. He had objected to Emma's relationship to Joseph with such vehemence that when they wanted to marry they had been forced to elope. Joseph, on an earlier visit, had promised

Isaac that he would give up using the seer stone, digging for buried treasure, and so on. Arriving again at Isaac's threshold, Joseph had not only *not* abandoned his questionable activities but he had arrived with their *culmination* in the form of a fabulous book written on golden plates, retrieved from a hole in a hill between Manchester and Palmyra.

Isaac wished, of course, to see the plates. If Joseph was to be believed, Isaac would have to revise his opinion of his son-in-law. Joseph said that no one except himself was to see them for now—and indeed, thus far Joseph was the only person to have seen the plates. In due time, Joseph said, the first person other than himself to see the plates would be his (as yet unborn) first son. Joseph offered to let Isaac heft the box containing them. Isaac said that if the plates were to stay in his house, then he should have the right to see them. Joseph said later that he then began to keep them hidden in the woods.

Be that as it may, the translation got under way in Isaac's attic. A blanket was hung to divide the room, separating Joseph from his scribe. Joseph dictated the translation as it was given to him via the Urim and Thummim.[1] The wrath of God, said Joseph, would strike down anyone who attempted to see the plates. The plates continued to remain unseen, throughout the translation, by anyone but Joseph. His first scribe was Emma. One must wonder at her thoughts as she listened to the flow of narrative from her husband. Joseph and Emma shortly moved into a small house of their own on Isaac's property, where the enterprise could be conducted with more privacy. In February 1828 Martin Harris, who had been persuaded to underwrite the project, came to Harmony to see how the work was going. Harris was a successful farmer, a substantial member of the Manchester–Palmyra community, though a man of flighty religious background. Joseph had solicited his aid in the translation process, and Harris had listened sympathetically. Further, and to the consternation of his wife, he had provided financial support. And now *he* wanted to see the plates.

Joseph refused to show them, but he did provide Harris with what he said was a copy of some of the "reformed Egyptian" characters he was working on, together with a translation. These Harris carried to New York to a classicist at Columbia University, Charles Anthon; this visit leads us into murky territory. Harris reported that Anthon had declared the translation to be the most correct from the Egyptian that he had ever seen.[2] Anthon's report differed considerably:

He requested an opinion from me in writing, which of course I declined.
. . . This paper was in fact a singular scrawl. It consisted of all kinds of
crooked characters disposed in columns, and had evidently been prepared
by some person who had before him . . . a book containing various
alphabets. Greek and Hebrew letters, crosses and flourishes, Roman letters
inverted or placed sideways, were arranged in perpendicular columns, and
the whole ended in a rude delineation of a circle divided into various
compartments, decked with various strange marks, and evidently copied
after the Mexican Calendar given by Humboldt, but copied in such a
way as not to betray the source whence it was derived.[3]

After his visit to the classicist, Harris returned to Manchester, then
went to Harmony in April, this time accompanied by his troublesome
wife, who distrusted the project. She was persuaded to leave after a
two-week stay. Harris then began to act as Joseph's scribe as the
translation continued. After two months they had produced 116 pages
of text, and Harris now began to press for a new concession from
Joseph. He wanted to take the manuscript to Manchester to show it
to the skeptical. It is likely that Harris hoped to silence his wife's criticisms
by showing her something tangible. By this time, mid-June 1828, Joseph
was frequently making direct contact with the Lord via the Urim and
Thummim, and he put forward Harris's request. After two refusals
Harris's wish was granted, provided that the pages be shown only to
five members of his immediate family—his wife, brother, parents, and
sister-in-law. Disaster struck forthwith; the manuscript disappeared. It
was never recovered.

Joseph's immediate reaction was as if in response to total catastrophe.
"All is lost!" he cried, weeping.[4] He was in his parents' house when
he learned the news, having come to Manchester to find out why he'd
heard nothing from Harris. The house was filled with lamentation. The
eventual solution, when it came, was nothing short of brilliant, and
represented a decisive turning point in Joseph's life. The answer to the
problem came in the form of a direct communication from God. The
essence of it was that the work would go on. He had transgressed,
certainly, and would be punished by the temporary withdrawal from
him of the Urim and Thummim. He remained, however, the one chosen
to do this work, and in due course the translation would continue.
As for the lost pages, the translation would resume using a *different*
set of plates in his possession, not yet translated.

Clearly, there could be no retranslation of the first set of plates. Should the 116 pages reappear later, inconsistencies would cloak the enterprise in suspicion.

During the winter of 1828–29 Martin Harris returned to Harmony, and the work of translation was resumed, with Harris as scribe. Early in April 1829, Oliver Cowdery, a schoolteacher who had boarded for a time with the Smiths in Palmyra, came to visit Joseph. His curiosity had been aroused by the tale of the golden plates. Two days after his arrival he superseded Harris as Joseph's scribe, thereby becoming another key figure in the early history of the church.

As the translation continued, Joseph's methodology changed considerably. He no longer needed the privacy provided by the hanging blanket; nor did he need the Urim and Thummim. He did not even need the plates! The process was described by David Whitmer, a friend of Cowdery. As Whitmer reported it, Joseph put one of his old seer stones in a hat and brought the hat closely around his face to exclude the light. Something like a piece of parchment would appear to Joseph, bearing upon it a hieroglyph, together with its translation into English. This Joseph would dictate to his scribe.[5]

By some point in the early spring of 1829 it had become apparent, both to Joseph and to those about him, that they were involved in something larger than the production of a book; they were engaged in no less an undertaking than the founding of a new church. Or rather, according to Joseph's revelations, they were reestablishing the true Christian church of old. In token whereof Joseph and Cowdery baptized each other into the Aaronic priesthood on 15 May 1829.

As the translation of Mormon's book neared completion, Joseph was well aware that the work he was doing had been met with skepticism in many quarters. The book would surely not be accepted by any sizable public if no one but he had seen the plates. Witnesses were necessary. Joseph assembled Harris, Cowdery, and David Whitmer, and took them into the woods to pray. Cowdery and Whitmer, together with Joseph, shortly beheld a vision in which an angel appeared with the plates, turning them one by one, showing the hieroglyphs. Harris was unable to share this experience, and went off in the woods by himself to pray. Joseph went to pray with him, and soon Harris said, " 'Tis enough, 'tis enough, mine eyes have beheld." Joseph had his witnesses.

Later, in Manchester, as the preparations were being made for publication, Joseph assembled eight additional witnesses, perhaps hoping that this would increase credibility. These were his father, his brothers Hyrum and Samuel, four Whitmers—Christian, Jacob, Peter Jr., and John—and one Whitmer in-law, Hiram Page. After lengthy prayer and exhortation they were, in Thomas Ford's phrase, "persuaded that they saw the plates."[6]

Now publication could begin. A Palmyra printer, Egbert B. Grandin, agreed to produce an edition of 5,000 copies for $3,000, a sum guaranteed by Martin Harris. Joseph remembered well the loss of the first 116 pages, and the printing of the book began under conditions of tight security. Cowdery copied the entire manuscript, which was delivered to Grandin only a few pages at a time. The natives of Palmyra were offended at the presumption of an unschooled lad from their midst bringing forth a book in apparent competition with the Bible. They banded together, expressed their indignation to Grandin, and let him know they proposed to mount a boycott of the book. The frightened printer refused to continue unless paid. Joseph had no funds. The printing stopped. The solution came in the form of a searing revelation addressed directly to Martin Harris; he must not covet his worldly goods and must impart them freely to the Book of Mormon lest he *and* his property be destroyed. Harris sold his farm, and the book came from the presses in late March 1830.[7]

The book was not well received by the popular press. The *Rochester Daily Advertiser* called it "a vile imposition . . . an evidence of fraud, blasphemy, and credulity, shocking both to Christians and moralists."[8] Mark Twain didn't think much of it. "Chloroform in print," he called it.[9] Religious leaders of the day didn't welcome it. Alexander Campbell (cofounder, with his father, of the Disciples of Christ) reviewed the book cogently, pointing out that the geography was confused (it placed the birth of Jesus in Jerusalem) and that the problems discussed in the book seemed more like those of contemporary than of ancient times.

Thus the question of the authorship of the Book of Mormon arose immediately upon publication—and has remained open. Some speculated that Joseph had not translated the book from ancient plates, but made it up. Others wondered if Sidney Rigdon had written it. Members of the Spaulding family came forward with the suggestion that the book had been cribbed from a missing manuscript entitled *Manuscript Found,* which had been written by one Solomon Spaulding. Some critics pointed out that the book might have been plagiarized from Ethan Smith's (no relation) *View of the Hebrews*—a book published in nearby Poultney, Vermont, in 1823, with a second edition two years later. In this book Smith set forth the view, then widely held, that the American Indians, found in the New World by the early explorers, were descendants of one or more of the lost tribes of Israel. We shall not consider these speculations here, though we shall later have a closer look at *View of the Hebrews.*

The date formally celebrated as that of the founding of the church is 6 April 1830. On this day a group of Joseph's followers assembled in Peter Whitmer's house, in Fayette, New York. Six of those present joined the church on this occasion: Joseph and his brothers Hyrum and Samuel, Oliver Cowdery, and David and Peter Whitmer, Jr. They blessed and took bread, and they blessed and took wine. They "rejoiced exceedingly." As I put it in *Trouble Enough,* "Never, perhaps, has a mighty empire begun from such a small, homely, domestic, and cheerful beginning."

Various groups of Joseph's followers had been meeting before this date—indeed, since the completion of the translation. At the time of the church's *formalization* there were already three branches of it, all in New York State—in Fayette, in Colesville, and in Manchester. Before long the young church began to demonstrate what was to be a persistent inability to live in harmony with its neighbors.

It is not difficult to understand why, in the vicinity of these events, considerable resentment was directed at Joseph and at his followers, which numbered more than 40 within a month of the church's formal establishment. Joseph's money-digging activities were well-remembered, and large segments of the local population found it impossible to accept him as the founder and prophet of a new church. Joseph was subjected to severe harassment. On one occasion he was arrested, charged with being disorderly, tried in Colesville, and, after a measure of maltreatment, was acquitted. The atmosphere surrounding the young church as it strove to grow continued hostile, however, and it gradually became apparent that a move was indicated. In December 1831 and January 1832 such a move was specifically commanded by divine authority, in the form of revelations received by Joseph. Ohio was to be the gathering place, and this brings us to Sidney Rigdon.

From its very beginnings, the Mormon Church has vigorously

proselytized. In October 1830, Parley Pratt and three other church members were sent west by Joseph to preach to the Lamanites of the *Book of Mormon*—that is, to the American Indians. Parley Pratt had been a Campbellite preacher, together with Sidney Rigdon. Pratt was an early convert to Joseph's new church. Rigdon had become dissatisfied with the Disciples of Christ, and was preaching to his own separatist congregation in Mentor, Ohio. Pratt and his fellow missionaries visited Rigdon and gave him a copy of the Book of Mormon. Rigdon read it and was converted—thus comprising a one-man demonstration of the power of the book. Not only was *he* converted but he also took a goodly number of his own congregation into Joseph's church with him, almost doubling its membership. Rigdon, accompanied by a good friend, Edward Partridge, soon traveled to Fayette to visit Joseph, and Joseph recognized at once that Rigdon was no ordinary convert. Rigdon was told, by revelation, that he was designated for "greater work," and he became Joseph's scribe forthwith. Partridge was warmly welcomed as well, though with a less fulsome revelation. Both men would play important roles in the early history of the church.

Time, then, to move west. Two revelations had specified Ohio, where Rigdon's already existing congregation awaited them. However, some of Joseph's members thought that Rigdon was having an undue influence upon Joseph. In due course, though, they would uproot themselves and their families, abandon their farms, and follow their prophet westward.

Joseph and Emma, traveling by sleigh in the company of Rigdon and Edward Partridge, arrived in Kirtland, Ohio, in late January or early February 1831. Kirtland was a small town, a close neighbor of Rigdon's Mentor. These towns lay just to the east of Cleveland, on the southern shore of Lake Erie. The rest of Joseph's following was expected to follow in the spring.

If Joseph had been subjected to harassment and a measure of ridicule in Manchester and Palmyra, in Kirtland—where his early history and recent troubles were not common knowledge—he was at first an immediate success. He and Emma were quickly taken into the home of Newell K. and Elizabeth Ann Whitney. The Whitneys were recent converts to the church and felt honored to have the prophet and his wife living with them during their first weeks in new and strange surroundings.

Joseph was no doubt pleased to discover that his ready-made

congregation numbered about a hundred, a considerable increase over those he had left behind, but its organization was not to his liking. This had been Rigdon's following, and Rigdon had attempted to create a microcosm of communality, or community, in which everything was owned by everyone. In consequence, the group was in some disarray. Joseph sought to remedy this, in the process beginning to create his own kind of community. In this task he was assisted by a comprehensive revelation setting forth the Law of Consecration, whose principle was that members' goods and property were to be consecrated—that is, given to the church—thus forming a common store from which each would be given to according to his need. This would be managed by a bishop of the church. Needless to say, this was not as agreeable to those relatively well off as it was to those less favored.

The main body of Joseph's followers from New York, now identified as the Colesville branch of the church, arrived in Kirtland in the early spring of 1831, but they were not to remain there long. They settled first on land belonging to two men, Leman Copley and Ezra Thayer, who soon wanted the New York Mormons off their land—a desire occasioned in part by Thayer's excommunication from the church for "unseemly behavior." The church held its first conference in Ohio during the first week of June; this conference was, by all report, a disaster.[10] Thus, only four months after Joseph's promising arrival in Ohio it was time to begin a second migration still further west. A revelation received on 7 June left no doubt: ". . . let my servants Joseph Smith, Jr., and Sidney Rigdon take their journey as soon as preparations can be made to leave their homes and journey to the land of the Missouri."[11]

Joseph, Rigdon, and others named in the revelation went west, traveling in pairs, taking different routes, preaching along the way. Their goal was the then-frontier of the United States—Independence, in Jackson County, Missouri. This was rough country on the edge of the wilderness, but, as decreed by revelation, it was to be the land of Zion. A temple site was selected and dedicated, just west of Independence. The Colesville branch arrived and settled in the nearby township of Kaw. Joseph and Rigdon returned to the relative comfort of Kirtland. The church was now again in two principal locations, Ohio and Missouri—and events did not proceed smoothly in either.

In Jackson County the new settlers were an irritant to the established inhabitants; the Mormons were an industrious and cohesive lot who tended to keep to themselves. Their industry no doubt shamed some of the locals, and in addition they preached the doctrines of a new church, setting forth, in effect, that they had the answers and that unless the natives joined them they were lost.

Nor were things going smoothly in Kirtland. Joseph's life was repeatedly threatened, and both Joseph and Rigdon were tarred and feathered by a mob on 24 March 1832. One member of the mob was convinced that Joseph was carrying on with his sister; he pressed for surgical remedy but the doctor in the crowd declined to perform the operation. Rigdon was dragged about by his feet and was eventually found by his wife in a state of incoherence. Later, in a delirium, he asked for a razor, threatening to kill both his wife *and* Joseph. It has been suggested that Rigdon's later zeal, thought by some to be excessive, was attributable to a head injury, with brain damage, received on this occasion, but that does not seem likely.

Joseph's alleged adultery aside, these attacks were probably caused by the reaction of some new converts to the church to the Law of Consecration.[12] As they interpreted it, the church was going to take away their property, and they protested by doing violence to its leaders. Also, the church (together, as it happened, with the nation) would soon face a serious financial crisis—the Panic of 1837. In the meantime, however, there was work to be done in Kirtland, and a grave crisis was brewing in Missouri.

In Kirtland a temple must be built. Joseph received revelations in 1833 demanding that this be done, and the work was started in the summer of that year. Out in Jackson County tension between the Mormons and the earlier settlers increased, culminating in mob violence during this same summer. The Mormon press was destroyed, men were beaten, houses were burned. As the earlier settlers saw it, the Mormons were threatening to take over the entire county as their "inheritance," promised them by their religion. They must, proclaimed the mob, leave. The governor of the state, Daniel Dunklin, was ineffective in curbing the violence, and most of the Mormons fled northward into adjoining Clay County, whose residents granted the Mormons at least provisional permission to remain.

The Missouri members felt neglected by their prophet in this time of great trouble. Although Joseph had received a revelation in December 1833 to the effect that his flock had brought their difficulties upon themselves because of transgression, a further communication received the following February directed him to raise an expeditionary force and march to the rescue of his beleaguered followers. They would engage the Missourians in battle and regain possession of that from which they had been driven.

The effort to recruit men and collect arms began at once, but it proceeded slowly. The expedition, which came to be known as Zion's Camp, did not leave Kirtland until 5 May. It numbered about 100 men and 20 wagons. Progress westward was slow; the wagons were filled with supplies, and the men marched on foot. News of their identity and purpose traveled ahead of them. The Jackson County Missourians, in consequence, burned the few Mormon houses remaining in the county.

The expedition reached the northern banks of the Missouri River, in Clay County opposite Jackson County, in late June. Zion's Camp had been harassed along the way, and now they learned that *three* mobs had collected on the other side of the river, intending to cross it and rout the outnumbered Mormons. A violent storm providentially intervened and defused the attack. And then, on 22 June, the march of Zion's Camp ended in abrupt anticlimax. Joseph received a revelation that again placed the blame for the problems of the Missouri Mormons upon their transgressions: they hadn't learned to be obedient and were still filled with all manner of evil.

This couldn't have been easy for the Missouri church to hear, particularly since the leaders of the expedition, including their prophet and Brigham Young, were directed by the same revelation to return to Kirtland. The redemption of Zion would have to wait. Further disaster immediately struck the area in the form of an epidemic of cholera, which eventually claimed the lives of 14 of the Camp's members.

The abortive trek was formally disbanded on 3 July. Though it had been a costly failure, Joseph thought affectionately of Zion's Camp thereafter, and many future leaders of the church were drawn from its roster. Brigham Young said later that the experience gained during the expedition had been invaluable. His tutelage in leadership had begun, he said, by observing all that Joseph said and did during the long march.[13]

Joseph returned to Kirtland during the first week of August 1834. Three years and five months later, on 12 January 1838, leaving behind a disintegrated church, he fled the city, never to return. Three weeks before, Brigham Young had similarly fled—to escape the fury of a mob. How had this come to pass? What had happened? We shall briefly examine this stormy period.

On the constructive side, the Kirtland church built the first Mormon temple—a handsome edifice that still stands and that is still used.[14] As for the troubles, these were essentially of two kinds: moral and economic.

The moral-personal-social difficulties were the allegations of sexual misbehavior persistently leveled at Joseph. The rumors were discussed mostly in whispers, but were sufficiently widespread to lead to an alarming apostasy. The other problem was rooted in economics.

The splendid temple had been built, and all good Mormons were rightly proud of it—but it hadn't been paid for. The Mormons needed money, and so they established a bank and printed it. This was not so outlandish at the time as it may sound now. This was 1837, and a wild banking boom (later panic) was on. Joseph and Rigdon established the Kirtland Safety Society Bank Company and, having obtained plates from Philadelphia, printed banknotes. The bank's application for a charter was denied, however. Undaunted, they changed *Bank* in the title to *Anti-Banking,* and overprinted the banknotes to that effect. Prosperity briefly reigned until the house of cards inevitably collapsed. Joseph was taken to court on numerous counts, and Rigdon was charged with issuing false money. The failure of the nonbank, together with allegations of Joseph's sexual misbehavior, caused many of his flock to wonder if they had been following a false prophet. There was strife and turmoil within the church, bitterness, apostasy, and disillusionment. Joseph, Brigham, and others headed for the hills of Missouri.

The Missouri Mormons, driven from Jackson County, had gone first to Clay County, immediately to the north. Their welcome there had worn thin, and by the time Joseph and the others arrived from Ohio they had moved to a recently incorporated county, Caldwell, just northeast of Clay County. Here more than a thousand Saints were established in the county seat of Far West, a flourishing community. All was far from well, however. There was trouble both within the church and between the Mormons and their neighbors. Internal dissension followed the breakdown of the Law of Consecration. Some of the earliest Saints, including Oliver Cowdery, William Phelps, and David Whitmer, who had sold their property in Jackson County, now had substantial holdings in Caldwell County, and had no intention of turning them over to the church. Eventually, in consequence, they were "cut off." Be it noted that two of these three were two-thirds of the original Book of Mormon witnesses.

The trouble with their neighbors was caused by a number of factors, perhaps the most powerful of which was fear of Mormon political power, as they continued to pour into Caldwell *and* surrounding counties, "Mormonizing" the region. On the Fourth of July—the day set for laying the cornerstone of the temple to be erected in Far West—Joseph organized a parade, and put on display such armed troops as he was able to muster. The overzealous Rigdon then delivered an impassioned speech, in which he declared that the Mormons had had enough of persecution.

> . . . And that mob that comes on us to disturb us, it shall be between us and them a war of extermination; for we will follow them till the last drop of their blood is spilled or else they will have to exterminate us. . . . We will carry the seat of war to their own houses and their own families, and one party or the other shall be utterly destroyed. . . . We this day then proclaim ourselves free with a purpose and determination that never can be broken.[15]

It is arguable that the "Mormon War" began on this day. Because there were non-Mormons (Gentiles) in the audience, word of Rigdon's oration spread. The Gentile press mounted a bitter attack, and tensions rose

Election day came that year a little more than a month later, on 8 August, and attempts were made to prevent the Mormons from voting. There was a bloody battle in Gallatin in Daviess County, just north of Far West. A report spread that two Mormons had been killed, and a band of Mormons from Far West hastened to Gallatin, where they discovered that though there had indeed been violence, there had been no fatalities. They also learned that a number of Mormons had cast their ballots. Nevertheless, they surrounded the house of Justice of the Peace Adam Black, and obtained from him, apparently under duress, his agreement to keep the peace and not molest the Mormons.

And so it went, one event leading to another, tension and hostility always increasing: men (and boys) killed, women and girls fired upon, houses burned by both sides, violence rampant, culminating in Governor Lilburn Boggs's infamous "extermination" order. At the end of it all, the Mormons laid down their arms and agreed to leave Missouri. Their leaders, including Joseph, surrendered and went to jail, pending trial. This first Mormon War was over, but there would be others.

Joseph, together with his brother Hyrum and others of the church hierarchy, was remanded to Liberty Jail, in Clay County, on 28 November. Here they would spend the next 132 days. During this time the Missourians saw to it that the Mormons were forced to leave the state. They fled to Illinois, gathering on the eastern bank of the Mississippi. In early April 1839 Joseph and the other prisoners were taken, under guard, to Gallatin for trial before a grand jury, which brought in a true bill on an impressive array of counts including, among others, theft, arson, murder, and treason.

Since everyone in the county had been involved in the war in one way or another, a change of venue was granted. The prisoners set out, again under guard, for Boone County, more than a hundred miles to the southeast. It seems apparent that on the second day of their journey, under circumstances cloaked in mystery, money changed hands and liquor was consumed by the guards. As the guards slept that night, the prisoners rode away on horse toward Illinois, where they soon joined their families and the rest of the church in Quincy. The church would now establish new headquarters.

Most of the Mormons driven from Missouri had settled in and around Quincy, but the city was too small to accommodate them all, their number now exceeding 5,000. It was obvious that they would have to move on. About 50 miles north of Quincy, near a high bluff overlooking a bend in the Mississippi River, was a small settlement named Commerce, and the Saints settled in this area. They soon changed the name of the place to Nauvoo, which, Joseph said, meant "beautiful plantation" in Hebrew. And indeed this bluff, high above a gentle bend of the big river, is one of the most attractive city sites in the nation. Here Joseph and his followers established a bustling community that soon rivaled Chicago as the most populous city in the state.

The city was duly chartered by the Illinois state government, as was the Nauvoo Legion. This military force must necessarily be, administratively, a component of the state militia, but Joseph considered it his private army. Further, as the city grew the citizens of Illinois saw what the Missourians had seen before—that they now had within their midst not just a new, and quite different, church, but a growing political power as well.

The few Nauvoo years preceding Joseph's assassination were eventful. They shall not be examined in detail here, but two signal events must be noted. The first of these relates to the doctrine of plural marriage, the source of no end of conflict and dispute. This doctrine was formally proclaimed in August 1843, when Joseph went public with the revelation establishing it. This public statement did not initiate the practice, which had been going on for some time, supposedly secretly, within the higher ranks of the hierarchy. The establishment of polygamy was opposed by many—first and foremost by Emma, the prophet's first wife.

The second consideration to be noted here is the establishment, within the city of Nauvoo, of an opposition press, the *Nauvoo Expositor*. This paper was published by a group of Mormon apostates, led by William Law, a man who had been friend and Second Counselor to Joseph. Law had been particularly outraged by Joseph's revelation on plural marriage, an irreparable rift had developed between him and Joseph, and Law, his wife, and Law's brother had been excommunicated in April.

Law and his followers proposed to form a reorganized church of their own, in opposition to Joseph's, and to establish their own paper. Their printing press arrived in Nauvoo on 7 April, and the first and only issue of the *Expositor* appeared on 7 June, a Friday. It created a furor. The Mormon rank and file had heard only whispers of the active practice of polygamy—Joseph's public statement of the revelation notwithstanding—but here it was out in the open. The tone of the paper was not unrestrained. Despite an almost moderate stance, however, its text did challenge other sensitive issues, including Joseph's political ambitions and his control of land in and around Nauvoo.

Joseph was confronted with a formidable crisis, in the face of which he was curiously indecisive. At one point he confided to an old friend, William Marks, his thought that polygamy would ruin the church and would have to be put down. (But how could he square this with the revelation commanding it?) He also suggested to Marks, who was president of the High Council, that those practicing plural marriage should be brought before the Council and cut off if they did not repent and renounce the practice. Joseph was clearly making wild stabs at solutions to problems beyond his ability to resolve.

The city council met twice to consider the matter on Saturday, before everything shut down for the observance of Sunday. It met again on Monday, and in the end declared the *Expositor* to be a public nuisance, "worse than a dead carcass," and ordered the mayor (Joseph) to eliminate it. Whereupon Joseph made one of the biggest mistakes of his life; he sent the city marshal and others under his command to destroy the offending press and burn its stock of paper. One of the participants, Madison Daniel Hambleton, described the events:

> In the evening I was called upon by the City Marshal to go help abate. About sunset we met at the Temple, the City Police and many others under the charge of the City Marshal, who selected fourteen of the Police, myself one of the number. With sledges and other necessary tools we went into the printing office and piled and tipped the fixtures into the street and burned them, broke the press and throwed it into the street and set fire to them and burned all that would. We obeyed the order of the City Council with delight. When done we marched to the Prophet's home under command of the City Marshal and reported to him our doings. The Prophet said he was glad of it, and blessed us in the name of Jesus Christ.[16]

The job had been done—and the last 17 days of Joseph's life had begun.

Did the destruction of the *Expositor* lead directly to Joseph's assassination before the month was over? There is no question but that this event was the precipitating cause. Certainly it provided a rationalization, were any needed. Nauvoo was, by and large, surrounded by hostile territory, including particularly the communities of Carthage and Warsaw to the south, both in the same county. A good number of people there were eager enough to seize upon any opportunity to make mischief for their Mormon neighbors, and now Joseph had provided them with a justification: he had violated the freedom of the press, one of the building blocks of the Constitution of the United States.

Tension in the area, already high, escalated after the destruction of the *Expositor*. The anti-Mormon editor of the *Warsaw Signal* published an inflammatory call to arms. In Carthage a warrant was issued for the arrest of Joseph, Hyrum, and others on the charge of riot. Joseph seized upon a technicality and appeared before a friendly Justice of the Peace in his own city of Nauvoo. He was honorably discharged, to the further fury of his enemies. The citizens of Warsaw sought the intervention of Governor Thomas Ford, and Joseph wrote to Ford in an attempt to justify the destruction of the press. Ford knew he was headed for trouble no matter what he did. In Nauvoo Joseph declared martial law, closed the city, and assembled the Legion, which was seen by the surrounding populace the same way Joseph saw it— as his private army.

Governor Ford wrote, from Carthage, that Joseph and the others involved would have to submit to the law of the State of Illinois. Joseph and Hyrum and two old friends fled across the Mississippi. After considerable discussion, and in part at least in response to a message from Emma, they returned to the Illinois side of the river and gave themselves up. Ford demanded that they submit again to the same warrant and appear in Carthage, though he refused to provide safe conduct. On the morning of 24 June, Joseph and the others named in the warrant set off for Carthage. They were met, en route, by a company of mounted militia, whose commander displayed an order, signed by Ford, demanding that the Mormons return all state arms held by them in Nauvoo. Joseph and party returned with the militia to accomplish this, finally reaching Carthage near midnight. They spent the rest of the night in the hotel and tavern in which Ford and his party were also staying.

The next morning Ford addressed the companies of militia that had gathered in the town and cautioned them against violence. He then paraded Joseph and Hyrum before them. Later that day the parties named in the warrant were released on bail, except for Joseph and Hyrum. They were taken to jail that night, escorted there through a rowdy throng.

The jailer, George W. Stigall, lived on the ground floor of the two-story stone building. Above were two rooms for the detention of prisoners. Joseph and Hyrum spent the night in the larger of these, in the company of eight friends. There were no bars on the windows, and the door did not latch. The next morning Joseph expressed to Governor Ford his fears for his and Hyrum's safety. Ford reassured him and made promises.

In the afternoon they were escorted by militia—the Carthage Greys— to the town courtroom. Their counsel asked for a delay to provide time to subpoena witnesses, and the case was put over to the next day. The prisoners, with their friends, returned to the jail. As they were going to sleep that night a shot rang out near the jail. The next morning Joseph sent one of his friends, Dan Jones, to inquire about it. He was told by the captain of the militia that neither Joseph nor Hyrum, nor any friends remaining with them, would live to see the sunset. Joseph sent Jones at once to Ford with this disquieting information. Ford dispensed more reassurance and promises of nonviolence. When Jones returned he was denied admission to the jail. Another friend went out for medicine, and when he returned with it, he was ridden out of town at bayonet point.

Soon there were but four left in the room—Joseph and Hyrum, Willard Richards, and John Taylor. For defense they had a single-shot pistol, a six-shooter, and two canes. Their spirits were low, and in the late afternoon they sent out for wine. They had begun to drink it when a shout to surrender came from below. Shots were fired from both sides. Hyrum was struck fatally almost at once. John Taylor was seriously injured. Joseph emptied the six-shooter down the stairs and then sprang to the window. He saw an armed mob, with painted faces. He tried to jump from the window, and was shot both from in front and behind. Mortally wounded, he fell to the ground. Richards was unscathed, except for the grazing of an earlobe. The mob fled. The attack had lasted two or three minutes. Joseph's life was over, and with it ended the first chapter in the history of the church he had founded.

Notes

The purpose of this chapter is to provide the reader with a brief history of the Church of Jesus Christ of Latter-day Saints from the supposed finding of the golden plates to the assassination of its founder, Joseph Smith, Jr. I have drawn freely from my own *Trouble Enough*, in which this history was considered in more detail. Thus the present volume may stand alone. The reader interested in more detail of early Mormon history may consult either my earlier work, Fawn Brodie's *No Man Knows My History*, or Donna Hill's *Joseph Smith, The First Mormon*. Brodie's book was sufficiently controversial to cause her excommunication from the church; Hill's study is a thoughtful assessment from the Mormon point of view. Both are well worth reading. Any book in which the Mormon movement is discussed will be challenged from one quarter or the other. My own approach has been to be as objective as possible. Full publishing information for each citation appears in the Bibliography.

1. The Urim and Thummim are curious items. They were discussed in *Trouble Enough* as follows: "These are mentioned several times in the Old Testament, almost always together, but never described in detail. They are appendages associated with the ephod of the ancient Jewish high priests, the ephod being a sacred upper vestment worn by the priest. 'And he placed the breastpiece on him, and in the breastpiece he put the Urim and Thummim.' (Lev. 8:8) Clear description of what the Urim and

Thummim actually were does not exist. They are described, for example, as stones of onyx; also as detachable objects that could be thrown like dice, their fall revealing the divine will. Whatever they were, they were consulted by the high priests to learn the will of God. The use of Urim and Thummim apparently ceased after the reign of David, not to reappear until Joseph received Mormon's at the Hill Cumorah."

2. Joseph Smith, *History of the Church,* vol. 1, p. 20. (Hereafter *HC.*)

3. Linn, pp. 39-40. Brodie reproduced in her biography (opposite p. 43) a reproduction of "Caractors" [sic] said to have been copied from the golden plates. In *Trouble Enough* (p. 37) I reproduced a different copy of such characters that had surfaced in May 1980. Because of a recent series of events in Salt Lake City, it is now known that this "Anthon transcript" is a forgery, sold by Mark W. Hofmann to the church under false pretenses. Hofmann, prior to his arrest in October 1985, was a rich source of purported early Mormon documents, most of which, if not indeed all, were forgeries. His arrest on two charges of homicide in the first degree and multiple charges of communications fraud (forgery) followed a series of bombings in Salt Lake that left two dead and Hofmann himself seriously injured. Hofmann was injured by the accidental explosion of a bomb of his own construction, intended to do mischief to a third victim. He was scheduled to come to trial in March 1987, but in late January plea bargaining resulted in pleas of guilty to second-degree murder, fraud, and theft. Hofmann thus escaped conviction on charges of first-degree murder, which could have led to his execution. It is interesting to note that Hofmann's father wished his son, if he were guilty, to be executed, in keeping with the Mormon doctrine of blood atonement. See the *Deseret News* (Salt Lake City) for 23 January 1987. Three book-length accounts of the Hofmann affair are Sillitoe's and Roberts's *Salamander,* Lindsey's *A Gathering of Saints,* and Naifeh's and Smith's *The Mormon Murders.*

4. This reaction seems disproportionate to the event, more appropriate to an author than a translator. With respect to translation, time is lost to be sure, but the work can be repeated. The *author* knows all too well he cannot reproduce, verbatim, more than a hundred pages of text.

5. See Whitmer's *Address to All Believers in Christ,* p. 12. Whitmer describes in this remarkable document the differences that later arose between Joseph and him.

6. See Ford's *History of Illinois.* Ford was governor of Illinois at the time of Joseph's assassination in 1844.

7. Harris was excommunicated from the church in 1837. He rejoined later, however, and outlived Joseph by many years. He is well remembered by the church, particularly at his grave site outside of Clarkston, a small town in Cache County, Utah. Just south of Clarkston's cemetery is the Martin Harris Memorial Amphitheater, where the annual Martin Harris Pageant is held. This is a beguiling spot, pleasantly situated on high ground overlooking the Cub River. When last visited by this writer in 1986 the empty amphitheater faced a stage setting showing part of Palmyra's Main Street, featuring Grandin's printing shop.

8. *Rochester Daily Advertiser,* 2 April 1830.

9. Twain, *Roughing It,* chap. 16.

10. Not much detail about this conference appears in church history, but apparently it was common knowledge at the time that Joseph tried unsuccessfully to heal the sick and in one sad case to raise the dead. He also prophesied rashly, giving the location of the lost tribes of Israel as somewhere near the North Pole, surrounded by impassable mountains of snow and ice.

11. *Doctrine and Covenants* (hereafter *DC*), 52, 3. This revelation named a large company, in addition to Joseph and Rigdon, to set out for Missouri.

12. See Simonds Ryder's letter of 1 February 1868 in Hayden's *Early History of the Disciples in the Western Reserve* (pp. 220-21).

13. Salt Lake High Council Record, 1869-72, cited in Arrington's *Brigham Young: American Moses*, p. 46.

14. See Taves, *Trouble Enough*, p. 111.

15. Rigdon's fiery diatribe was published by the Liberty Press and copies were distributed in pamphlet form. The Chicago Historical Society has a copy.

16. Journal of Madison Daniel Hambleton, unpublished, compiled and edited by Howard Ernest Hardy.

2

Brigham Young Takes Over

United we stand, divided we fall.

At the time of Joseph Smith's assassination, the leaders of the church were widely scattered, doing missionary work and, at the same time, furthering their prophet's bid for the presidency of the United States. Brigham Young, Orson Hyde, and Wilford Woodruff were in Boston. News did not travel swiftly then, and contemporary records suggest that Brigham and the others did not hear the first rumors of the murders of Joseph and Hyrum until 9 July, almost two weeks after the killings. In the days following, Brigham seemed almost hesitant about returning to Nauvoo.

On 11 July he and Orson Pratt went to Peterborough, New Hampshire, to conduct a church conference, and Brigham's journal for 13 July indicates that he had a "good time" all that day at the meetings. By this time he must have had Joseph's death on his mind, because he noted that he said in one of the meetings that the death of one, or of a hundred, would not destroy the priesthood or hinder their work. But again on the next day, Sunday, 14 July, he wrote that he was enjoying himself. Finally on 16 July Woodruff, in Boston, received definitive word of the murders in Carthage, and got the message to Brigham, who returned to Boston, where he remained at least until 23 July.[1]

If Brigham showed no haste to return to Nauvoo to fill the power vacuum caused by Joseph's death, the same cannot be said for Sidney Rigdon.[2] He arrived in Nauvoo on 3 August, three days before Brigham and his group. He brought with him a revelation indicating that he should serve as guardian of the church. He forthwith called for a meeting three days hence at which his claim might be voted upon, but Brigham and the apostles traveling with him nullified that when they arrived in Nauvoo on 6 August. The next day they held a meeting at the home of John Taylor, the ever-loyal apostle who had been in the Carthage jail with Joseph and who had himself been wounded. In the confused weeks following Joseph's death the affairs of the church had been principally in Taylor's hands.

At this meeting the apostles rejoiced in being able to meet together again after having been through such trying times. Later the same day, at 4:00 in the afternoon, the apostles met in the Seventies Hall with the High Council and the high priests. It shortly became apparent that there would be a contest between Brigham and Rigdon for leadership of the church. Rigdon said, in effect, that Joseph was still the leader of the church and that he, Rigdon, was commanded to speak for him, to see that the church was properly governed. He had had a vision, he said, on 27 June. "I have been ordained a spokesman to Joseph, and I must come to Nauvoo and see that the church is governed in a proper manner. . . . I have been consecrated a spokesman to Joseph, and I was commanded to speak for him."[3] Brigham said that he wasn't interested in who was to lead the church, but was indeed interested in what God had to say about it. He further stated that he and the other apostles had the keys of the kingdom, and thus the means of discovering God's thoughts on the matter. This would be discussed in public the next day.

The open-air meeting, attended by a gathering estimated at 5,000, convened at 10:00 A.M. Rigdon, usually an impressive orator, was curiously flat that day, making a rambling presentation that lasted an hour and a half. Brigham spoke briefly, and as he did so an odd phenomenon of mass psychology occurred. Many of those present swore that as he began to talk it was as if Joseph himself were addressing the multitude— the voice, the dress, and appearance unmistakably Joseph's. To many it was at this moment, during Brigham's brief remarks, that the mantle of Joseph fell upon his shoulders.[4] To some of the congregation it was as if Joseph had been restored to them from the dead. Not so, comments Bernard DeVoto. As he saw it, Joseph had been replaced by a much better man. In his view, Joseph had been "a man drunk on deity whose mind swooned with apocalyptic splendors but who could produce no effective leadership." By contrast, Brigham possessed one of the most formidable intelligences in the country, and knew how to get things done.[5]

The membership met again that afternoon, at which time Brigham spoke at length, declaring that they must not be overanxious to hurry matters now. "You cannot take any man and put him at the head; you would scatter the saints to the four winds . . . so long as we remain as we are, the heavenly Head is in constant cooperation with us; and if you go out of that course, God will have nothing to do with you."[6] The membership voted overwhelmingly to sustain the Twelve as against the claims of Rigdon. (At the same time they voted to uphold Rigdon's continuing membership in the First Presidency.) Though the vote was technically in support of the Twelve, it seems clear that there was no doubt in anyone's mind that Brigham Young was indisputably the new leader of the church.

It is important now to examine the context within which Brigham assumed the mantle of leadership. The general situation in Nauvoo was far from healthy. All contemporary journals and other accounts give ample evidence of tremendous anti-Mormon sentiment in the surrounding countryside. Nauvoo was a troubled island in a threatening sea of hostility. The Mormons and the Gentiles were forever taking pot shots at each other, burning each other's houses, and stealing from each other. In addition there was the occasional murder. Near-anarchy prevailed in the region, and dissolution of the church was a possibility, one that Brigham saw clearly, and he spoke forcefully to prevent fragmentation. Speaking to a Sunday meeting as early as 18 August Brigham delineated the situation with clarity. He spoke of the disturbing discovery he had found on his return—a disposition of the sheep to scatter now that the shepherd was gone. He thundered against such a course in no uncertain terms. "I wish you to distinctly understand that the counsel of the Twelve is for every family . . . to *stay here in Nauvoo,* and build up the Temple and get your endowments; do not scatter; 'united we stand, divided we fall.' "[7] The only exception, stated in the ellipsis in the above quotation, was that a group would go north into the pine country to obtain timber for the temple.

The completion of the temple was of surpassing importance here. It is fair, I think, to say that Brigham was truly obsessed with the need to complete it. If the writing on the wall was not yet clear, it soon would be—the Mormons were going to have to move on. Never mind, the temple *would* be completed, if only to be left behind. In the meantime it would serve a purpose: the granting of endowments, about which more will be said later. Anyone who thought they could flee into the wilderness and yet be endowed was in error. They would, said Brigham, in this same address, "sink and not rise;—go to hell and not to the bosom of Abraham."

Brigham berated those who would leave because of fear, at the same time noting that he was, himself, fearless. Possibly he was—though that would seem a somewhat irrational response, for one of his intelligence, in the situation in which he found himself. The record shows that his house was regularly guarded nightly by the Nauvoo police.[8]

In addition to the anti-Mormon hostility in the counties surrounding Nauvoo, there was also dissension within the church. Emma Smith, Joseph's widow, had never been fond of Brigham. To the already existing antipathy between them, further injury was added when Brigham, tactless and thoughtless here, failed to call upon her when he first returned to Nauvoo from Boston. Emma would eventually leave Brigham's church altogether and her son, Joseph III, would become the leader of the "Reorganized" church, with headquarters in Missouri. (There were those within the church who considered that Joseph III was, in any case, the rightful successor to the leadership of the church.)[9] Arrington suggests that Brigham was sad to lose Emma and Joseph III, but my guess is that he didn't mind much.

Another problem, a minor one, was James Jesse Stang. Shortly after the apostles had consolidated their position, Stang sent to Nauvoo, from Wisconsin where he was looking for possible places for the church to move, a letter that he claimed had been dictated by Joseph. The letter named Stang as church president, and said that their new gathering place was to be Voree, Wisconsin. Brigham declared the letter a fraud. Stang succeeded, however, in gathering a few followers around him, and these followed him to the northern country. His splinter group was never a serious threat to the main church. He was later murdered by a disaffected follower on Beaver Island, in northern Lake Michigan, to which he had led his flock.[10]

Brigham was troubled also by the behavior of other citizens of Nauvoo. Addressing the brethren from the open-air stand in Nauvoo on a Sunday in January 1845, he scourged the congregation for the evil doings amongst them, including thieving, gambling, "bad houses," and the use of liquor. They must root out the evil in their midst, he said, or the evil would root them out. (It is of interest to note, in passing, that the proscription against the use of alcohol was viewed much more liberally during this period than it is now. There are repeated references in the journals of Hosea Stout—the chief police officer—of many festive occasions upon which beer and spirits were freely consumed. But, one hastens to add, no reports of drunkenness.)

But the larger evil remained outside—the unremitting hostility of the Gentile inhabitants of the area—and it became increasingly apparent that the Mormons would have to move on. Reports had come eastward, of course, from mountain men, trappers, and explorers, and Brigham was aware that there were large areas, essentially unpopulated, in the Great Basin. By mid-year in 1845 the decision had been pretty well made—they would go to the country of the Great Salt Lake. They would not go to the areas then called Texas, California, and Oregon, although they would establish outposts beyond the Great Basin. Gentiles were already establishing themselves in the Far West. The Mormons had been unable to live with the Ohioans, the Missourians, and the people of Illinois, and they hoped to do better on the far frontier. They must go to a place where they would be the first settlers and could establish their own church and way of life. They would strike out for the northern part of the Great Basin.[11]

Before they went anywhere, however, they had to complete the temple. Brigham had inquired of the Lord in January of that year whether they should remain in Nauvoo until the completion of the temple, and the answer had been yes. The capstone thereof was laid on 24 May of the same year, and the work went on. One can wonder why it was so important to finish this structure, with the certain knowledge that it would shortly be abandoned. The answer lies in the function of the temple in the Mormon religion. It is not equivalent to a church, chapel, meeting house, synagogue, or cathedral. It is not, that is, a place in which sermons are delivered and ordinary religious services conducted. It is not open to the public. After dedication, only church members in good standing may enter. The Mormon temple is the place in which the most sacred ceremonies are performed, including those of the granting of endowments, the baptism of the dead, and the rites of celestial marriage.

Let us consider each of these briefly. The granting of endowments was, and is, a matter of some importance. (See Brigham's warning, p. 37). The rituals are extensive and complex; they have changed and evolved over time and cannot be considered in detail here, because they are secret. Yet many accounts have been published over the years. The non-Mormon has no way, obviously, of knowing the accuracy or inaccuracy of these reports. Still, the general nature of the rites can be perceived.

The endowment, said President David O. McKay when dedicating a Mormon temple in Berne, Switzerland, is "an ordinance pertaining to man's eternal journey and limitless possibilities and progress which a just and loving Father has provided for the children whom he made in his own image—for the whole human family." Those to be endowed are first washed, then anointed with oil, then shown a reenactment based upon Biblical themes. Covenants are entered into, vows are made, blessings are pronounced in what appears to be essentially a purification process. These ceremonies can be performed only in a temple.[12]

There are points of similarity between these rituals and those of Freemasonry, and the charge has been made that Joseph borrowed most of the substance of his ceremonies from the Masons. Joseph and Brigham and other church leaders were Masons, and they had maintained an active Masonic lodge in Nauvoo. Mormons deny any significant influence of Freemasonry upon their religion.[13]

Baptism for the dead is the process by which one is baptized as proxy for an ancestor, thus saving him or her from damnation, admitting him to the kingdom. This practice goes hand in hand with the intense Mormon interest in genealogy, the consequence of which is that the church has the most extensive genealogical library in existence.[14]

As for celestial marriage, this is a ceremony in which marriage partners are "sealed" for eternity—as distinct from the " 'til death do you part" of conventional marriage vows. Parents and children are similarly sealed. These rites can also be carried out for one's ancestors posthumously, by proxy. Indeed, the dead so outnumber the living that the larger part of temple ordinance work is performed by proxy in their behalf.

Even before the Nauvoo temple was finished, some of its upper rooms were put to use for endowment ceremonies, of which more than 5,000 were completed before the exodus began. But even as that work continued, it was becoming increasingly clear that time was running out. The last weeks in September were a terrible time in the City of Joseph. Bands of anti-Mormons were plundering outlying settlements, driving the Mormons out of their homes, then burning them down.

There was nowhere for the dispossessed to go except Nauvoo, whose population grew to 15,000 (as populous as Chicago at that date). The town was turned into an armed camp, as the inhabitants worked to bring together the materiel needed for mass migration. Wagons were built by the hundreds. Farms and houses were sold at distressed prices to raise funds with which to buy cattle, horses, oxen.

Perhaps the mood of the times may be appreciated by examining a dream of Brigham Young. On the night of 9 September he dreamed that he was pursued by a mob into a barnlike building, so closely followed by one person that he got into the barn before Brigham closed the door. This mobster was Thomas Ford, governor of Illinois, standing, in the dream, about two and a half feet tall. Brigham took him by the wrist, carried him to the door, and used him as a club to knock down the other members of the mob, one after the other, until he discovered that Ford was dead.

I understand full well the danger in the analysis of dreams at a far remove, but here the temptation is too great. Any analyst worth his salt would be pleased to have Brigham on his couch for an hour or two to have a look at this one. Let us examine it now, with the proviso that we cannot be scientific.

First, Brigham is being pursued by ruffians. Let us be careful to read no paranoia into this, for this was truly how it was for him and his church. The highest governmental official in the State of Illinois is one of the pursuers, but he is drastically cut down in size. Brigham's hostility and contempt for Ford are clear enough, but note how he uses him: one component of the villainous mob is used against the rest of it, leaving Ford dead and the others presumably scattered and in disarray. Brigham's resort to physical violence comes as no surprise to one familiar with his ferocious brand of exhortation. Arrington suggests that Brigham's verbal ferocity was a cover beneath which he concealed his basic kindheartedness and tenderness, being essentially a nonviolent person.[15] This dream does not lend credence to that hypothesis.

Let us examine one more aspect of the dream. Brigham, the leader of the church, triumphs over the highest government official at hand. Though all Mormons weren't aware of it then, the Council of Fifty could understand that Brigham's victory was a graphic portrayal of the way things were eventually supposed to turn out. The Mormon edifice was composed of two components, the Church of God and the Kingdom of God. The Kingdom of God, the political, governmental arm of the last dispensation would, in the vision of the Fifty, in due course govern all the earth. In the dream Brigham takes a small step in the right direction. The dream may be seen, then, as a crafty, if minor, work of art, presenting within its small confines an illuminating glimpse of Brigham's mind at work. This is, granted, a facile look at the dream, but it is a look worth taking.

One fracas outside the city during this troubled time brought the Mormons a small degree of comfort. A non-Mormon, Jacob Backenstos, was now sheriff of Hancock County. He had been elected by the votes of the Mormons. Though not a member of the church, he liked the Mormons and favored their cause. He had established his headquarters in Carthage, the scene of the assassinations of Joseph and Hyrum, and had mounted a guard there. The anti-Mormons seized every opportunity to harass the sheriff with the same energy they devoted to the Mormons. On this occasion he was headed toward Nauvoo, fleeing in a buggy from a group of mounted mobsters, when he passed two Mormons, Orrin Porter Rockwell and John Redding, resting by the roadside. The sheriff stopped, hastily described the situation, and commanded their assistance

"Fear not," Rockwell said. "We have fifty rounds."

Backenstos turned and ordered the mob to halt. They continued to advance, waving guns. Rockwell took aim and fired. One man fell dead, and the mob retreated. The dead man was Frank Worrell, who had been in command of the guards at the Carthage jail and had, in effect, permitted the murders of Joseph and Hyrum. There was some satisfaction at Nauvoo in this encounter—and no doubt on the part of Rockwell as well. He had been one of Joseph's bodyguards and one of his most fiercely devoted supporters.[16]

This violent episode exemplifies the anarchic situation in Hancock County. Governor Ford was well aware of the problems there. As he would later write in his *History of Illinois:* "Civil war was on the very point of breaking out more than a dozen times. . . ." Late in September Ford directed Brigadier General John J. Hardin of the Illinois militia to gather a force and go to Hancock County to establish order. He arrived in Nauvoo on 30 September. In addition to his troops he also took with him a group of dignitaries to assist in the peacemaking; these included Congressman Stephen A. Douglas, who would soon rise to national prominence. Acting under Ford's instructions, Hardin held discussions with both factions in the conflict, and from these talks emerged a general agreement. Acts of violence on both sides would cease, and the Mormons would leave Nauvoo and the state in the spring—an arrangement that worked reasonably well as the Mormons prepared to depart.

It was 1 January 1846. The beginning of a new year, and not just any new year, for this was, in DeVoto's phrase, the year of decision. Hosea Stout noted in his journal that it began disagreeably in Nauvoo, the weather being very warm and rainy. As for the nation, the year began with a considerable sense of impending crisis, for the United States faced the possibility of war with both Mexico and England. Not only was this a year of decision, but this was the year in which the nation's "manifest destiny" was becoming clear for all to see: the United States would expand westward. California and Oregon were where settlers were headed, although these were not the present states with precise boundaries but vast territories generally unmapped. In this press toward the west the Mormons would play a not inconsiderable part.

It was important that their exodus not begin before spring, so that the animals could feed on grass along the way—not to mention that the humans would be more comfortable. But their actual departure turned out to be precipitous and premature. First of all, a rumor spread (and was given credence) that the federal government was going to step in by sending troops from St. Louis to Nauvoo to drive the Mormons out forthwith, and with violence. But it is likely that the proximate precipitating cause was that the law threatened to take Brigham into custody; he (and others) had been indicted on charges related to counterfeiting.

Be that as it may, the exodus began on 4 February. Before traveling west with the Saints, we must first turn eastward, to New York City, where we meet Sam Brannan. An elder of the church, he had been publishing a church organ, *The Prophet,* in New York. Brannan was energetic, resourceful, opportunistic, and, at times, irresponsible. He had been given the responsibility of transporting the Mormons on the east coast to California, and for this purpose he chartered a ship, the *Brooklyn.* He would shepherd 235 (some accounts say 238) Saints to San

Francisco Bay, taking with him everything needed to establish a new city, including a printing press,

The press is worthy of note, because the enterprising Brannan used it to publish the first paper on the Pacific Coast, the *California Star.* Brannan and his flock were the first American emigrants to settle in California. "Indeed, it is not a little singular that the Mormons were not only the pioneers of Utah, but also the pioneers of California, the builders of the first houses, the starters of the first papers . . ."[17] The *Brooklyn,* by coincidence, sailed from New York on 4 February, the same day the Mormons began to cross the Mississippi.

The exodus from Nauvoo would slowly progress across the Great Plains, over the Rockies, and down into the Great Basin, not in the sense of a single discrete movement but more like a continuous stream that would eventually involve more than 15,000 men, women, and children. There were wagons by the hundred, horses and oxen to pull them, herds of cattle, and the people all uprooted, leaving behind everything that couldn't be taken along. Eventually, in July of the following year, the lead party would see lying before them the great lake and the site of the city to which it would give its name. While those Saints would be finishing their journey to the Great Basin, others in the east would be beginning theirs.

The trials, difficulties, hardships of the first to leave Illinois cannot be imagined easily. In early February there was ice in the Mississippi, and the ferry crossings were perilous. Some of the first to leave fell into the icy and treacherous river, rescued only with the greatest difficulty. And the weather was very cold. The first camp was established about eight miles east of Nauvoo, at Sugar Creek. No comfortable homes here, with warm hearths. The Mormons camped as best they could, cutting firewood, pitching tents, erecting primitive shelters and lean-tos, sleeping in wagons.

By 13 February the Mississippi was frozen solid, ice all the way across sufficiently thick to bear the weight of traffic, and the crossing became easier. Brigham crossed on the 15th. The general idea was that the trek westward would be in groups—50 families in each, these further divided into units of 10. Each group and subgroup had a leader, head, or captain, the organization of the whole being along military lines. There was precedent for this—in the abortive march of Zion's Camp in 1834. Brigham Young would never agree that that march had been

without profit. He proclaimed many times that the experience gained
on that expedition had been invaluable. It was now time to put that
experience to use.

Notes

1. Both Brigham and Woodruff kept journals during these days, and some of
the entries are quoted in Smith, *HC*, vol. 7, chaps. 15 and 16, *passim*. Dates of different
events are not always in agreement however.
2. Sidney Rigdon had been with Joseph since the founding of the church. At
the time of Joseph's murder he was a member of the First Presidency. He and Joseph
were at odds with each other at the time of Joseph's death. Joseph had, indeed, in
October 1843 tried to dislodge Rigdon from the Presidency, but Rigdon's impassioned
defense had carried the day.
3. Smith, *HC*, vol. 7, pp. 229-30.
4. I make no attempt to account for this phenomenon on scientific grounds.
Arrington suggests it might have been caused, in part, by a longing to be comforted
by their fallen leader. In any case it is known that Brigham did possess a certain gift
for mimicry.
5. DeVoto, *Year of Decision*, p. 77. DeVoto's accounts of Mormon history are
lively and full of interest, in part (at least) because he could not escape an emotional
involvement. His mother was Mormon, his father Catholic, and he grew up amongst
the Mormons in Utah. His attitude toward both his parents' churches was antagonistic,
and he was convinced that Joseph Smith was a paranoid psychotic. His writings of
America's westward expansion are definitive and make for profitable and enjoyable
reading. I am indebted to Avis DeVoto for interesting conversations about her distinguished husband's thoughts on Mormonism.
6. Smith, *HC*, vol. 7, pp. 232-35.
7. Ibid., pp. 254-60.
8. Hosea Stout was chief of the Nauvoo police force at this time. His meticulously
kept diary (see Bibliography) is an invaluable primary source, not only with respect
to police affairs but also to many aspects of Mormon history through which he lived,
the diary being kept until 1861.
9. A document surfaced in 1981 that supported the view that Joseph Jr. intended
that his son Joseph III should succeed him. The document read in part, "For he shall
be my successor to the Presidency of the High Priesthood and a Seer, and a Revelator
and a Prophet unto the church which appointment belongeth to him by blessing and
also by right." That seems straightforward enough. However, the document was shown
to be one of the many forgeries of Mark Hofmann.
10. Arrington, *Brigham Young: American Moses*, p. 119; for an expanded account,
see Quaife, *Kingdom of St. James*.
11. DeVoto, *Year of Decision*, pp. 86-89.
12. For a comprehensive discussion of the role of the temple in Mormon theology,
see Talmage's *House of the Lord*. Talmage also presents a good number of photographs
of interiors of several Mormon temples, primarily the one in Salt Lake City.
13. See Ivins, *The Relationship of Mormonism and Freemasonry*.
14. The Genealogical Library in Salt Lake is now housed in its own new and
well-equipped building just across West Temple Street from Temple Square. Its facilities

are freely available to the public, Mormon and non-Mormon alike. A branch library system makes many of its records available in many locations throughout the United States.

15. Arrington, p. 407.

16. Smith, *HC,* vol. 1, pp. 439, 446-47, and Stout's Diary, vol. 1, p. 64. *John Redding* in *HC* is in Stout's Diary amended by Juanita Brooks to *Return Jackson Redden.*

17. Tullidge, *History of Salt Lake City,* pp. 15-17. Before leaving New York harbor, Brannan became involved in complex negotiations with some politicians with respect to getting permission for the Saints to go west without interference from the federal government. This was at the time the Mormons in Nauvoo were hearing rumors about federal troops prepared to force them westward. For an extended account of Brannan's expedition, see Bancroft, *History of California,* vol. 5.

3

Nauvoo to the Great Salt Lake

I am anxious to go . . . to be about my errand.

As we watch the Mormons fleeing Nauvoo, crossing the frozen Mississippi, we must remember that they weren't just getting out of Illinois, they were fleeing the United States of America. On the opposite shore lay Iowa, a territory. It would not become a state until the following year, when it would be the 29th to join the union. The Saints would have to pass through that territory, and they were apprehensive. The church authorities, before the start of the exodus, had written to the governor of the territory for protection.

> We, the presiding authorities of the Church . . . in behalf of several thousand suffering exiles, humbly ask Your Excellency to shield and protect us in our constitutional rights, while we are passing through the Territory over which you have jurisdiction. And, should any of the exiles be under the necessity of stopping in this Territory for a time, either in settled or unsettled parts, for the purpose of raising crops, by renting farms or upon public lands . . . we humbly petition Your Excellency to use an influence and power in our behalf, and thus preserve thousands of American citizens, together with their wives and children, from intense sufferings, starvation, and death.[1]

As the westward trek began, what did Brigham Young and the Council of Fifty have in mind? They would establish the Kingdom of God on earth, to be sure, but what manner of entity would it be? One conjecture, subscribed to by some historians, is that they dreamed of establishing an autonomous governmental state that would *not* become part of the expanding United States. The Oregon Territory was under joint occupation by the British and by Americans, and the future of Texas was unclear. The Mexican War lay months ahead. California was in Mexican territory, as were the areas of the present states of New Mexico, Nevada, Utah, Arizona, and parts of Colorado and Wyoming. The Great Basin was inhabited only by Indians, and it was not altogether far-fetched to dream of setting up an independent theocracy there. In due course the Mormons would, indeed, establish the sovereign state of Deseret, but the record shows that, by the time the Pioneers had made their first trip to the Great Basin and back, the Mormons wanted their Zion eventually to become part of the United States. In a long General Epistle sent to the brethren throughout the world, dated 23 December 1847, this intention was made clear: ". . . notwithstanding all our privations and sufferings, we are more ready than any other portion of the community to sustain the constitutional institutions of our mother country. . . . We anticipate, as soon as circumstances will permit, to petition for a territorial government in the Great Basin."[2] The historian Hubert H. Bancroft later wrote: "The Mormons did not . . . hope to remain an independent republic, nor did they probably wish to do so."[3]

What they did dream of, beyond all doubt, was traveling westward toward open regions, without other Anglo-Saxon settlers, where they would build a shining city and be left alone to prosper while awaiting the final days—a dream it must not have been easy to hold close as they moved through the snows of Iowa, trying to keep warm, trying to keep themselves and their animals fed, sleeping in tents, in wagons, or on the cold ground.

Nor were the brethren always governed by brotherly love. Some found the privation too much and wanted to leave. There were squabbles about equitable distribution of food. Some of those who had more were disinclined to give to those who had less. The dissension between the older policemen and the newer recruits was not left behind in Nauvoo; it continued on the trail and in camp. Then, again, the emigration was not a simple movement of one mass of people from one place to another; they were spread out over a long stretch of territory. Chains of command and authority in the paramilitary organization were confused, and it was not always easy to maintain discipline. However, though all was not peace and light in the Camp of Israel, the movement did manage to hold together, bound by a religious communality.[4] Underlying the disputes there still was a genuine sense of brotherhood—of pulling together, as it were—as the families moved westward. As spring came things improved to a degree, though there was still trouble enough to go round. Children died in their parents' arms, wives and husbands were buried in lonely graves. And, in predictable counterbalance, men and women married, children were born.

Possessions brought from Nauvoo were sold for food. Hosea Stout, intrepid head of the police, exchanged a bedstead for corn.[5] Spring brought mud, wagons mired to their axles, horses in the muck up to their bellies. Sickness and death, poverty and privation, had traveled thus far with the Camp of Israel, and would continue to do so, but now and again there came the inevitable exhilaration: this thing is *working,* this vast congregation is *moving* westward! In the Mormon vision the place for the shining city lay out there, somewhere, and they expected to get there and build it. Hosea Stout, not one given to poetic expression, writes on the evening of 14 April 1846: "It formed a beautiful sight to see so many wagons and tents together and could be seen for miles on the prairie."

This was mid-April, and Hosea and his family had been on the trail for three months. They were about two-thirds of the distance across Iowa Territory, and the Missouri River was less than a hundred miles ahead. Winter quarters would be established on the banks of that river, and that was as far as they would go in 1846, though they didn't know that yet.

The first group of emigrants arrived at the Missouri in mid-June. En route the Camp of Israel had established two settlements, to which they had given the names Garden Grove and Mount Pisgah. Though these place names have not survived, the settlements were important way stations for many emigrants following. Now at the Missouri, the Mormons began, on both banks of the river, to establish two more permanent camps. The site was about 15 miles north of the present city of Council Bluffs, Iowa. The settlement on the east bank of the river became known as Kanesville, honoring the Mormons' influential friend Thomas L. Kane; the one on the west side was Winter Quarters, the present location of Florence, Nebraska, a suburban community of Omaha.[6]

Two weeks after arrival at the Missouri, Brigham was planning to send a body of men out to the Great Basin, without their families, but this plan was soon abandoned as Brigham and others came to understand that more preparation was necessary. Departure would eventually be put off until the following spring, while in the meantime the two camps buzzed with preparatory activity. Wagons were built, crops were planted, food supplies were gathered, herds of livestock were assembled.

One group of Mormon men, however, did not have to wait until spring to head westward. The United States was now at war with Mexico. President James K. Polk was well aware that there were now camped upon the banks of the Missouri a considerable body of Mormon men who had cause enough to harbor hostile feelings toward the United States. Polk was uneasy about this number of disaffected emigrants on the right flank of his troops.

At the outbreak of the Mexican War, Stephen Watts Kearny had been given command of the Army of the West, and in June 1846 his rank had been elevated to that of brigadier general. He and his troops were now stationed at Fort Leavenworth, Kansas, preparing to move westward. Polk now ordered Kearny to enroll some Mormons into his army—not in numbers sufficient to cause trouble or endanger the rest of his infantry but enough to redress the balance of that army, which was long on cavalry but short of infantry. The Mormons, instructed Polk, were to be brought into a more harmonious relationship with the government they were leaving behind.

Kearny's offer was taken to the Mormons at Mount Pisgah, on 26 June, by Captain James Allen, who rode into camp accompanied by three dragoons. The arrival of men in uniform was a minor sensation, but the excitement subsided when Allen revealed his mission. He met with the High Council of the camp and presented them with a *Circular to the Mormons,* a document which set forth the offer to accept some 500 Mormon men into the Army of the West. They would march with Colonel Kearny to California, where they would be discharged. They would receive the same pay as regular army soldiers, and upon discharge would be given, gratis, their arms and all equipment supplied them at Fort Leavenworth, which would be the staging area. In short, he was offering "an opportunity of sending a portion of their young and intelligent men to the ultimate destination of their whole people, and entirely at the expense of the United States government."[7]

Captain Allen proceeded forthwith to Winter Quarters, where he made the same offer to Brigham and his advisors. It is probable that Brigham had also conceived, at about this time, the idea of using United

States military forces to facilitate the movement of a body of Mormons to the west. Soldiers' pay would provide the Camp of Israel with much-needed hard cash. As early as January 1846 he had instructed the president of the eastern mission, Elder Jesse C. Little, to do what he could to obtain federal help for the movement of the church. Now, Thomas Kane, a man very well connected in Washington, heard Little speak in Philadelphia, was impressed, and became friendly with him. He also became and would remain an important friend and advocate for the Mormons. (Kane's father was John Kenzer Kane, political ally and friend of President Polk, an elder statesman in the government, and at this time attorney general of Pennsylvania.)

Armed with letters from Kane and others, Elder Little gained access to President Polk, and at the end of their meeting Little offered to raise a battalion of men to march west with the army. Polk accepted, and Little hurried the news to Brigham. Polk failed to mention to Little that a week earlier he had ordered Colonel Kearny to approach the Mormons for the purpose of raising such a battalion. This was a typical Polk maneuver, according to DeVoto.[8]

Back at Winter Quarters and at Mount Pisgah, Brigham set to work collecting and persuading the necessary number of brethren—500—to form what would become known as the Mormon Battalion. This was no simple matter; after all, the church had been railing against the United States for a long time, and the brethren had serious reservations. Was it now gospel that the Saints should join an army of the United States, under whose administration they had suffered such severe persecution? Brigham convinced them that this was so—that in this course lay political as well as practical wisdom. They were patriotically answering a call to duty, he said, for which they would be paid, and other benefits would follow. Would not the Army of the West help them conquer the very land, part of which they intended to make their own? He collected his hundreds of "volunteers," and on 18 July, before they marched off to Fort Leavenworth, Brigham gave them his blessings and many words of advice, not the least of which were to burn their decks of playing cards and to be sure to wear their holy temple under-garments, which would protect them against enemy weaponry.

The Mormon Battalion would march with Kearny first to Santa Fe, then onward to San Diego—at that time (indeed, if not until now) the longest sustained march by infantry in U.S. history.

The formation of the Mormon Battalion brought needed cash into the coffers of the Camp of Israel, but not much of it went to the families of the soldiers. Brigham diverted a considerable part of the initial payment made at Fort Leavenworth into the purchase of goods for the mercantile store he, together with Albert Rockwood and William Clayton, operated in Winter Quarters. The goods thus purchased were sold to the brethren at substantial profit. Later, John D. Lee would return from Santa Fe with more funds, and most of these would also be diverted to Brigham's personal use. Some of these funds were used to pay off bills incurred during the construction of a grist mill, which was Brigham's personal property. Lee expressed his concern about this to Brigham on 27 January 1847. Brigham told him not to worry, it was all for the best, pointing out that the mill should net about $20 per day, perhaps meaning to imply that the funds would eventually be restored from these proceeds.[9]

If the decision to delay the exodus of the Pioneer companies to the Great Basin until the following spring had not yet been finally fixed, the departure of the Mormon Battalion had put the seal upon it. The Saints would remain in Winter Quarters until spring, and on 31 August 1846 they signed a pact with the Omaha Indians, upon whose land they were camped, giving them permission to do so. The agreement was signed, with their "x" marks, by Big Elk, Standing Elk, and Little Chief. The Omaha Nation graciously gave the Mormons all the time they needed to prepare for their trek west—providing only that their great father (President Polk) didn't counsel them to the contrary.[10]

The Mormons continued to be very busy indeed—building wagons, assembling livestock, gathering foodstuffs, preparing for mass migration. While doing so, they listened avidly to every scrap of information arriving in camp from travelers returning from the west. One of those passing through, to whom the Mormons listened with great attention, was Pierre-Jean De Smet, a transplanted Belgian Jesuit priest, a zealous missionary doing good works in the western mountains. Though De Smet would later refer to the Mormons as a sect of fanatics, they now had a friendly meeting on the banks of the Missouri. He apparently gave Brigham an attractive description of the Great Basin; indeed, some historians have stated that De Smet's discussion with the Mormons was decisive in their ultimate selection of the Salt Lake valley as "the place," but other evidence suggests that the choice had already been made. While in Nauvoo they had avidly absorbed all reports of western exploration that came to hand, including those of John Charles Frémont. Be that as it may, when De Smet fortuitously appeared in camp the Mormons were, of course, eager to learn all they could, at first hand, from this experienced traveler.[11]

As winter approached, the town was a beehive of activity, with Brigham ever exhorting the brethren to get on with vital preparations, reading the law to them, holding the community together, leading them in prayer, lecturing them on how they should go. And the community did hold together, although there were always problems. It became apparent, for example, that a few of the young men were sporting with some of the young ladies on warm September evenings until the early hours of the morning. This was not to be tolerated. Hosea Stout saw to it that the guilty ones were taken into the woods and whipped, after the young men were first led to believe (in at least one case) that the punishment was to be nothing less than castration.

On the fifth day of the new year, 1847, came the first real snow, bringing gloom and misery to many of the shanties of the makeshift town. It was time for something definitive to happen, and it did so on 14 January. Brigham called together a council of his twelve apostles, plus Hosea Stout, chief of police, and brought forth his first and last *formal* revelation. Here was "the Word and Will of the Lord"; its subject was the organization for the move west. Now the brothers and sisters had something to look forward to; soon they would be going to Zion, the Promised Land.

The document, whose tone is reminiscent of a military directive, was explicit. The migration would be divided into companies of 100, with a captain as head of each. Beneath him would be captains of 50 and, further down the ladder, captains of 10, the entire assemblage to be under the direction of the Twelve and of the President and his two councilors. A number of individuals, including Ezra T. Benson and Erastus Snow, were specifically designated to form companies. Wagons, clothing, and provisions sufficient for the journey were to be assembled. Those lacking resources, widows with children, and the families of those marching with the Mormon Battalion would be divided up amongst the various companies, "that the cries of the widow and the fatherless come not up into the ears of the Lord against this people."

Those preparing to leave in the spring would also work on housing, and on the preparation of fields for raising grain for those who would, for now, be left beind. The brethren were commanded to stop bickering among themselves, to cease from drunkenness, to pay back what they had borrowed. Be humble and contrite, and keep the commandments. "So no more at present. Amen and amen."

The circulation of the Lord's Word and Will brought comfort and hope to many in the 'Camp of Israel. Certain elements would have to fall in line. Part of Hosea Stout's journal entry for 14 January is revealing. Writing of being one of the few present at the initial reading of Brigham's revelation, he declared:

> It was to me a source of much joy and gratification to be present on such an occasion, and my feeling can be better felt than described, for this will put to silence the wild bickering and suggestions of those who are ever in the way and opposing the proper council. They will now have to come to this standard or come out in open rebellion to the Will of the Lord, which will plainly manifest them to the people and then they can have no influence.[12]

As preparations continued during the winter of 1846–47 for departure in the spring, Brigham frequently issued specific instructions to the faithful. He addressed the women in mid-February:

> If you expect to call me Brother Brigham I want you to be cleanly, keep your faces and hands and skin clean from head to foot, your clothes, dishes and houses clean and nice, also your children, and learn them manners, and when you mix up bread don't have a dozen flies in your tray. . . .

As for the place of women in the community and the church, there was no doubt: "The man is the head and God of the woman." This was not to say they should be abused. "Treat them kindly, do their heavy lugging, but don't wash their dishes, as some do."[13]

As the Pioneers' time of leaving approached, Brigham appointed a number of men (John D. Lee, Isaac Morley, John Vance and about 20 others) to remain behind specifically to raise crops—to provide for those now in Winter Quarters and to supply other companies that would follow. The site selected was some 13 miles north of Winter Quarters, situated in flat land near the Missouri shore. It became known, appropriately, as Summer Quarters.

The westward trek of the Mormons to the Great Basin—later to be memorialized in innumerable histories, and to become a part not only of Mormon but also of United States history—got off to a shaky start, a little less than three months after Brigham's revelation. The initial Pioneer band was comprised of 149 Saints, including three women and two children.[14] The men making the Pioneer trek were by no means a random selection; they were chosen because they possessed a wide variety of skills—stonecutters and masons, blacksmiths and carpenters, hunters and teamsters.

The first contingent, a company of six wagons led by Heber C. Kimball, left on 5 April. Kimball was a self-taught scientist of considerable accomplishment. Brigham remained behind preparing for a church conference the next day. Many from the first group returned for the conference, and Brigham headed west with them the day after that, 7 April, but news shortly arrived that Parley Pratt had returned to Winter Quarters from England. His return was of sufficient importance to cause Brigham again to return to Winter Quarters, accompanied by some of the Apostles. By 11 April they were back at the camp on the far side of the Elkhorn River—the initial staging area, about 18 miles west of the Missouri. Then came news that John Taylor had also returned from England, and again Brigham and others returned to Winter Quarters to welcome him. And welcome he was, for he brought funds collected in England, as well as useful items for the journey to the Great Basin, including sextants, barometers, and a telescope. Finally, then, on 15 April Brigham and the others joined the spearhead group, now on the north shore of the Platte River, a few miles from the present site of Fremont, Nebraska, and the trek began in earnest the next day.

At first the company traveled westward along the north bank of the Platte. The Oregon-California Trail was already established on the other side of the river, but the Mormons had no wish to mingle with the Gentile overlanders headed in the same direction.[15] Mormons following this same route later would, working under Brigham's direction, continue to improve the trail, establishing permanent ferries and building bridges, to such extent that by the 1850s the "Mormon Trail," on the Platte, became more popular then the Oregon-California Trail on the other side.

Now, however, reports from mountain men and explorers notwithstanding, they were venturing into a very great unknown, although they did carry such maps as were then available, including Frémont's of his 1843 route to California via the Great Salt Lake. Brigham established a paramilitary organization, with himself with the rank of lieutenant general at the head of it. Beneath him were Colonel Stephen Markham, second in command, and Majors John Pack and Shadrach Roundy. All of the men were divided into companies of nine to thirteen. One group, the 13th, included two black men; these were slaves of Mississippi Mormons who were part of the Pioneer party. The 14th company also included one black man. Each group was led by a captain.

The terrain over which they would pass was presumed to be hostile, and discipline was to be strict. The horn would sound at 5:00 A.M. and all would be ready to move by 7:00. The men would not leave their wagons, unless otherwise assigned to special duty, and weaponry and ammunition were to be ready for instant use. Despite the Omahas' graciousness, the assumption was that *all* Indians were thieves, with a particular penchant for horses and other livestock. At night the wagons would be driven into a circle, with the horses inside.

One of the more thoughtful and intelligent men in the Pioneer party was William Clayton, an early convert from England. Joseph Smith had recognized his quality and had made him his friend, confidant, and scribe. On 19 April, no more than three days after the real start of the journey, Clayton suggested to Orson Pratt that a device be constructed to be fixed to the hub of a wagon wheel in order to have an accurate measure of the distance traveled. He had the foresight to see how valuable a reasonably precise map would be to those to follow. Pratt agreed that this was a good idea, did some thinking about how such a device could be constructed, and put Appleton Harmon to the job of making it. By 8 May, before the device had been completed, Clayton was sufficiently concerned about the differences between his and others' estimates of the distance traveled during a day that he determined to measure rather than estimate.

He measured the circumference of the left rear wheel of the wagon in which he slept and found it to be 14' 8". Making calculations to discover how many revolutions would be made in traveling one mile, he found to his astonishment that it was exactly 360. He tied a piece of cloth to the wheel, and on 8 May counted 4,070 revolutions—making the distance traveled just over 11¼ miles.

Needless to say, this was a tedious business, and he was pleased to note in his journal for 12 May that "Brother Appleton Harmon has completed the machinery on the wagon so far that I shall only have to count the number of miles, instead of the revolutions of the wagon wheel."[16]

Earlier, on 21 April, the Pioneers had met their first large body of Indians, as they passed a Pawnee village. The Mormons camped a short distance beyond the settlement and were soon joined by about 70 braves in search of gifts. They bore certificates from overlanders who had preceded the Mormons, stating that the Pawnees were friendly. Some of the wary Mormons gave small gifts to the Indians who, though they had the reputation of stealing horses, were protective of the buffalo roaming the prairies. The Indians issued a stern warning to leave the buffalo alone—a warning that later had to be repeated by Brigham when some of the men began shooting the animals for sport. If you shoot them now when we don't need them, Brigham warned, there won't be any to shoot when we do. Using them for food was all right; indeed, George Albert Smith wrote that the meat was better than beef.[17]

Two days after meeting the Pawnees, the Mormons made the first of a number of difficult river crossings. From the point where the Loup River enters the Platte, the Pioneers had traveled some 25 miles along the north bank of the Loup. This stream now had to be crossed in order to return to the Platte. They were about 110 miles from Winter Quarters, near the present site of Fullerton, Nebraska. The Loup had a maximum depth of about four feet, but it was broad and swift. It took two days to get all the wagons across. The sandy bottom made it strenuous work, and at first they had to partly unload the wagons and use double or triple teams. Once across, they continued a short distance along the Loup before turning southwest toward the Platte. They would soon be on the other side of the river from the Oregon Trail, which ran on the south bank, but the Mormons wouldn't cross over until they got to Fort Laramie, in Wyoming Territory.

It is not surprising that disciplinary problems arose as the move to the west continued. Here was, after all, a body of men far from home and family, not really knowing where they were going, and (except for three of them) without the satisfactions and diversions that might have been provided by friendship, companionship, love, or only dalliance with the opposite sex. So, after a weary day, they liked to play cards, checkers, and dominoes, and even have a drink on the rare occasion when opportunity arose. Brigham considered this behavior reprehensible (morale-supporting though it no doubt was), and toward the end of May called the reprobates together and threatened to leave the company and take with him a few God-fearing men. Brigham knew how to deliver a scorching reprimand, and the chastized men were quieter after that.

Continuing on the north bank of the North Platte, they met another large group of Indians on 24 May. These were Sioux, and they were a new experience for the Pioneers, who described them as well-dressed and noble in appearance. They wore robes decorated with beads and paintings. Clayton recorded that for cleanliness and neatness they would "vie with the most tasteful whites."[18] Some of the men, long deprived of feminine contact, found the squaws attractive. The Sioux were all about them as they camped that night, and to their surprise no one reported anything missing the next morning.

The Camp of Israel was now within sight of a famous landmark, Chimney Rock, and two days later they were opposite the spectacular formation. This provided a morale boost; the rock was considered a halfway mark between the Missouri and the mountains. Clayton would later show, in his *Emigrants' Guide,* that at this point they were 452 miles from Winter Quarters and 578 miles from their destination in the Great Basin.

Three days later, on 1 June, they camped on the north side of the Platte, opposite Fort Laramie, on Laramie Creek near the river. (This site is not to be confused with that of the present city of Laramie, Wyoming. See endpaper map.) They had traveled from Winter Quarters, according to Clayton's record, 543 miles. Here they were happy to meet a group of Mormons from Mississippi, who had arrived some two weeks earlier, and were waiting for the arrival of the Pioneer company.

No doubt the Mormons were pleased to arrive at this outpost on other grounds as well; the numerous forts scattered here and there on the overland trails were of no small importance to the overlanders. As increasing numbers of emigrants followed the earlier travelers, the forts became places where goods could be traded, horses and oxen shod, and news, tall tales, and lies exchanged. Fort Laramie was owned by the American Fur Company, and was an important part of the empire-monopoly-trust founded by John Jacob Astor. A number of Mormons crossed over to the fort on the day of their arrival on the opposite river bank, and on the following day, 2 June, Brigham Young and others had a friendly meeting with its then major-domo, James Bordeaux.

During the next two days the Mormons crossed to the south side of the Platte, using a boat rented to them by Bordeaux, thus joining the Oregon-California Trail. At this time almost everyone going westward from Fort Laramie went along the south side of the river—no doubt in part because of tales, told by Bordeaux, of danger and an impassable mountain on the other side. Later on, after the fort had been acquired by the Army in 1849, the soldiers operating the ferry repeated the same tales, this in aid of keeping the ferrying business there. This was to become a busy crossing point indeed, and running the ferry was a money-making enterprise, a point noted by Brigham Young at the Fort Laramie crossing. In the early 1850s adventuresome overlanders began taking the north side and reported that it was a pleasant route, as well as a time-saving one.[19]

This time, however, the Mormons continued to travel west, south of the river and out of sight of it. They now had company on the trail, and during their first two days of travel they overtook one company of Oregon-bound emigrants and were in turn overtaken by another. On 8 June they met a company, led by James H. Grieve, eastward bound from Fort Bridger. Grieve gave the Mormons useful information, telling them that when they reached Fort Bridger they would be within a two-day ride of the Great Salt Lake, and he further cheered them by describing the Utah country as beautiful. More importantly, he told them of a boat made of buffalo hide that his company had hidden at the North Platte crossing, and this generous traveler gave them permission to use it.

Brigham immediately detached a group from the main body to go ahead rapidly and retrieve the leather boat before it might be found by others, to make rafts as well, and to do all they could to prepare to ferry the Pioneers across the river. The main body of the camp advanced more slowly, and Clayton reported the first sighting of the North Platte on 10 June, 77 miles from Fort Laramie. The North Platte would soon turn south, and they must cross it again, but for now they continued along its south bank. They reached the site of the North Platte ferry two days later, there catching up with the advance group sent ahead to secure the leather boat.

And they found that their brethren had been putting the boat to good use indeed: they were ferrying the goods and persons of Gentile

Independence Rock. (Photo by W. H. Jackson, 1979, courtesy Utah State Historical Society.)

emigrants over the river for $1.50 per load, being paid in flour, valued at $2.50 per hundred pounds. They were hauling the empty wagons across by using ropes, but the stream was so swift that the wagons rolled over and over, causing considerable damage. Nevertheless, the operation netted the Mormons a total barter value of $78, which included 1,295 pounds of flour, plus odd quantities of meal, beans, soap, and honey.[20] With a nice sense of humor, the leather boat was appropriately referred to as the *Revenue Cutter*.

The ferrying job done, the Pioneers now had to get their own company across. They had the *Cutter* for the goods and people but the wagons, as they had discovered, were a problem. They tried to solve it by lashing two wagons together to prevent them rolling over, but that didn't work. They tried tying four together, and that was better, but still considerable damage was done to one wagon. The eventual solution was to build a raft of sufficient size and stability to carry one wagon at a time safely across. The last wagon was ferried on 17 June, and they spent the next day on the north side of the river. Clayton went fishing, and caught so many he needed help carrying them back to camp. On the 19th they continued westward toward South Pass and

Recent photograph of Independence Rock, by the author.

Fort Bridger, leaving behind a body of men to continue to run the profitable ferry service.

The first day of their renewed progress toward their goal was not encouraging, although the distance traveled, 21½ miles, was the greatest distance covered thus far in one day. They passed through a place known as Soda Springs (nothing to do with the town later established further west in Idaho) that Brigham said could aptly be called Hell's Gate. They continued onward to a barren and sandy area where they camped near two small streams of water; the water in one was undrinkable, in the other "not very bad." Clayton wrote that it was the worst camping site yet. Of one of the streams he said the banks were so soft that the horses and cattle had to be kept away from it, else they would be mired over their heads. And there were multitudes of mosquitoes. Heber Kimball wrote that the place was gloomy, cheerless, and filthy. It was, Clayton wrote, "one of the most horrid, swampy, stinking places I ever saw."[21]

The trail improved the next day, and by 21 June they were opposite another famous landmark, Independence Rock, 175 miles from Fort Laramie, 700 miles from Winter Quarters. A number of the brethren climbed the Rock.[22] Two days later later they saw for the first time the Wind River range of the distant Rocky Mountains. The company had passed through some terrain they had found very pleasant and some they thought entirely uninhabitable, and here at last were the mountains before them—visible, undeniable confirmation that they were approaching their goal.

They reached the Continental Divide, at South Pass, on 27 June. This Pass, the gateway to the west over the Rockies and now an officially designated Historic Landmark, is a broad and almost level plain, about 7,500 feet in elevation—nothing like terrain usually associated with a mountain pass. No doubt the Pioneers were not surprised by this, for they had been reading Frémont's reports in December 1845, before leaving Nauvoo. Frémont described the Pass thusly.

It will be seen that the Pass in no way resembles the places to which the term is commonly applied, nothing of the Great St. Bernard's and Simplon passes in Europe. Approaching it from the mouth of the Sweetwater, a sandy plain, 120 miles long, conducts, by a gradual and regular ascent, to the summit, about seven thousand feet above the sea; and the traveler, without being reminded of any change by toilsome ascents, suddenly finds himself on the side from which the waters flow into the Pacific Ocean.[23]

The Sweetwater River, which they had been following to its headwaters, was now left behind. Ahead lay the Green River, the next major challenge, and the Pioneers now made their way toward that stream, fording a number of smaller creeks—Dry Sandy, Little Sandy, Big Sandy—that would empty into it. At the Big Sandy crossing they had, by chance, an important meeting; here, on 28 June, the day after crossing the Continental Divide, they met Jim Bridger, toward whose fort they were making their way. Bridger, traveling eastward to Fort Laramie, was arguably the most celebrated of the mountain men, and the Mormons were eager indeed to talk to him. Happily, he also wanted to talk to Brigham Young, and so a meeting was arranged. Clayton was in attendance, and gives us the best report.

Bridger impressed his audience in different ways. Howard Egan didn't believe he was a man of truth. Wilford Woodruff was awestruck— if Bridger was telling the truth, and Woodruff had some reservations about that. Clayton described his way of speaking as "very imperfect and irregular." He did, apparently, try to give the Pioneers a good idea of what to expect between their present site and the Great Salt Lake, and he specifically warned them about the Indians around Utah Lake, a freshwater lake that empties into the Great Salt Lake. They would rob, abuse, and perhaps kill a white man found alone but would not bother white men in numbers. He also said he thought it imprudent to bring many people to the Great Basin until the ability to raise grain there had been demonstrated. A monument commemorating this meeting now stands at the site, where State Highway 26 crosses Big Sandy Creek.

The Pioneers reached the Green River just before noon on 30 June. The river was about 100 yards wide and far too deep for fording, so rafts had to be made; there was plenty of timber along the river banks with which to do this. And now, on the afternoon of the 30th, Sam Brannan appears again in our narrative—and not for the last time.

Brannan was a most interesting fellow, destined to become a man of legend. It will be recalled that in 1846 he had chartered the *Brooklyn*, the ship upon which he had taken 238 Mormons to California, via Cape Horn. They had settled in Yerba Buena (later San Francisco) under the leadership of the energetic Brannan who had, among other accomplishments, established the first newspaper there, the *California Star*. Such was his pressing need to talk to Brigham Young that he, together with two companions, one of whom was Charles Smith, had crossed the Sierras in early April before the spring thaw, over the snow, which was probably 200 feet deep in some places! During this hazardous adventure they traversed the Truckee Pass, site of the Donner disaster, where they saw some distressing remains of frozen bodies, some of them partially cannibalized. (At the time of the disaster Brannan had publicized the plight of the entrapped emigrants, thus helping to stimulate a rescue effort that succeeded, in February, in saving about half of the members of the party.)

Arriving safely at Fort Hall, Brannan there intercepted a letter from Brigham for him, a letter on its way to California. Brigham had written it on 6 June. The letter brought Brannan up to date on events since the Saints had left Nauvoo, and indicated that the company would not be continuing to California, that their goal was the Great Basin. This discouraged Brannan, because the main objective of his dangerous trip was to tell Brigham of the glories of California and to persuade him that *that* was where the future of the Saints lay. Brannan and his two companions met the Mormons at the Green River on 30 June.

There was much news to be exchanged on both sides. That finished and the amenities observed, Brannan produced the 16 copies of his paper he had brought with him and tried to persuade Brigham to lead the Saints to California. He praised the gentle climate and the lush fertility of the soil. He spoke of the harshness of the Great Basin, through parts of which he had just passed. His hazardous trip, however, had been in vain. Brigham pointed out that God had made the decision to settle in the valley of the Great Salt Lake and that with a touch of the Lord's hand added to some Mormon brawn they could make an Eden anywhere. Brannan was unconvinced.

The last wagon was ferried over on 3 July. The next day it was decided to send five men back along the trail to assist in ferrying emigrant companies that would be following later. This group was accompanied back to the Green River by Brigham, Heber Kimball, and Willard Richards. There they were amazed and delighted to find a party of 13 horsemen, who turned out to be an advance guard, of James Brown's invalided detachment of the Mormon Battalion. The detachment had not yet been discharged or fully paid.

It was now decided to send one of these men, William Walker, back along the trail with the five from the lead camp, while the rest returned to the main camp. At a council meeting it was further decided that Brannan and one other of the Mormon Battalion, Thomas Williams, would also go back on the trail to bring the rest of the Battalion to the Great Basin, whence Brannan would pilot them to California for discharge and the balance of pay due them. Brannan was still unconvinced of the finality of Brigham's decision to settle in the Great Basin; after all, he had seen it and Brigham hadn't. He was accordingly pleased at the opportunity to guide at least the Battalion band of his brethren back to his beloved California. As it turned out, they met Brown's troops in mid-July and conducted them to the valley of the Great Salt Lake.

Meanwhile the main company continued westward, and as they neared the mountains many of the company fell victim to what was called mountain fever, probably Rocky Mountain Spotted Fever, a viral disease carried by ticks. On 12 July, the day they crossed the Bear River, Brigham became seriously ill, and that evening he was delirious. His recovery was slow and on the 19th, unable to travel, he sent the rest of the camp onward, only a few remaining behind to care for him.

Brigham had earlier, on the 14th, sent out an advance party of more than 40 men under the direction of Orson Pratt. These men carried axes and shovels and did what they could to make the tortuous passage through the canyons easier for those soon to follow. The canyon roads, with mountains to either side, were mostly very narrow, crooked, filled with shrubs and trees, and so rocky that wagons frequently broke down, making it necessary to stop for repairs. Still, they were getting close to the site of Zion.

Nearing the long-sought valley, Pratt and Erastus Snow went on ahead, and on 21 July were the first to sight the broad valley below, the Great Salt Lake shining in the distance. Seeing Zion spread out before them, they shouted for joy. Pratt recorded the proud moment in his journal: "After issuing from the mountains among which we had been shut up for many days, and beholding in a moment such an extensive scenery open before us, we could not refrain from a shout of joy which almost involuntarily escaped from our lips the moment this grand and lovely scenery was within our view."[24]

The rest of the advance party reached the site the next day, and on the 24th Brigham's wagon reached the canyon, known ever since, appropriately enough, as Emigration Canyon. Raising himself from his pallet he beheld the view. "Yes," he said, "this is the place."[25] Finally down on level ground, below the foothills of the Wasatch Mountains, Brigham arrived at a camp humming with activity. Planting had top priority, followed by building shelters and surveying.

The Mormons were not, of course, the first white men to come to the Great Basin. They had been preceded by a considerable and motley crowd: Jim Bridger, Etienne Provost, Jedediah Smith, William Ashley, William Sublette, Father de Smet, and a host of others. They were Americans, Britons, Frenchmen, and Spaniards for the most part— river men, mountain men, explorers, traders, mappers, trappers, missionaries, tellers of extravagant lies, some of them creators of myth. Although the Mormons weren't the first here, they were the first to come with the thought of permanent sanctuary, with the dream of building a shining city, of making the desert blossom as the rose.

Not all of the first band of Pioneers experienced great joy upon their arrival at Zion. The Snows, Lorenzo and Harriet, were particularly disappointed. Harriet bemoaned the absence of trees—not yet holding

"This Is the Place" monument. At top are Brigham Young, Heber Kimball, and Wilford Woodruff. (Photo by the author.)

within her vision a desert colorful with flowers—and said she'd rather go another thousand miles, if necessary, to find a more congenial landscape. Clayton saw it somewhat differently:

> There is an extensive, beautiful, level-looking valley from here to the lake which I should judge from the numerous deep green patches must be fertile and rich. . . . There is but little timber . . . which is about the only objection which could be raised in my estimation to this being one of the most beautiful valleys and pleasant places for a home for the Saints which could be found.[26]

In any case, here was the valley in which Zion would be established.

It was 15 to 20 miles wide, 20 to 40 miles long. To the west were the Oquirrh Mountains and the lake, to the east the Wasatch range of the Rockies. Here they would settle, apart from the Gentiles. Brigham made this clear in a talk to the settlers on his second day in the valley. He said that they had no intention of trading or engaging in commerce with the Gentile world. Such trade, he said would make them dependent. "I am determined to cut every thread of this kind and live free and independent, untrammeled by any of their detestable customs and practices."[27]

He could not have foreseen that precisely six months later to the day gold would be found at Sutter's Mill, that the date of the discovery would be established by the diary of a Mormon working at the site. This signal event led to the gold rush of 1849, wherein Salt Lake City would become a halfway house, and trade and commerce with the Gentile world would flourish.

By 28 July Brigham was sufficiently recovered to make a decision of paramount importance, to determine the site upon which the temple would be erected. To understand the importance of thinking so immediately about the temple we must understand, as Stegner indicates, the *literalness* of Mormon belief. The Saints had come not just to a new country, not just to a new life, "but to a new Dispensation, to the literal Kindom of God on earth."[28]

Joseph had been an urban planner before Brigham, and though Brigham did not follow Joseph's basic plan altogether, he followed it in spirit.[29] The initial temple site, the first designated spot on the plan of the new city, was a grandiose 40-acre superlot, which was shortly reduced to a more manageable ten acres. The city would be laid out square to the compass, with large blocks separated by broad streets, and the large blocks would be sectioned into eight lots of 1¼ acres. Houses would be set back 20 feet from the street, and in alternate blocks the houses would face east and west, and north and south, providing outlooks unimpeded by directly facing houses. Joseph's original plan had been that each Mormon settlement would be one mile square. Whether Brigham thought to maintain that limit in the Great Basin is not known, but such a plan would have been, in any case, shortly violated by expansion as the following emigrants poured in. And the original Salt Lake City lots were indeed soon subdivided, with more houses appearing where one had originally been intended. Be that as

Salt Lake Base and Meridian, placed 3 August 1847. Latitude 40° 46′ 04″, longitude 111° 54′ 00″. Southeast corner of Temple Square. (Photo by the author.)

it may, the present-day first-time visitor to downtown Salt Lake City is impressed by the length of the blocks, the width of the streets. Indeed, throughout the West the size of lots in towns first settled by Mormons is significantly larger than those of non-Mormon towns.[30]

Now, however, at the very birth of what would become Salt Lake City it was a different matter altogether. The first crude cabins and adobes were arranged closely together, fortresslike. They were intended as temporary structures. The Pioneer trek had been essentially exploratory, the long-sought-for location in which to establish Zion had been found, and Brigham and others would return to Winter Quarters, there to work through the winter, preparing for the large mass movements that would begin in the spring.

The return journey to Winter Quarters began in mid-August. Two companies departed the Great Basin a few days apart. The first, which comprised 72 men with 33 wagons, left on 17 August. In this group was William Clayton, who would carefully monitor a newly constructed "roadometer" throughout the journey. (This one, redesigned, and constructed by William A. King, had additional gears and a total capacity of 1,000 miles.) From this group those men with horses to ride were given the responsibility of going on ahead, fixing the trail where it was needed, so the wagons and oxen could follow. They were also to locate suitable camp sites. The plan was that this group would later be caught up with by Brigham's company in the vicinity of Grand Island, and they would return from there to Winter Quarters together. That plan went awry, however, when William Clayton, in the leading group, decided on his own to forge ahead. His journal makes it quite clear that he made this move because of internal conflict within his company and because of scanty food supplies, caused at least in part by the behavior of some of the men.

On 14 September Clayton noted: "In consequence of some things which have passed and some which at present exist, I have concluded to go on as fast as circumstances will permit to Winter Quarters and I intend to start tomorrow." Others would go along with him, including at least one of the troublemakers. John Pack caused many "unpleasant feelings," Clayton wrote. ". . . He takes . . . all the best meat and has now got more than will serve him home while many of the rest have scarcely any, and that of the poorest pieces."

Clayton thought Pack's conduct disgraceful; nor did he have anything good to say of Thomas Cloward, whose behavior he considered "worse than the general run of gentiles and unworthy of a saint." He would remember what these men had done, he wrote, for a long time. "Such little, selfish, unmanly conduct as has been manifested by them, is rarely exhibited except by the meanest classes of society. A man who will openly and boldly steal is honorable when compared with some of their underhanded conduct."[31]

Clayton arrived in Winter Quarters on 21 October, ten days ahead of Brigham Young and his party. He had kept a meticulous record of the journey, troublesome though it had been, and computed the distance to Salt Lake from Winter Quarters as 1,032 miles. He now prepared a complete guide for the travelers to follow. *The Latter-day Saints' Emigrants' Guide* was published in St. Louis in 1848. It found much favor with the forty-niners and other emigrants; it was, by general consent, the most accurate guide available for the part of the trail it covered.

The group traveling with Brigham apparently had a less disputatious journey. Certainly Brigham would not have tolerated the kind of behavior recorded by Clayton. Their return trip was brightened as they met at least five companies of Mormons headed toward Salt Lake, and thus had reunions with groups led by Parley Pratt, Daniel Spencer, Jedediah Grant, Joseph Horne, and John Taylor. On 4 September they met Parley Pratt's group; this was not an altogether happy occasion, as Brigham felt compelled to chastise Parley Pratt for "disarranging" the plans agreed upon by the Twelve. It will be remembered that Pratt and Taylor had been abroad during most of the planning of the move west, and no doubt there were some misunderstandings. Pratt at first resisted Brigham's reproof but finally acknowledged his error.

Two days later, on 6 September, they met the companies led by John Taylor and Joseph Horne, and although Brigham had the same complaint against Taylor that he had had against Parley Pratt, this meeting was of an altogether different character. As veteran diarist Thomas Bullock described it, "they had killed the fatted calf to make merry."[32] Further, there was something here in the nature of a surprise. While all the leaders present were consulting together in private, the women were preparing a gala. "Game and fish were prepared in abundance; fruits, jellies and relishes reserved for special occasions were brought out until truly it was a royal feast. . . . The Pioneers knew nothing of what had taken place until they were led by Elder Taylor through a natural opening in the bushes fringing the enclosure, and the grand feast burst upon their astonished vision."[33] One hundred and thirty sat down to this emotionally charged festive table. After due compliment had been paid to the sisters, there was music and dancing.

There is something quite touching here. Two parties meeting on a wild and mostly comfortless trail, one returning to a temporary home, the other headed toward the beginning of a new one, discomfort and hardship both ahead and behind, and they get together and have a ball. Whatever lay ahead, how could people with this kind of spirit lose?

Shortly after this extraordinary reunion Brigham greeted, in Jedediah Grant's group, two of the wives he had left behind in Winter Quarters, Margaret Pierce and Eliza Snow. Thus three of his wives would be spending the winter in Salt Lake—Clara Decker having been left behind when Brigham departed. That first winter spent in Zion would not be an easy one, but this community would survive, as does one of the cabins from that first winter. It may be seen today just west of Temple Square near the genealogical library building. It is 15 by 20 feet, built of Douglas fir and lodgepole pine, the home of Osmyn and Mary Deuel. (This is not its original site.)

Brigham and the others of his group continued on toward Winter Quarters, with food running low at times and bands of Indians stealing their horses. On 18 October they were met by a welcome group riding out to meet then, bringing horses (which were badly needed), grain, and provisions. Things were looking up. Two weeks later, almost home, they were met by another large group. The next day the journey ended, as they came into Winter Quarters an hour before sunset. Within sight of the settlement Brigham called his company together, thanked them for all they had done, and set them free to join their families. Families had been separated for a long season, and there was much joy in the town that evening. Problems faced them, indeed, but they could wait until tomorrow.

Notes

1. Tullidge, *History of Salt Lake City,* pp. 18-19.
2. Roberts, *Comprehensive History of the Church,* vol. 3, p. 309 (hereafter *CHC*).
3. Bancroft, *History of Utah,* p. 444.
4. The movement generally, and particularly in Winter Quarters, was called the Camp of Israel. It should be remembered that Mormons considered their church not a new one but rather the reestablished, original church of Jesus Christ.
5. Stout was one of many diarists on the trek westward. Their day-by-day writings are the primary source for the history of the move to the West. In using such primary sources, I make minimal changes in spelling and punctuation for ease of reading.
6. A Visitor's Center has been established at the site of Winter Quarters and is well worth a visit. Many interesting publications are available, and the vistas are beguiling.
7. Tullidge, pp. 23-24.
8. DeVoto, *Year of Decision,* p. 238.
9. John D. Lee, *Journal* for 1846, pp. 34-60, *passim.* Lee's journal entries clearly indicate his embarrassment about the uses to which the Mormon Battalion money was put.
10. Tullidge, pp. 34-35.
11. De Smet's views of the Mormons and the Utah settlements, which he expressed later, were not entirely consistent. In 1851 he wrote a glowing description of Salt Lake City. But in 1957 he wrote: "The place where they live, the Great Salt Lake country, is most miserable. . . . The region would never allow a heavy settlement. . . . Sonora offers all kinds of advantages, and the Mormons, after they have done all the harm they can, will take refuge there." Chittendon and Richardson, vol. 4, pp. 1407ff. De Smet apparently fell victim here to wishful thinking; the removal of the Mormons to Mexico at that time would have solved lots of problems.
12. Stout, *Diary,* vol. 1, pp. 227-29.
13. These are Brigham Young's remarks as reported in Lee, *Journal,* 16 Feb. 1847, pp. 81-90.
14. Brigham's brother, Lorenzo, wanted to take his wife, Harriet, along because the Missouri lowlands were bad for her asthma. Harriet said she needed womanly company, and Brigham allowed her daughter by an earlier marriage, Clara Decker, to make the trip, as well as Heber Kimball's wife, Ellen. Clara Decker was also a plural wife of Brigham. The two children were Lorenzo's son and stepson, both about six years old. Thus the initial party represented a considerable departure from the master plan of the January revelation, in which each company would include a proportionate number of widows and fatherless children.
15. The usual starting points for those intending to travel the Oregon Trail were Westport (now Kansas City), Independence, and St. Joseph. From these outfitting stations emigrants traveled generally northwestward, reaching the Platte River at Fort Kearny, continuing along the south banks of the Platte and the North Platte. The Mormons were on the other side.
16. The odometer worked as follows: a cog on the hub of the wagon wheel engaged a spoke upon a vertical rod, topped with a worm gear. There were six spokes on the bottom of the rod, so the rod turned once for every six revolutions of the wheel. The worm gear on the rod engaged a 60-tooth gear that rotated once for every 60 rotations of the rod. Thus each rotation of this gear represented travel of one mile. The concept of the odometer was not new at this time (the *Oxford English Dictionary*

indicates use of the word as early as 1791), but it was a noteworthy achievement to construct an accurate one under the conditions of Pioneer travel. See William Clayton, *Journal*, pp. 81-143 *passim,* Wright, *Pioneer Odometer,* and Stringham, *The Pioneer Roadometer.*

17. Indiscriminate shooting of buffalo inevitably endangered the species. Now that their numbers have been brought back, with reference to George Smith's comment it is interesting to note that the meat has become a fashionable and popular item on the menus of many restaurants.

18. Clayton, *Journal,* p. 181.

19. Diary of Brown Nathan McKinstry, cited in Unruh, *The Plains Across,* p. 272. A microfilm of this diary is in the Bancroft Library of the University of California, Berkeley.

20. Roberts, *CHC,* vol. 3, pp. 195-97.

21. Clayton, *Journal,* p. 245.

22. Independence Rock is now surrounded by a protective fence. The visitor may stand at the fence within a few feet of the Rock, upon which many of the inscriptions left by early emigrants are visible.

23. John Charles Frémont, *Report of the Exploring Expedition . . . ,* pp. 19–56, *passim.*

24. Tullidge, p. 41.

25. See Note 81, p. 459, in Arrington, *American Moses.* Where—and, indeed, whether—Brigham said these words has been a matter of some disagreement. Nevertheless, an imposing This Is the Place monument now stands on the site, commanding a fine view of the city below. See photo on p. 68.

26. Clayton, *Journal,* p. 308.

27. Arrington, p. 169 (citing "Norton Jacob's Record").

28. Stegner, *Gathering of Zion,* p. 2.

29. Taves, *Trouble Enough,* p. 83.

30. Richard Jackson, "The Mormon Village . . . ," provides a wealth of information comparing Mormon with non-Mormon towns in the West.

31. Clayton, *Journal,* pp. 362-67.

32. Bullock, *Journal,* cited in Arrington, *American Moses,* p. 148.

33. Roberts, *CHC,* vol. 3, p. 297.

4

Exodus

The time has come for the Saints to go up to the mountains.

The all-important task confronting Brigham and his followers at Winter Quarters—once the many happy reunions of friends and families had been duly celebrated—was to plan and make preparation for the larger emigration of the church that would begin in the spring. The 1847 harvest had been remarkably abundant, so that was one large concern the leaders of the church didn't have to worry about. But there was much other work to be done, and Brigham began by proposing a major reorganization. The church should now consider, he said, whether the time had not come to return to the structure the church had before Joseph's assassination. It had been functioning since that time under the guidance of the Twelve, in an Apostolic Interregnum. During the past three and one half years the Twelve had attended to the tasks at hand and had, by and large, succeeded. Was it not now time to free the apostles to return to their original function—going forth to the corners of the earth, spreading the gospel? The time had come to select a Prophet and a First Presidency to lead the church. Brigham had, he said, been reluctant to set this forth until the proper time. He said that it had been revealed to him during the return journey to Winter Quarters that the time was now.

There was some resistance to this reorganization, particularly on the part of Orson Pratt, but they came to unanimous agreement on 5 December. They elected Brigham president; Brigham selected Heber Kimball and Willard Richards as his counselors. Brigham left no doubt in the minds of the apostles that he was going to be their leader. He knew, he said, that he was too harsh and critical at times, and would try to improve. But he was not going to consult the Twelve at every turn. He would not be trammeled. He felt toward the Twelve, he told them, as he did toward his children and his wives. He wanted them in his "pocket" (Brigham's phrase) so when he wanted to talk to them he could take them out and do so.

He wanted to talk to all the brothers and sisters spread over the globe as well, and on 23 December he and the Twelve sent a long General Epistle giving no end of advice and instructions as to how to gather at the appointed place (Kanesville) and prepare to move to the mountains. Brigham's writing was not often felicitous, and no doubt his prose owes a considerable debt to Willard Richards, a Dartmouth graduate and a strong writer. (Later he would be the first editor of the *Deseret News*.) In any case, there is in this document some interesting and fetching writing, and I give herewith a substantial quotation:

> Let all Saints . . . gather without delay to the place appointed, bringing their gold, their silver, their copper, their zinc, their tin, and brass, and iron, and choice steel, and ivory, and precious stones; their curiosities of science, of art, of nature, and every thing in their possession or within their reach, to build in strength and stability, to beautify, to adorn, to embellish, to delight, and to cast a fragrance over the House of the Lord; with sweet instruments of music and melody and songs and fragrance and sweet odours, and beautiful colours, whether it be in precious jewels, or minerals, or choice ores, or in wisdom and knowledge, or understanding, manifested in carved work; or curious workmanship of the box, the fir and pine tree, or any thing that ever was or is, or is to be, for the exaltation, glory, honour, and salvation of the living and the dead, for time and for all eternity . . . for the time has come for the Saints to go up to the mountains of the Lord's house, and help to establish it upon the tops of the mountains.[1]

The reorganization that the Twelve had agreed upon was placed before the brethren at a general meeting on 27 December, in a spacious log tabernacle constructed for the purpose, and the actions taken were sustained by the membership. Brigham said, after a loud Hosanna, that it was the happiest day of his life.

There was also the problem of vacating Winter Quarters. The settlement was on land reserved for the Omaha Indians, and the Mormons were under pressure to leave. It was, accordingly, decided they would depart in the spring. As many as could be provided for would go west to Salt Lake, while the others would move across the river to Kanesville, by which name that settlement was now known.[2]

Another problem was caused by disunity within the camp and internal dissension, some of which was related to the uses to which the funds paid to the Mormon Battalion had been put. We have already seen that most of these monies did not wind up in the purses of the wives and other family members left behind. There was acrimony about this, and we shall now examine one trial proceeding based upon this problem to see how Brigham dealt with it, and how in doing so he revealed something of himself, his way of relating to men, and—by no means least—some of his thoughts on relations between men and women.

John D. Lee was one of the good strong members of the church who had been left behind on the first trek in order to grow grain at Summer Quarters for subsequent emigrations. On 11 March 1848 he was in Winter Quarters, both to arrange for the grinding of grain and to appear as plaintiff in a trial to be heard before one Bishop Clark. Brigham told Lee to have the trial held back until he could be in attendance. For Brigham's convenience the trial was delayed until 7:00 P.M., and was held in the Council House. Lee's complaint was that while Andrew Lytle had been away, presumably in the Mormon Battalion, Lee had provided Lytle's wife with clothing and provisions to the amount of $56.76, and he wished to be reimbursed. The Bishop asked Lytle if he acknowledged Lee's bill, and he denied it. The Bishop then asked Lytle's wife if she would acknowledge or deny the bill, and began to read it to her, item by item. She was in the process of denying most of the items when Brigham interrupted.

He asked Lee if he had a record of the account, and Lee said that he had and would stand by it. Brigham proclaimed that he knew how Lee did business, and that he was careful in keeping accounts. He said further that what he, Brigham, would do were he in Lee's place would be to forgive the debt to prevent the arousal of hard feelings. Lee promptly arose and offered to burn it, and said, in effect, that if Lytle had come to him as a brother should, had said he was grateful for what Lee had done but couldn't pay now, then Lee would have said (again, in effect) so pay me later, if you can. Instead of which he had acted meanly and insulted him (Lee) and his wife in his own house.

Now Brigham took the stage:

> Brother Andrew, I am sorry to think that your feelings should be so
> trammeled by your wife. She is a stranger to me, yet I know that she

possesses a nasty little whining peevish devilish spirit. . . . The soldiers' wives have lied and tattled about me . . . and said that we have cheated and wronged them out of their money and thereby poisoned and soured the feelings of their husbands. . . . Great God! Could women trammel me in this manner? NO! All their counsel and wisdom (although there are many good women) don't weigh as much with me as the weight of a fly turd. Excuse me for my vulgarity. It is not common for me to use such language, but I know of no language too mean to suit the case before us. It is not woman's place to counsel her husband, and the moment a man follows a woman he is led astray and will go down to hell unless he retracts his steps. I could have a perfect hell with my wives were I to listen to them, but whenever one begins to strut and lead out, I say go it and show your wisdom, and soon she gets ashamed and curls down, but still my wives stick to me.[3]

Lee adds that Brigham spoke for three hours on this occasion and then invited Lee to spend the night at his house, which he did. They continued to chat, over bread and milk, until almost midnight.

By way of a pleasing counterpoint let us now interrupt the narrative briefly by making a jump back to the Great Basin and ahead in time. Again someone is speaking to a group of Mormons, a large group this time, in the Tabernacle in Temple Square in March 1892. The speaker is a distinguished non-Mormon visitor.

Did it ever occur to you what is the most heroic part of planting a colony of people which moves into a wilderness to establish a civilized community? You think, perhaps, it is the soldier, the armed man, or the laboring man. Not so; it is the women who are the most heroic part of any new colony. [*Applause*] Their labors are the less because their strength is less. Their anxieties are greater, their dangers greater, the risks they run are heavier. We read that story in the history of the Pilgrim and Puritan colonies of Massachusetts. The women died faster than the men; they suffered more. Perhaps their reward was greater too. They bore children to the colony. Let us bear in our hearts veneration for the women of any Christian folk going out in the wilderness to plant a new community.[4]

So spoke Charles William Eliot, President of Harvard University. On a trip to the West his train had been delayed for a time somewhere in the wilds of Rocky Mountain country, a detention that had caused him to reflect upon the treks of the pioneers, upon the difficulties of establishing new colonies in the wilderness.

Another responsibility the leaders of the church had to address was to see to it that as many Mormons as possible gather at Kanesville, which would be the point of assembly whence they would travel to the west. There were Saints all over the world—in the British Isles, Australia, China, and in Pacific outposts, including the Society Islands. These must be gathered at Kanesville. Instructions were dispatched to the far corners. The Mormons in the British Isles could reach Kanesville entirely by water, via New Orleans, and were advised to do so. Those in China, Australia, and the East Indies should come to the most convenient port. And what were they to bring, in addition to themselves? The instructions were far-reaching and specific, and they reveal that a lot of thought had gone into them. This is from the General Epistle already noted:

> All kinds of choice seeds, of grain, vegetables, fruits, shrubbery, trees, and vines—everything that grows upon the face of the whole earth that will please the eye, gladden the heart, or cheer the soul of man. . . . The best stock of beasts, bird, and fowl of every kind; also the best tools of every description, and machinery for spinning, or weaving, and dressing cotton, wool, flax, and silk, etc., or models and descriptions of the same, by kinds of farming utensils and husbandry, such as corn shellers, grain threshers and cleaners, smutt machines, mills, and every implement and article within their knowledge that shall tend to promote the comfort, health, happiness, or prosperity of any people.

The leaders—and no doubt the rank and file as well—gave plenty of thought to their children and their education, and to the generations that would follow them. Where they were going there would be no schools except ones they established, there would be no libraries other than those they built, no books except the ones they carried. The General Epistle asked that every good available treatise on education should be taken with them, together with "every book, map, chart, or diagram that may contain interesting, useful, and attractive matter, to gain the attention of children, and cause them to love to learn to read." Writings from diverse disciplines were to be taken: historical, geographical, geological, astronomical, scientific, and so on. There would be no museum where they were going so they must build one. The brethren were instructed to bring "all kinds of mathematical and philosophical instruments" and, in addition, works of art and specimens of natural curiosities. The point of all this? From such matters the rising generations would receive instruction. The Saints would build, if their vision was realized, the most useful and attractive museum on the earth.

Preparation was ceaseless as summer neared in 1848, and by the end of May no fewer than 623 wagons were assembled at the Elkhorn. This company comprised two groups, one led by Brigham, the other by his counselor Heber Kimball—1,891 men, women, and children in all. Accompanying them were 2,012 oxen, 983 cows, 904 chickens, 654 sheep, 334 loose cattle, 237 pigs, 134 dogs, 131 horses, 54 cats, 44 mules, 11 doves, 10 geese, 5 ducks, 5 bee hives, 3 goats, and 1 squirrel! The first two groups would be followed shortly by another large company led by Willard Richards and Amasa Lyman.

The first wagons pulled out of the Elkhorn staging area on 3 June. Some of the emigrants had made the trip before, but this trek would be a different matter. Many more people would be involved, including women and children. Though the route and problems to be solved were now better known, the general progress of the larger company was slower. Brigham's company would not reach the Salt Lake valley until 20 September, preceding Kimball's group by a few days. Some of the problems that arose were the same as those encountered by the earlier group. For example, when Brigham's company first sighted a herd of buffalo, some of the men shot them indiscriminately, against Brigham's orders and to his considerable disgust.

The presence of women, of entire families, though no doubt a tre-mendous boon in most ways, also caused problems. On 5 July, to cite an instance, the wagon of Hiram Gates overturned. No one was in the wagon and there were no injuries but the contents were dumped all about, revealing the presence of a (forbidden) bottle of wine. Gates blamed his wife for this, and a quarrel of considerable magnitude ensued. That night the guard, when it came time to cry (that all might know it was time to be properly abed), cried thusly: "Eleven o'clock and all is well, and Gates is quarreling with his wife like hell."[5]

Brigham's and Kimball's groups arrived in the valley on 20 and 24 September 1848. Another large company led by Willard Richards and Amasa Lyman, arrived on 11 October. The population of Zion was now something like 5,000.

Those members of the three parties that had been in the valley the preceding year found that the brethren had altered the landscape.

They had fenced in an area of about 5,000 acres, including most of the original city plat. A good deal of this had been seeded with fall wheat. The winter weather had been quite mild, and they had been able to plow during parts of each month; in the spring they had planted acre after acre in the expectation of a healthy fall harvest. Pending that harvest, however, provisions were running so low that rationing was in effect.

Further, the spring planting had been followed by crisis and by miracle. The crisis was an overwhelming invasion of the newly planted fields by hordes of black crickets. They ate their way through the fields destroying the crop, and the community—already on rations—was in despair. The miracle was the appearance, from over the lake, of flight after flight of gulls, who promptly set about devouring the crickets. The crop was saved. Priddy Meeks recorded this history:

> Now everything did look gloomy, our provisions giving out and the crickets eating up what little we had growing, and we a thousand miles away from supplies. When Sunday come we had a meeting. Apostle Rich stood in an open wagon and preached out of doors. At that instant I heard the voice of fowls flying overhead that I was not acquainted with. I looked up and saw a flock of seven gulls. In a few minutes another flock passed over. They came faster and more of them until the heavens were darkened with them and they would eat crickets and throw them up again. A little before sundown they left for Salt Lake, for they roosted on a sandbar. In the morning they came back again and continued that course until they had devoured the crickets and then left. . . .[6]

Later the imposing Sea Gull Monument was erected in Salt Lake to commemorate the event. On 9 August those of the Twelve in the valley wrote that "our wheat harvest is over, and grain is splendid and clean. . . . We can raise more and better wheat to the acre in this valley than in any place any of us ever saw; and the same with other grains, vegetables, etc., that we have tried."[7] So is the tale usually told, and I remember being told it by my grandfather, while being shown the monument.

There may have been a little exaggeration here, or poetic license, or whatever, or natural embellishment of a surprising happening, because after the First Presidency arrived their evaluation was not quite so glowing: "Most of their early crops were destroyed (in May) by crickets

Sea Gull Monument, erected to honor the sea gulls who devoured the crickets that threatened the crops in 1848. (Photo courtesy Utah State Historical Society.)

and frost. . . . The brethren were not sufficiently numerous to fight the crickets (and) irrigate the crops." No mention of miraculous intervention. Still, prospects were not gloomy; ". . . the experiment of last year is sufficient to prove that valuable crops may be raised in this valley by an attentive and judicious management."[8]

Shortly after the arrivals of Brigham and Kimball the lots of the city were distributed to the brethren, both the lots of the central city proper (one and one quarter acres), and the larger ones, to the south and west (five, ten, and twenty acres), which went to those who intended to farm. A lottery was set up to determine who got which lot. There was no charge for these lots—except each recipient had to pay $1.50, one dollar as a surveying fee, and 50 cents for recording the deed. Those with plural wives received plural lots. A widow with children received one lot. Unmarried men received no lot. As noted earlier, restrictions were strict: one house on one lot, the house properly set back from the street, no subdivision.

We cannot know whether Brigham and Kimball and the others were thinking, as the land was being distributed, of who had been using the land before they took it over. It was the Ute Indians. One of the reasons this particular area had been chosen was because it was where the Utes were. According to the sketchy information available it appeared that they would be easier to get along with than those to the north (Shoshones and Gosiutes) or south (Navajos and Piutes). It must be remembered that the Mormons were, because of the history set forth in the Book of Mormon, under a particular obligation to the Indians— the Lamanites of the Book of Mormon. They were the remnants of one of the fallen lost tribes of Israel—a bad lot, degraded, and given to warfare and sin of every kind. They were to be redeemed by the Mormons, whereupon they would, in time, become a "white and delightsome" people. But now, in the fall of 1848, Brigham and Kimball were apportioning out their land to themselves.

Later Brigham would acknowledge that this had been the Utes' land, the land that they and their fathers had walked over, where they had buried their dead. "This is their home and we have taken possession of it."[9] That was all right, however, because they, the Mormons, were there because of the providence of God. Not that they didn't have responsibilities, however. They were to raise enough grain to feed the

Indians, and they were to be kind to them, and bring them the gospel. We hasten to add here that the Mormons were no different from everyone else in taking it for granted that it was all right to take over the land from the natives. The palefaces were doing that all over the continent, would continue to do so until they had it all except for small reservations set aside here and there, creating grievances that are still a matter of concern to many Native Americans today.

The Indians generally—and not just in the Great Basin, but everywhere—claimed that the land was theirs. The white man, for the most part, and again not just in the Great Basin, didn't take that view seriously. Actually, Brigham said in one discussion of the matter that the land belonged not to the Indians or the Saints, but to the Father in Heaven, and they, the Saints, intended to plow and plant it.

Notes

1. *Millennial Star,* vol. 10 (March 1848), pp. 81-88. The General Epistle here cited was addressed, from the Twelve, to "The Church of Jesus Christ of Latter-day Saints abroad, dispersed throughout the earth, Greeting." B. H. Roberts, in *CHC,* was apologetic about what he referred to as the turgid prose of the letter. No such apology was needed.

2. Thomas L. Kane, never a church member, was a lifetime friend of the Mormons. His first exposure to them was in Philadelphia in 1846 at a church conference conducted by Jesse C. Little, who was in the East, on the way to Washington to seek governmental assistance for the emigration from Nauvoo. Little made a favorable impression upon Kane, who became friendly to their cause. Kane later had a distinguished military career as a Union officer in the Civil War, in the course of which he achieved the rank of general.

3. Robert B. Cleland and Juanita Brooks, eds., *A Mormon Chronicle: The Diaries of John D. Lee, 1848-1876,* vol. 1, pp. 5-8.

4. *Deseret Evening News,* 17 March 1892, cited in *CHC,* vol. 3, p. 291.

5. Diary of Oliver Huntington, p. 31, cited in Arrington, *American Moses,* p. 161.

6. Autobiography of Priddy Meeks, manuscript in the Library of the Utah State Historical Society.

7. *Millennial Star,* vol. 10, p. 370.

8. *Millennial Star,* vol. 11, p. 228.

9. Clayton, *Journal,* pp. 327-30.

5

Gold Rush

This was a miraculous providence.

"We do not intend to have any trade or commerce with the Gentile world," said Brigham, addressing the brethren on his first full day in the valley of the Great Salt Lake—25 July 1847. Six months later, on 24 January 1848, John Marshall found gold in the American River, at a site about 25 miles northeast of the present center of downtown Sacramento, California. The exact date of that momentous find is determined by an entry in the diary of a Mormon, Henry W. Bigler.[1] This find would later turn Salt Lake City into something of a halfway house for hordes of forty-niners, and there would be commerce aplenty with sizable numbers of westbound Gentiles. Indeed, the proceeds of this commerce would contribute mightily to financing the Mormon emigrations of the 1850s.[2]

Our examination of the interaction between the Salt Lake Mormons and the outside world, particularly the forty-niners, begins with an introduction to John Augustus Sutter, born Johann August Suter in Baden of Swiss parents. He came to the United States in 1834, became a trader in the Oregon country, and eventually settled in the Sacramento valley, where he became highly successful. He established a thriving colony, New Helvetia, on land he owned from a Mexican land grant. Here he also built a fort, and soon Sutter's Fort became the designation for the settlement. In 1848 he was engaged with a partner, John W. Marshall, in building a saw mill on the American River. Marshall and twelve others were building the mill, and at least six of these—possibly as many as nine, accounts vary—were discharged members of the Mormon Battalion. Following instructions from the Twelve, they were working while they waited for spring to make their way over the Sierras to Zion. One of these was Henry Bigler, and this is his entry for 24 January 1848: "This day some kind of metal was found in the tail race that looks like gold." What appears to be a later addition— in the same hand—follows, giving credit where it was due: "First discovered by John Marshall, the boss of the mill."[3]

The next entry is for 30 January: "Our metal has been tried and proves to be gold. It is thought to be rich. We have picked up more than a hundred dollars worth this week."

A considerable effort was made to keep the discovery quiet, but inevitably the news did spread—slowly at first, but then all at once. Here we meet again the zealous Californian Mormon, Sam Brannan, leader of the east coast Mormons to Yerba Buena, who had tried to convince Brigham that he should move the church there. Brannan ran a store at Sutter's Fort, not far from the mill, and he visited the site of the discovery and collected a small quantity of the yellow metal. It was Brannan who let the cat out of the bag. After first informing his Mormon brethren, he then appeared, in May, in San Francisco, waving his hat with one hand. In the other he held a bottle containing a quantity of yellow powder. Through the streets he paraded, shouting "Gold! Gold! Gold from the American River!" According to contemporary accounts—possibly somewhat exaggerated—the city was deserted within a week.

The news traveled swiftly to the East, where the reports were at first greeted with disbelief. "Many believed it to be some cunning device of interested persons to decoy thither immigrants and thereby stimulate the growth of that sparsely populated territory."[4] The first accounts were supported by later ones and eventually substantiated by official governmental reports, and by the beginning of 1849 ships were being outfitted in Atlantic ports to carry the forty-niners westward. The California gold rush was on. Brigham's initial wish for zero traffic and commerce with the Gentiles had already been violated—as, for example, in the establishment on the Oregon-California-Mormon Trail of profitable ferry service for other overlanders headed west—and now the gold rush escalated that commerce as prospectors, merchants, adventurers, camp followers, and other opportunists scrambled to the gold fields. Salt Lake City stood squarely on one of their paths, and the Mormons put that invasion to good use. (The other routes were by ship via Cape Horn; by ship to Panama, across the isthmus by boat and pack train, and again by ship to California; and, by land, by the California Trail via Fort Hall, bypassing Salt Lake City.)

Did Brigham and his followers want the gold-seekers to travel through Zion? Well, there were a lot of Saints in the area by then, and there were differences of opinion. Many saw opportunity for profit here, and Brigham himself must have been of two minds about it. Certainly he issued many public statements suggesting to the forty-niners that it would be best if they did not pass through Salt Lake City. By way of contrast, consider the experience of Kimball Webster, a member of a company of 29 men from New Hampshire and Massachusetts, who started west in April 1849 to look for gold. Though they had a guide of sorts, they became lost in the mountains north of Salt Lake City and after wandering for some days they came down into the Bear River valley. "We saw an old Mormon here who tried hard to induce us to go by way of Salt Lake City. He said it would be no further than to follow the California trail, and offered us his services as a pilot."[5] A trader told the New Englanders that the Mormon was lying, and they continued toward Fort Hall.

But whether Brigham or the community in general wanted the gold-seekers to pass through Salt Lake City, pass through they did, by the thousands. And thus they played a very large part in bringing needed supplies from long distances, in bringing an almost miraculous salvation to Zion in a time of great need. Arrington goes so far as to suggest that without the gold rush the Mormons might have had to abandon, or at least postpone, the establishment of their city in the Great Basin. He uses, with significance, "The Harvest of '49" as the title of a chapter on the gold rush.[6]

Consider the plight of Zion before the influx of forty-niners. Here we shall examine what Benjamin Brown had to say about it. Brown had been the bishop of two of the 22 wards at Winter Quarters. He had arrived in the valley in September 1847, and was made a bishop of one of the Salt Lake City wards. He sets forth the condition of the Saints in early 1849:

> There we were, completely shut out from the world, with scarcely any knowledge of its proceedings, and it equally ignorant of ours. Our boots, shoes, hats, coats, vests, and material to make them of, were either fast going or altogether gone through wear. Our picks, shovels, spades, and other farming implements were also getting used up, broken, or destroyed.

> Our wagons were becoming scarce, many had been broken in the canyons, and we had no timber suitable for making more, and if there had been, from where were we to get the iron work necessary for making them, or for making ploughs, shovels, etc., for cultivating the ground, without which, of course, food would cease, and starvation ensue. . . . Things looked alarming, and just calculated to dry up our hopes, and fill us with fears.[7]

During this somber time, notes Brown, Heber Kimball prophesied that in a short time the Saints would be able to buy clothes and utensils cheaper in the valley than back in the States. And then came the gold-seekers, accompanied by companies formed to supply the gold fields with food, clothing, and implements with which to pursue their quest. They brought, Brown reported, clothing of every kind, spades, picks, shovels, chests of carpenters' tools, tea, coffee, sugar, flour, and fruits. "In fact, these persons procured just the things they would have done, had they been forming companies purposely for relieving the Saints, and had they determined to do it as handsomely as unlimited wealth would allow."[8]

Why were these entrepreneurs willing to trade their goods to the Mormons at reasonable prices? Because they had a problem; they had heard as they approached the valley that many ships were taking the same kinds of merchandise to California, and they feared the market would be glutted by the time they got there—that the expense of transporting their goods to the presumptive market would not be covered by what they could get for them. What the entrepreneurs lost, the Mormons gained.

We have noted Arrington's "Harvest of '49" chapter title. Unruh entitles a corresponding chapter "The Mormon 'Halfway House,' " and uses as an epigraph, "It cost nothing to get in, but a great deal to get out."[9] We shall shortly take a look at the halfway house in operation, but first another question needs to be considered.

Here were thousands of gold-seekers passing through the Mormons' major city (and through many smaller settlements to the south), seeking their fortunes in California, hoping to acquire vast wealth. Most of them didn't, of course—though some did—but the question that naturally arises is, Why didn't the Mormons—a number of them, at least—join them? Why didn't the Mormons who were there at the moment of discovery of gold make more of their opportunity? Many Mormons, mostly discharged members of the Battalion, were working in the vicinity of Sutter's Mill in January 1848. Had they put their minds to it they could have established early claims, encouraged their brethren in Zion to join them, gotten in on the ground floor, and presumably brought rich reward to themselves, their church, their kingdom.

No doubt the principal reason for the relative nonparticipation of the Mormons was Brigham Young's wish that they not join the rush. He wouldn't keep anyone from going to look for gold—they could go and be damned, he said. As for himself, he would stay where he was and build up the kingdom. Further, he thought, those staying in the valley would be better off financially, as well as spiritually, than those who went looking for gold.

"I will . . . pick out twenty-five of our inhabitants as they average," he said, "and another man may take fifty of the gold diggers . . . and they cannot buy out the twenty-five men who tarried at home . . . and again, look at the widows that have been made, and see the bones that lie bleaching and scattered over the prairies."[10]

Further, it seems to me that, by and large, the Mormons simply didn't want to go to California to look for gold. Their history to now has shown clearly that they were a socially cohesive community, and they wanted so to continue, they wanted to be together. Though settlements were rising in all directions from Salt Lake, they were all together in Deseret, the Great Basin Kingdom, and they wanted—again, by and large—to stay there.

The beginning of the influx of the forty-niners, who did indeed want to go to California to look for gold, was well noted and recorded by the Mormons living in the city. On 8 July 1849 Parley Pratt wrote to his brother Orson:

> The present travel through this place, or near it, will, it is thought, amount to some thirty or forty thousand persons. All will centre here another year, as much of it does this year. This employs blacksmiths, pack-saddlers, washing, board, etc., and opens a large trade in provisions, cattle, mules, horses, etc. Scores or hundreds of people now arrive here daily, and all stop to rest and re-fit.[11]

The influx was also noted in the diary of John D. Lee:

> After about the first of July, 1849, the emigration for California or gold regions commenced rushing into the valley, bringing in with them groceries, clothing, and provisions in great abundance, much of which were sold and exchanged to the Saints for butter, cheese, milk, garden vegetables, etc., at a very low rate. Wagons that was rating from 50 to 125 dollars before the emigration commenced rolling in, were sold and traded during the summer and fall of 1849 from 15 to 25 dollars.[12]

Lee goes on to tell of the eagerness with which the gold-seekers who hadn't already abandoned their wagons (many had done so, back on the trail, back toward South Pass) did so now, in order to obtain pack animals, with which they hoped to increase the speed of their passage westward. Such were the tales reaching Salt Lake City of property abandoned along the trail that in mid-July Lee and his wife, Rachel, together with George W. Pitkin, set off eastward on a salvage expedition. Prepared to bring back a heavy load, they headed for the Sweetwater with five yoke of oxen, two horses, and a wagon. After traveling about 60 miles they met a group of Mormons who had been sent to South Pass to check on rumors of a gold strike *there* (false rumor, no gold), and were given the impression that not much of value would be found along the trail. This discouraged Pitkin, who turned back.[13]

Lee wasn't willing to quit without giving it a fair trial, and he and Rachel continued eastward—and were glad they had. They found the trail lined with discarded material and with the stench of decomposing animal carcasses. "Destruction of property along the road was beyond description, consisting of wagons, harness, tools of every description, provisions, clothings, stoves, cooking vessels, powder, lead, and almost everything, etc., that could be mentioned."[14]

Lee and his wife continued to travel east along the trail, filling their wagon with abandoned property that would command good prices in Salt Lake City. He mentions, for example, finding an excellent Premium No. 3 stove that would be worth 50 dollars in the valley. And they met people along the way, lots of people headed west, many of them in trouble. They were, he recorded, hailed by overlanders almost every 15 minutes. Their wagon would be surrounded by eager, desperate questioners. "Is there any feed by the way? What will be the chance to get fresh animals, provisions, vegetables, butter, cheese, etc., and could we winter in the valley. Do pray tell us all you can that will benefit us, for we are in great distress."

These encounters caused Lee to muse that the love of money was indeed the root of all evil, for that was what had caused thousands to leave their pleasant homes and comfortable firesides and thus plunge into unnecessary suffering and distress. Lee and Rachel arrived back home on 17 August, having been on their expedition a full month.

We have seen, then, through the eyes and words of John D. Lee a sample of the forty-niners. What was their reception when they got to the valley? How were they treated? What kinds of relationships developed between the Saints and the gold-seekers? All kinds of relationships developed, and we have many reports of many different kinds. The impression I get from contemporary accounts is that the visitors were treated as they deserved to be treated. Many complained loudly, and many others wrote of their treatment in glowing terms. Some of the "golden pilgrims" stayed in Salt Lake City only for a night, while some tarried for more than a month. Some, indeed, became "Winter Mormons," and stayed until spring before going on. And some of these married into the community and remained.

It must be noted here that some of the forty-niners passing through were from Missouri and Illinois, and the attitude of many of them toward the Mormons was still as it had been in Missouri. They treated the Saints with disrespect, paid scant attention to local laws, made hostile remarks, and trespassed—and were treated accordingly. Those who came to town without a chip on their shoulder were treated with hospitality. At the same time it must be pointed out that the Mormons were particularly interested in identifying specific Illinoisans and Missourians who had been active in their persecution, for they intended to deal with them harshly if they came through Salt Lake City. This became known, and many overlanders from those two states traveled via Fort Hall and the California Trail, thus avoiding passage through the city.

By contrast, many friendly gold-seekers boarded with Mormon families during their stay, and were delighted to obtain excellent meals for, say, 50 cents. One such sojourner, Ansel McCall, who passed through in 1849 wrote:

Our hostess, with dispatch, set before us a sumptuous meal of new potatoes, green peas, bread and butter, with rich, sweet milk. It is needless to say that the hungry wayfarers, who for months had not seen these

> delicacies, did ample justice to this bountiful repast. The memory of this feast will live with me forever.[15]

Apart from those from Illinois and Missouri, wherever Gentile and Mormon got together there was frequently conflict. Friction developed along the trails on the way to Salt Lake City, as did disputes between Gentiles. A legal system had to be developed for seeing justice done. In 1849 the State of Deseret, part of which would later become the State of Utah, was not yet a territory; that would not come until 1850. (It would not become a state—the 45th—until 1896.) In Deseret the church and state were virtually inseparable, so we must be curious about the nature of justice dispensed in the city. Here, then, is a case that arose when one thieving Mormon, William Bird, stole a pair of boots from a Gentile passing through. Hosea Stout's account demonstrates that Bird was not treated with favoritism. He was found to be guilty, was required to return the boots, to pay the owner four times their value, to pay the costs of the court, *and* he was fined 40 dollars "to be applied on the roads."[16]

Many emigrants, particularly "Winter Mormons," complained bitterly of their treatment, and declared they had been exploited. These reports were given wide circulation on the Pacific coast. One of the most hostile accounts was published by Nelson Slater in 1851. The title indicates the nature of the contents: *Fruits of Mormonism; or a Fair and Candid Statement of Facts Illustrative of Mormon Principles, Mormon Policy, and Mormon Character, by More than Forty Eyewitnesses.*

Typical of emigrant complaints was one of harassment by local ordinances and regulations. In early 1851 an antiswearing statute was put into effect, and any Gentile heard to say "God damn" was promptly whisked off to court and fined. And there were accusations of breach of contract. A Winter Mormon would be promised a certain remuneration for work performed during the winter, but when it was time to settle accounts he might be paid in overvalued produce instead of cash or in considerably less cash than he had been promised. According to Slater's account, one of the Twelve, Ezra Benson, was particularly guilty of this practice, and Slater's treatise warned emigrants to have absolutely nothing to do with Benson. The Winter Mormons were also subjected to a property tax which they found vexing, to say the least. In short, the general impression was spread, by numerous hostile reports, that the Saints were cordial and friendly with the gold-seekers until it was too late in the season for them to continue. Then they did their best to see that when they did leave they took as little cash as possible from the valley.[17]

All of the Winter Mormons did not view their stay in Salt Lake City in that light. J. W. Gunnison, for one, gives quite a different impression. He spent the winter of 1849–50 in the city, having arrived there as a member of an exploring team led by Captain Howard Stansbury, a topographical engineer ordered to survey the valley of the Great Salt Lake in preparation for the eventual construction of a transcontinental railroad. Brigham did not welcome this intrusion, suspecting hidden purposes inimical to Zion, but Stansbury disabused him, and the topological engineers were made welcome. The Saints had been planning such a survey themselves, but hadn't been able to afford to mount the project yet.

Gunnison was a lieutenant in the Topographical Engineers, and wrote of his impressions of the valley, the city, and the Mormons. With particular respect to the gold-seekers, he noted that the great majority of emigrant parties broke into fragments as they crossed the plains and arrived in Salt Lake City to settle their differences.

> Many of these litigants applied to the courts of Deseret for redress of grievances, and there was every appearance of impartiality and strict justice done to all parties. Of course, there would be dissatisfaction when the right was declared to belong to one side alone; and the losers circulated letters far and near, of the oppression of the Mormons.[18]

It is a very even-handed view that Gunnison presents. In contrast to reports of exploitation and price gouging, Gunnison wrote:

> . . . Provisions were sold at very reasonable prices, and their many deeds of charity to the sick and broken-down gold-seekers, all speak loudly in their favor, and must eventually redound to their praise. Such kindness and apparently brotherly good-will among themselves, had its effect in converting more than one to their faith, and the proselytes deserted the search for golden ore, supposing they found there pearls of greater price.[19]

Bancroft, prolific historian of the west, considered Gunnison's book to be one of "the most valuable and impartial works yet published [about Mormonism] by a Gentile writer," and that seems a fair judgment.[20] Gunnison himself said that his purpose in writing was "to dispel, by the light of knowledge, the mists of prejudice on one side, of fanaticism on the other."[21]

We must consider now a particularly curious phenomenon of the relationship between the Mormons and the discovery of gold in California, and of Brigham Young's ambivalence about the situation in which he found his kingdom. He had made many, many statements discouraging his followers from participating in the hunt for the precious metal. "Go and be damned," he had said on one occasion. (Those already working there, mostly members of the Battalion, could remain, at least until spring; their tithings would be welcome.) But in the fall of 1849 Brigham organized a covert operation wherein two groups of young Mormons were sent to the gold fields on behalf of certain church officials, including John Smith, the Patriarch.

Most of those sent were Battalion members who had already been there, including Henry Bigler. The arrangement was that the Patriarch would provide Bigler with what he needed to get to the gold fields, where he would go to work. The eventual profit, after all expenses were paid, would be divided evenly between the two.

I earlier expressed my view that, by and large, the Mormons didn't want to go off looking for gold; they wanted to stay in the Great Basin with their own kind, building up their cities, settlements, and farms, living in a cohesive group relatively free from controversy. Bigler was by no means pleased to receive this summons to go prospecting again. His journal entry for 7 October 1849 states that President Young had told the Patriarch that (in effect) his condition was such that he should fit out someone to go look for gold on his behalf, that he might be comfortable in his old age. "After I had consented to go I could not help feeling sorrowful and a reluctance to go for I feel attached to this place and to this people for they are my brethren and dear friends and it was with some struggle with my feelings that I consented to go."[22]

Another chosen to go on the secret gold mission was George Q. Cannon, who would later be First Counselor to the First Presidency. He was no more pleased than was Bigler by this assignment. He wrote, 20 years later: "There was no place I would rather not have been at the time than in California. I heartily despised the work of digging gold. . . . There is no occupation I would not rather follow than hunting and digging for gold."[23]

Nor were the emigrants free of the Mormons when they left Salt Lake City heading southward. It had never been Brigham's intent that the kingdom be limited to the valley of the Great Salt lake. As soon as possible he directed the establishment of small settlements in all directions from home base. In 1849 he envisioned "Mormon country" as comprising about one-sixth of the area of the United States and the Territories. It extended southwest to San Bernardino in California, north to Fort Lemhi in Idaho, northeast to Fort Bridger in Wyoming, and southeast to Moab, Utah. When the Utah Territory was established in 1850 it contained 187,928 square miles. The maximum east-west span was 720 miles, the corresponding north-south distance was 347 miles. Different parts of this region later became parts of different states, and the area of the State of Utah was finally, after several reductions, fixed at 84,916 square miles.[24]

Notes

1. Creer, *Founding of Empire,* p. 264ff.
2. Arrington, *Great Basin Kingdom,* p. 64.
3. A facsimile of this page of Bigler's journal is in *CHC,* vol. 3, p. 362.
4. Webster, *The Gold Seekers,* p. 17.
5. Ibid., pp. 71–72.
6. Arrington, chap. 3.
7. Benjamin, Brown, *Testimonies for the Truth,* pp. 27–28. This is a rare publication. The Huntington Library has a copy, and the writer is grateful to that library for providing a photocopy.
8. Ibid., p. 28.
9. Unruh, *The Plains Across,* chap. 9. The epigraph is from an entry on 25 July 1852 in Barry, ed., *Overland to the Gold Fields of California,* p. 277.
10. *Journal History of the Church,* 6 September 1850, cited in Arrington, pp. 65–66.
11. Tullidge, *History of Salt Lake City,* p. 67.
12. Cleland and Brooks, eds., *A Mormon Chronicle,* p. 110.
13. Pitkin had earlier become a part of the documentary history of the Church. In 1843 the State of Missouri made a strenuous effort to extradite Joseph Smith from Illinois to try him for treason. Legal battles followed. Pitkin was one of a number of Mormons, including Brigham Young and Hyrum Smith, who testified in the Municipal Court of Nauvoo, regarding the persecution of the Mormons by Missourians. The attempt to drag Joseph back to Missouri failed. See *HC,* vol. 3, pp. 403–66.
14. Cleland and Brooks, p. 111.

15. McCall, *The Great California Trail*, p. 55. This glowing description is cited in Unruh, p. 311.

16. Brooks, ed., *On the Mormon Frontier*, vol. 2, p. 354.

17. See Unruh, pp. 325–27.

18. Gunnison, *The Mormons, or Latter-day Saints in the Valley of the Great Salt Lake*, pp. 64–67.

19. Ibid., p. 65.

20. Bancroft, *History of Utah*, p. 463 ff. Gunnison in 1853, by then promoted to captain, was again sent to the Great Basin to survey a possible southern route. He and most of his party were massacred by Piute Indians, while camping on the Sevier River.

21. Gunnison, p. v.

22. Bigler, *Journal, Book A,* cited in Arrington, p. 73.

23. Cannon, "After Twenty Years," in *Juvenile Instructor,* vol. 4 (1869), pp. 13–14. I was led to this source by a citation in Campbell, *A History of the Church,* p. 149.

24. These data are from the *Encyclopaedia Britannica,* 8th edition (1860), vol. 21, p. 498, and the *New York Times Encyclopedic Almanac,* 1970, p. 293.

6

The State of Deseret

We the people . . . do ordain and establish a free and independent government, by the name of the State of Deseret.

A small band of Mormons came to the valley of the Great Salt Lake in 1847 to found the Kingdom of God on earth. The first contingent numbered fewer than 200. A small company by most measures, and minuscule when measured against the territory they proposed to make their own. Some of this group returned to Winter Quarters to spend the winter there, preparing to lead a larger migration in the spring. Those remaining in the Great Basin were joined by a few others; these were the first Mormons to winter in the valley—a tiny colony in a vast space. Yet even such a small group must be governed; there must be rules, regulations, laws, standards of conduct in the mini-state. There was no commerce with Gentiles here; the Mormons were a cohesive group on their own, living alone in the wilderness except for the Indians and, in a sense, the latter didn't count. So the first government was essentially a theocracy—or, as some called it, a theodemocracy.

Brigham Young took the first step in establishing a government in the Great Basin when, speaking for the Twelve before returning to Winter Quarters, he addressed the brethren to the effect that their affairs should be presided over by a president. He suggested that this authority should be John Smith, if he arrived in the valley before winter. As the uncle of the slain Joseph, John commanded great respect. He would later be formally sustained as Patriarch of the church.

As it happened, on the way back to Winter Quarters, near South Pass, Brigham and his party met a group that included John Smith. Eight apostles being present, a formal meeting was held, during which were nominated a president, a High Council, and a marshal. Three days later Brigham incorporated these nominations in an epistle that they sent to the brethren in the Valley. They put forth John Smith for president, said that he should appoint two counselors, and they suggested Charles Rich and John Young for those positions. And they nominated twelve men for the High Council.[1]

To the extent that government and church could be differentiated, the High Council was to be the governmental authority. They would formulate and pass such laws and ordinances as were found to be necessary for the peace and prosperity of the community. The Twelve hoped that few of these would be required, since the brethren knew what was right and what was wrong. After John Smith had arrived in the new settlement a church conference was held, on 3 October 1847, and the recommendations of the Twelve were sustained. An officer of the law would be needed for enforcement, and John Van Cott was nominated and sustained as marshal. Until the return of Brigham, the High Council would be the governing authority in the settlement.

Two apostles, John Taylor and Parley Pratt, were spending the winter in Salt Lake and, in actual practice, they took the lead and ran things. They were, nonetheless, subject to the authority of the High Council. Thus there was a shadowy definition between church and state, but essentially they were one. "Pragmatically, the needs of the community, spiritual or political, were met without conscious concern for the principle of separation of church and state."[2] It was, as Dale Morgan put it, "a spontaneous government immediately responsive to popular needs, and accreting such laws and functions as the public good required."[3]

The Twelve may have hoped that few laws and ordinances would be required to maintain order in the new community, but it shortly became all too apparent that this was not the case. A committee was formed to put the regulations into written law, and laws were drawn up as the need arose. And, since the Kingdom of God contained within it a number of members who now and then committed ungodly acts, that need did arise—and frequently. Most of the first regulations were prohibitory of such acts; they related to disorderly conduct, disturbance of the peace, stealing, housebreaking, malicious destruction, adultery and fornication, drunkenness, and the like. Horses were not to be ridden without leave, cattle were not to be driven from the feeding range. There was no jail in Salt Lake, and punishment was by monetary fines, compulsory work, or public whipping—up to a maximum of 39 lashes on the bare back. Trade with the Indians was regulated, and the selling of firearms to them was prohibited.

When the top of the church hierarchy returned to the valley in September 1848, the First Presidency took over as the highest authority in the settlement, though the High Council did continue to have a hand in running its affairs. Contemporary records do not make it clear what is meant by references to High Council, but John D. Lee's diary entries for the time suggest that legislative affairs just before the Deseret constitution was voted upon were in the hands of the (secret) Council of Fifty, which Lee, in the interests of discretion, usually refers to as the Ytfif. It was, after all, Joseph's original intent in establishing the Council that it be the legislative branch of the kingdom.

It is interesting to note that a goodly share of offenses against the community that the Council had to deal with was related to the behavior of some of the members of the Mormon Battalion. Spirits ran high amongst some of these discharged veterans, as noted by Lee in his diary for 24 February. A group of six "soldier boys" came riding into the community on horseback, one of them holding a woman in the saddle before him, with his arms around her, while another was playing the violin! "This they called Spanish manners, or politeness." Judgment was swift and harsh; it was "voted by the council that they all be cut off from the church and fined twenty-five dollars each and that the marshal collect their fine forthwith."[4]

As the day-by-day events formed the new and growing community, Brigham's gaze probed the far horizons, for it had never been his intention that the kingdom be confined to the valley of the Great Salt Lake, or even to the vastness of the Great Basin; in his vision he saw its extension to the Pacific coast. From the very entrance of the Mormons into the valley Brigham was sending exploring and settling parties in all directions from Salt Lake.

When the Saints first arrived in the valley in 1847, there was no certainty about under whose governmental control they would eventually fall, though there is no question whatever that, from the time their thoughts first turned westward, the assumption was that their future lay with the United States—some anti-Mormon writings to the contrary notwithstanding. Indeed, they had hoisted the Stars and Stripes in the valley while it was still Mexican territory. The Treaty of Guadalupe Hidalgo, which was signed on 2 February 1848 and proclaimed on 3 July the same year, settled the question of who controlled what, and removed all serious doubt as to under whose aegis the Kingdom would eventually fall.

Meanwhile, a provisional government must be established, and on 1 February 1849 a call for a consitutional convention was issued:

> Notice is hereby given to all the citizens of that portion of Upper California lying east of the Sierra Nevada Mountains, that a convention will be held at the Great Salt Lake in said territory, on Monday, the fifth day of March next, for the purpose of taking into consideration the propriety of organizing a territorial or state government.[5]

The convention convened as scheduled, and a committee under the chairmanship of Albert Carrington was named to draft a constitution. They did so, and on 10 March the convention ratified the Constitution of the State of Deseret. The epigraph at the beginning of this chapter is from the preamble thereof. (*Deseret* is a Book of Mormon word signifying honeybee—symbol of industry and frugality.)[6] The statement preceding the one used as epigraph must be attended to: "Therefore, your Committee beg leave to recommend the adoption of the following CONSTITUTION, *until the Congress of the United States shall otherwise provide for the Territory hereinafter named and described, by admitting us into the Union.*" (Emphasis added.)

The intention to become one of the United States is once again made clear—but with a difference: the Mormons were bypassing the traditional and historic path to statehood that had been established by the Ordinance of 1787, also known as the Northwest Ordinance. That traditional procedure was first set forth to take care of the Northwest Territory, the first possession of the United States, comprised of what would later become the states of Ohio, Indiana, Illinois, Michigan, Wisconsin, and part of Minnesota. An area within the territory destined for statehood would be governed by the U.S. Congress, through a governor, a secretary, and three judges. When the population reached 5,000 voting members, the territory would set up its own elective legislature, which would include one nonvoting member of the U.S. House of Representatives. When the population reached 60,000, the territory could apply for admission to the States. In establishing the constitution of their own state the Saints were (for the time being, at any rate) skipping the territorial interim, during which they would have been under the jurisdiction of the U.S. Congress.

What were the dimensions, then, of the new state? Expansive, to say the least. Its boundaries were set forth in the preamble to their new constitution. They began at the intersection of 33° north latitude and 103° west longitude, proceeding thence to the Pacific Coast, following the Gila River and the northern boundary of Mexico. The boundary then followed the coast north until it reached 118° 30′ west longitude, then north along this line to the dividing ridge of the Sierra Nevada mountains. From here the boundary line followed the dividing ridges separating the waters flowing into the Great Basin from those flowing into the Pacific and the Gulf of Mexico; northward into what is now Oregon, generally eastward across the present southern boundary of Idaho, down the Wind River range of the Rockies, and southward following the mountains to the starting point. Thus the proposed State of Deseret was an area about one-sixth that of the entire present-day contiguous 48 states. (See outline map on p. 109.)

This nation, as the Mormons saw it, would begin in independence, and later become a state of the Union, with or without an intervening territorial status. All of these governments, together with all the other governments of the world, would give way to the Kingdom of God when the millennium arrived; after that the entire planet would be ruled by Jesus Christ as king. That the Mormons had had enormous troubles with the United States was no barrier toward their achievement of statehood, since it was (and is) Mormon doctrine that the Constitution of the United States is of divine inspiration. This is the Lord speaking to Joseph Smith in 1833: "Therefore, it is not right that any man should be in bondage one to another. And for this purpose have I established the Constitution of this land, by the hands of wise men whom I raised up unto this very purpose. . . ."[7]

The constitution proposed for the State of Deseret did not differ in any essential way from those of the states already admitted to the union. It is worth mentioning here, however, that it was particularly clear and forthright with respect to freedom of religion. I bring this forth in defense of Brigham Young's reputation regarding his intolerance of creeds other than his own; allegations of his essential bigotry are unfounded. He said more than once that anyone was free to worship as he chose, and must not be denied that freedom. Creeds other than his were *wrong,* of course, but those who wished to follow them would not be impeded by him.

> All men shall have a natural and inalienable right to worship God, according to the dictates of their own consciences; and the General Assembly shall make no law respecting an establishment of Religion, or of prohibiting the free exercise thereof, or disturb any person in his religious worship or sentiments, provided he does not disturb the public peace, nor obstruct others in their religious worship; and all persons . . . shall be equally under the protection of the laws; and no subordination or preference of any one sect or denomination to another, shall be established by law; nor shall any religious test be ever required for any office of trust under this State.[8]

Deseret's constitution was conventional in that the powers of government would be divided into three departments—executive, legislative, and judicial. The General Assembly was analogous to other such bodies, including the United States Congress, with a House and Senate. Other provisions were also generally in line with those of the constitutions of other states.

The first activities of the newly created legislative body were characterized by a certain informality. The constitution called for the first elections to be held on the first day of May following. The slates had, in reality, been fixed before the convention convened, and the first elections were held on 12 March, two days after the ratification. According to Morgan and others who had access, the church archives are silent as to how the members of the first General Assembly and the other officers were chosen, but J. D. Lee's diary appears to leave no doubt that this business was conducted by the Council of Fifty in early March.

The elections of 12 March were held at the "meeting ground" or "the Bowery," the place of religious services being known by both names. The slate included Brigham Young for president, Heber Kimball as chief justice, and Willard Richards as secretary of state. Brigham was, of course, president of the church, and Kimball and Richards were his first and second counselors. The same congruence continued downward into the church leadership, bishops becoming magistrates of their wards, and so on. Thus a relatively simple transformation of sorts had been accomplished; civil raiment had simply been added to the ecclesiastical structure of the church.

One of the first orders of business was to address the United States

Congress by way of petitioning for admission into the national structure. The church leaders had been working for months on a memorial to send to Congress, and a document was finally sent on to Washington in the hands of John M. Bernhisel, who was accompanied by Wilford Woodruff. The petition, or memorial, that they carried had been signed by more than 2,000 petitioners. The text noted that the petitioners had done more than any other equal number of citizens to secure the vast area they inhabited to the government of the United States, and they prayed to be granted a territorial charter, the territory to be known as Deseret.

They stopped in Philadelphia en route to the capital to consult with their non-Mormon friend, supporter, and political adviser, Thomas Kane. Kane suggested that they might be better off with *no* national government than with one of territorial status—unless they could be assured that the territorial officers would be chosen from their own midst. "You do not want corrupt political men from Washington strutting around you, with military epaulettes and dress, who will speculate out of you all they can. They will also control the Indian agency, and Land agency, and will conflict with your calculations in a great measure."[9] The memorial was never presented before Congress, no doubt due in part, at least, to Kane's persuasive comments. Other factors were at work as well, as will be seen shortly.

Bernhisel and Woodruff had set off for Washington from Salt Lake on 3 May. Two months later, on 2 July (coinciding nicely with the beginnings of the influx of gold seekers into the valley), the General Assembly of the State of Deseret met for the first time. Its principal business was to produce a different memorial to the Congress of the United States, again with the burden of seeking assimilation into the national government. The delegate selected to carry it to Washington was Almon W. Babbitt; as matters developed this proved to have been an unfortunate choice. The services of Orson Hyde, then in Kanesville, would also be called upon. On 19 July Brigham wrote to Hyde:

> We have now completed our organization so far as to elect a delegate with whom we expect your cooperation in obtaining our admission as a sovereign and independent state into the union upon an equal footing with the original states. That delegate is Almon W. Babbitt who is somewhat acquainted with many members of Congress especially on the other side

of politics [the Democrats]. This may prove beneficial to our cause, but we principally rely upon you, and consider that the Lord had directed you to pursue that course which is best calculated to give you influence with the present administration, our present object to accomplish.[10]

Babbitt left Salt Lake on his mission to Washington on 27 July 1849. After his departure developments relative to the achievement of statehood continued independently in the valley. Of particular importance was the arrival in Salt Lake, in August, of General John Wilson, on his way to California in his capacity as Indian Agent for that region. (Morgan gives the date as 30 August; Roberts, in *CHC,* gives it as 20 August.) Wilson brought to the Mormons a startling proposal from President Zachary Taylor. Before considering that proposal, it is important to note that all activities relating to admission to the union at this time took place under a darkening cloud of dissension over the issue of slavery.

In 1846, while the Mexican War was still in progress, a bill was passed by the House appropriating two million dollars for President Polk's use in settling accounts with the Mexican government. David Wilmot, congressman from Pennsylvania, added an amendment to the bill stipulating that no territory acquired from Mexico would be open to slavery. This was known as the Wilmot Proviso, and it immediately made a substantial contribution to the already fermenting bitterness between North and South. Though the bill passed the House, the Senate adjourned that year without voting upon it. The same bill, with the appropriation raised to three million, was passed by the House again in 1847. That year the Senate passed a similar bill, but excluded from it the Wilmot amendment. Nevertheless, feelings ran high about the Proviso, and the Mormons, engaged in the process of seeking admission to the Union, gave it considerable thought. They were mostly, though by no means exclusively, from the North and they opposed slavery, but they did not propose to become actively involved in controversy about it.

In the letter to Orson Hyde, already noted, Brigham continued:

In regard to the Wilmot Proviso . . . we wish you distinctly to understand that our desire is to leave that subject to the operations of time. . . . You might safely say that as a people we are averse to slavery, but that we wish not to meddle with this subject, but leave things to take their natural course.[11]

The proposal that General Wilson brought to Brigham was designed to avoid Southern opposition to the admission of new free states to the union. This would be done, in President Taylor's thinking, by admitting the entire California region as one state; this would include everything out west except the Oregon Territory, Texas, and Mexico. The question of free versus slave status would be decided by popular vote. The area was obviously large enough for more than one state, but the population of Deseret was as yet too small for such a division to be practical. The Mormons conferred with Wilson, and added to the original proposal a crucial one of their own: the constitution for the new "state" would really be a constitution for two states—the boundaries of one being those of Deseret, the boundaries of the other to be set by its inhabitants. The name of the state didn't matter much, and would be determined by general agreement. The kicker here, added by the Mormons, was that at the beginning of 1851 the pro tem union of the two areas would be dissolved, and each would become a sovereign state *without further action of the Congress.*

When the proposal reached California, it was received hostilely. The situation there was quite different from that in Deseret. There had been a non-Indian (Mexican, Spanish, American) population there for some time, and the last Mexican governor had been driven out in 1845. The Californians had been making attempts to establish their own government since at least 1846. The most recent such activity in the period under discussion was the establishment of a state legislature, which first met on 15 December 1849. In February 1850 the California governor, Peter H. Burnett, sent a message to this legislature condemning the Wilson proposal. Even without the governor's denunciation, the proposal never had a chance. California was clearly headed toward statehood; the population of the younger Deseret was far short of that traditionally required, and that was that. Under the provisions of the Compromise of 1850, California achieved statehood that same year. Deseret, with its name changed and its area drastically reduced, would have to wait another 46 years.

Our focus now turns to Washington, where the representatives of the church were putting forward the case for Deseret statehood. Bernhisel had proceeded toward Washington in no great haste, and had not held the meeting with Kane in Philadelphia until late November. He arrived in Washington on 30 November, and took up temporary residence at the National Hotel, which he found to be, as he later wrote, the very center of "politics, fashion, and folly."[12]

In the period now under our consideration the State of Deseret was represented by two men, Babbitt and Bernhisel, and their receptions by Washington insiders were altogether different. Almon Babbitt was a disaster. Friend Kane considered him to be both faithless and inadequate. Bernhisel would later wonder how it had been that the people of Deseret had chosen such an "immoral man" as Babbitt to serve as their delegate. Orson Hyde held him in low esteem; though granting that he might be "a good hand to manage a dirty law suit."[13]

Bernhisel's appearance upon the Washington scene was a different story. He carried with him important letters of introduction and lost no time in putting them to use. By his own account he had no difficulty in meeting all of the leading figures in both houses of Congress. One of the most important favorable impressions he made was upon Vice-President Millard Fillmore, who immediately granted him the privilege of the floor of the Senate during his stay in Washington. He was similarly granted access to the "privileged seats" in the House of Representatives.

The constitution of the State of Deseret and its accompanying memorial, or petition, were formally presented to the Senate on 27 December 1849 by no less a personage than Stephen A. Douglas. He asked that Deseret be either admitted to statehood or granted a territorial government, and left the choice to be made by the Senate. The matter was referred to the Committee on Territories.

The smooth flow of events was disturbed four days later when Joseph Smith's brother, William, together with Isaac Sheen, presented their own memorial to Congress. William Smith was no friend of Brigham Young and the Utah church; he was, indeed, spoken of as the renegade brother of the Prophet. The burden of the Smith-Sheen memorial was that Deseret should not be admitted to the union because, before being driven from Nauvoo, the Mormons had sworn eternal hostility to the United States. The publication of this charge created quite a stir in both houses of Congress, but it gave Bernhisel the opportunity to call upon many members of Congress to tell them of the history and beliefs of his church.

Bernhisel was an efficient lobbyist, a good public-relations man. He gathered letters sent back east from California emigrants who had

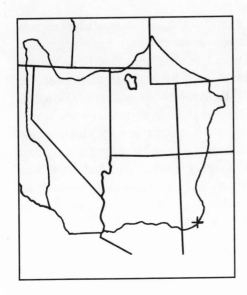

The state of Deseret, 1849-1851. The indicated point is 33° north latitude, 108° west longitude.

passed through the valley and who spoke well of their experiences among the Mormons. He saw to it that many of these letters were published, and to good effect, in the Washington press. And, again, Colonel Kane did what he could to help. On 26 March 1850 he delivered a lecture, "The Mormons," before the Pennsylvania Historical Society. This presentation, revised and reprinted many times, was "a powerful aid to the Mormons in the crucial matter of establishing themselves favorably before the public."[14]

As for Almon Babbitt, the Committee on Elections made its report to the House on its evaluation of his credentials and advised against seating him. He was, they said, a representative of a state, but not of a state of the union, and he should not be seated; doing so would, they argued, attribute legitimacy to the State of Deseret, and they weren't about to do that. The matter did not come to a vote until July, when the House voted 104 to 78 to adopt the report of the Committee on Elections.

Meanwhile, as national agitation over the slavery issue continued, Henry Clay was working on the question as it related to the territories recently acquired from Mexico. Clay, the Great Pacificator, frustrated by failure in his bids for the presidency, had emerged from retirement and, in 1849, had again been elected to the Senate. On 29 January 1850 he presented to the Senate a series of proposals that provided the means to stave off a national crisis, and helped to hold the nation together for a few more years. The major question was whether new states and territories were to be free or slave. Clay's basic suggestion was that California be admitted as a free state, and that New Mexico and Utah be given territorial status, with no mention of freedom or slavery, that choice to be decided by the respective populations. (Congress would have nothing to do with the name *Deseret;* the territory would be called Utah, after one of the Indian tribes therein.) This was the major component of the Compromise of 1850, and it passed both houses of Congress in September 1850. Zachary Taylor had died on 9 July of that year, and Millard Fillmore was now the president. Without delay he signed the various measures included in the Compromise of 1850, and the State of Deseret ceased to exist.

Notes

Far and away the best and most concise single treatment of the establishment of the first formal government of what would eventually become the State of Utah is Dale Morgan's *The State of Deseret.* This little-known work was first published in 1940 in the April, July, and October issues of the *Utah Historical Quarterly,* vol. 8. That publication was under the joint sponsorship of the Utah Historical Society, the city of Salt Lake, and the Utah Project of the Federal Writers' Project. It has recently (1987) been reissued by the Utah State University Press with the Utah Historical Society. Morgan references below are to this volume.

1. Morgan, p. 10. The men were Henry Sherwood, Thomas Grover, Levi Jackman, John Murdock, Daniel Spencer, Stephen Abbott, Ira Eldredge, Edison Whipple, Shadrach Roundy, John Vance, Willard Snow, and Abraham Smoot. A High Council is composed of twelve high priests, presided over by one or three presidents.
2. Melville, "Theory and Practice of Church and State During the Brigham Young Era," p. 43.
3. Morgan, p. 22.
4. Cleland and Brooks, vol. 1, pp. 96-99.
5. Morgan, p. 30.
6. Ether, 2: 3. Book of Mormon: "And they did also carry with them deseret, which, by interpretation, is a honey bee . . ."
7. *Doctrine and Covenants,* 101, pp. 79-80.
8. Morgan, Appendix A, pp. 124-25.
9. Roberts, *CHC,* vol. 3, p. 432.
10. Journal History, 19 July 1849, cited in Morgan, pp. 37-38.
11. Ibid., cited in Morgan, p. 38.
12. Ibid., Bernhisel Letter to the First Presidency, 21 March 1850, cited in Morgan, p. 71.
13. Ibid., Wilford Woodruff's journal entry for 19 July 1851, cited in Morgan, p. 71.
14. Morgan, p. 73.

7

The Territory of Utah

One may well wonder what course the history of the West would have taken had Deseret, like California, been admitted to the Union in 1850.

The death of President Zachary Taylor in July 1850 was, for the Mormons, a serendipitous timing. Taylor had manifested no particular sympathy for the Mormon cause, nor had he been in much of a hurry to settle the state/territorial questions that were then agitating the political air. Because of Taylor's death, when the Compromise of 1850 was passed by the Congress, the president of the United States was Millard Fillmore and he—particularly because of the diplomatic efforts of John Bernhisel—was well-disposed toward the Mormons, as was partly demonstrated by the officers he appointed to govern the new territory.

Before making his appointments, Fillmore conferred with Bernhisel, and asked him to provide written recommendations. In the letter accompanying these recommendations, Bernhisel made a strong plea that the officers of the new territory be chosen from the local community. "The people of Utah cannot but consider it their right, as American citizens, to be governed by men of their own choice . . ."[1] The names he set forth were: for governor, Brigham Young; secretary, Willard Richards; chief justice, Zerubbabel Snow; associate justices, Heber C. Kimball and Newel K. Whitney; U.S. attorney, Seth M. Blair; U.S. marshal, Joseph L. Heywood.

President Fillmore announced his appointments on 20 September. They were not all Mormons, but the most important one was. The Mormons had wished for a territorial government, if they couldn't yet be admitted to statehood, but they wanted the officers to be chosen from their own community. There was a measure of disappointment when news of Fillmore's selections reached the valley the following January. Fillmore's selections were: for governor, Brigham Young;

secretary, Broughton D. Harris of Vermont; chief justice, Joseph Buffington of Pennsylvania; associate justices, Perry C. Brocchus of Alabama and Zerubbabel Snow of Ohio; U.S. attorney, Seth Blair of Utah; U.S. marshal, Joseph L. Heywood of Utah.

Thus we find that of the seven appointees, three were from the local community, four from outside. There were four Mormons, and three Gentiles; Zerubbabel Snow, though an Ohioan, was a member of the church, as were Blair and Heywood. The choice of Brigham for governor was obvious, but a hostile president might have chosen otherwise. Buffington of Pennsylvania refused to serve as chief justice, and was replaced by another Gentile, also a Pennsylvanian, Lemuel H. Brandebury.

In addition to his appointment as governor, Brigham was also designated as the Indian Agent for the territory. Two non-Mormons, Stephen B. Rose and Henry R. Day, were named as Indian subagents.

John Bernhisel, his work in Washington done, left on 4 October. He had been in continuous residence there for more than ten months, and he carried with him the commissions for the appointed officials of the Territory of Utah. Dale Morgan wondered, as he concluded his book on the State of Deseret, what course the history of the West would have taken had Deseret, like California, been admitted to the Union in 1850. We may wonder, as well, what might have been different had President Fillmore given the Mormons what they wanted: a territorial government completely their own.

The Mormons were not overly pleased with the way things had turned out. They had wanted statehood; California got it and they didn't. They thought the population requirement was trivial and irrelevant. (Be it noted that the population of the Territory of Utah very shortly exceeded that of some of the younger states when they had been admitted to the Union.) What they wanted was a government, recognized in Washington, of themselves by themselves. This they had gotten only in part. Gentiles would be coming in to participate in the conduct of their affairs, and the Saints were resentful. Not only had the boundaries of their turf been sharply reduced, but their cherished name, Deseret, had been taken away to be replaced by the name of a tribe of Indians they didn't have much respect for. What they had gotten from Washington was a mixed bag. Let us now observe the comportment of some of these Gentile officials as they addressed their new assignments in a strange and alien environment.

News of Fillmore's appointments reached Salt Lake on 27 January 1851, by way of a copy of the *New York Tribune* for 11 October 1850. On 3 February Brigham was sworn into office as governor by his friend Daniel H. Wells, the chief justice of Deseret. The new chief justice of the territory, Lemuel H. Brandebury, arrived in the Valley on 7 June. The other Gentile officers didn't arrive until July and August—almost a year after the territory had been established. They brought trouble with them.

In early September a church conference was in progress in Salt Lake. The newly arrived associate justice, Judge Perry C. Brocchus, asked for permission to address the gathering. Brigham acceded to the judge's request. Hosea Stout's journal entry for 8 September is brief and to the point: "Conference. Judge Brocchus made a speech in defense of the Government and condemning this people. Prest. B Young replied warmly."[2]

A clear text of the Brocchus speech does not survive, but there is no question but that its thrust was to challenge the practice of polygamy. The point should be made that his challenge—attack, really—was by innuendo only. No direct reference to the institution of plural marriage was made in any account of his address. Brocchus was sufficiently bold, however, as to express the hope that the women in his audience would *become virtuous.* And Brigham's response was warm indeed; he replied with considerable heat both immediately after Brocchus's speech, and in a letter published in the *Deseret News.* Responding to those assembled in the Tabernacle, he said that Brocchus was either profoundly ignorant or willfully wicked. Brigham was indignant that such a corrupt fellow would lecture them on morality and virtue. He would, however, allow no discussion to arise then and there. That might, he said, lead to cutting of throats. He said the performance of Brocchus was an insult, and at that time said no more. He continued, later, in his letter to the paper:

Sir, your hope was of the most damning dye, and your very expression tended to convey the assertion that those ladies you then and there addressed were prostitutes—unvirtuous—to that extent you could only *hope,* but the probability was they were so far gone in wickedness you dare not *believe* they ever could become virtuous. And now, sir, let your good sense, if you have a spark left, answer—could you, had you mustered all the force that hell could lend you—could you have committed a greater indignity

and outrage on the feelings of the most virtuous and sensible assemblage
of ladies that your eyes ever beheld?[3]

Two years later Brigham was still enraged at his former associate
justice and referred to him as a mean ruffian, a poor miserable creature.
Had he, Brigham, crooked his little finger (as a signal) Brocchus would
have been "used up, but I did not bend it. If I had, the sisters alone
felt indignant enough to have chopped him in pieces."[4]

Brocchus's abrasiveness aside, another problem lay in Secretary
Broughton Harris's view that the legislature currently busily working to
run things was unauthorized. Brigham had learned during the previous
November that he was expected to take a census of the territory, in order
that the legislature would be properly proportionate. He had performed
the task to his satisfaction by July, had apportioned the legislature according
to population, and had conducted elections. This he had done without
the seal and signature of the new secretary, Harris, who thought that
these proceedings had not been legal and that therefore the legislature's
expenses should not be paid. He had brought to the territory with him
$24,000 for use in meeting these expenses, but because of what he per-
ceived as grave irregularity he intended to withhold the funds.

Harris had also brought his wife, Sarah, to Zion. Harris's relationships in the Mormon community were not made easier by his wife's
abhorrence of polygamy. She later told of one of her experiences in
Salt Lake, in which she had found herself, unexpectedly, at tea with
no less than six of Heber Kimball's wives. She held her feelings in as
best she could, but when she got home the dam broke: ". . . My pent-
up feelings of disgust, indignation and horror found vent in a severe
attack of hysterics, quite frightening my young husband, who at once
decided not to subject me to such a trying ordeal again."[5]

Harris also thought that Brigham had been sworn into office
prematurely, and that the census had not been properly taken. The
situation was intolerable. He announced his intention to return to the
eastern states, taking with him his seal, his wife, and the cash.

The legislature hastily adopted a resolution instructing U.S. Marshal
Heywood, a Mormon, to take Secretary Harris into custody until he
relinquished the money and documents in his possession. Harris applied
to the justices of the court for an injunction against such procedure; the
court was Gentile by two to one, and the injunction was granted. Secretary

and Mrs. Harris, the two Gentile judges, and one of the Indian subagents, Henry Day, left Salt Lake for the eastern states on 28 September. Harris later delivered the cash to United States officials in St. Louis.

The territorial government was getting off to a rocky start, which didn't keep the legislature from meeting the next day. Among other activities, they authorized the Mormon judge, Zerubbabel Snow, to act in the two judicial districts vacated the day before by the departing Brocchus and Brandebury. Business would continue as usual. This was the Territory of Utah, but the government thereof was essentially that of the State of Deseret.

Though the judiciary of Utah had been diminished by two-thirds, justice was still to be had and could be meted out swiftly, as we may show by noting one case, that of the murder of James Monroe by Howard Egan. While Egan was in California looking for gold, Monroe— a friend of the Egan family—seduced Egan's wife, after which she gave birth to his child. When Egan returned to Utah in September 1851 and discovered what had happened, he sought out his friend and, after a brief conversation, shot him dead. He made no attempt to conceal his crime, and he came to trial on 17 October.

He had acted, he said, in the name of the Lord. Monroe had seduced his wife, ruined his family, and destroyed his peace on earth. Egan was defended by William Phelps and George Albert Smith. The presiding judge was the only U.S. justice remaining in the territory, Zerubbabel Snow. Counsel for the defense argued that it was "mountain common law" that if a man seduced the wife of another, his own life was endangered. He must die, and the wife's nearest relative must kill him. If Egan did kill Monroe this was, they said, in accordance with the established principles of justice known in these mountains. They suggested that if Egan *hadn't* committed the murder, his peers would have considered him as an accessory to the crimes of Monroe!

Judge Snow, in his charge to the jury, delivered the next day, introduced a voice of moderation. "The safety of ourselves individually, and of society, depends on the correct and faithful administration of good and wholesome laws." Referring to Monroe, Snow noted that a man should not be punished "until he has had an opportunity of having a fair and impartial trial, for, peradventure, he may not be guilty as alleged against him." The jury deliberated for fifteen minutes, and delivered a verdict of not guilty.[6]

The reappearance of the "runaway officers" back in the United States aroused a good amount of comment and discussion. Letters were written to the major newspapers, and editorials appeared. The officers made their case in a letter to President Fillmore, published in the *Congressional Globe*. A particularly important letter stating the Mormon position appeared in the *New York Herald*. It was signed by Jedediah Grant, the first mayor of Great Salt Lake City, but it was apparently inspired and written by the Mormons' staunch supporter, Colonel Kane, together with George M. Dallas, who had been vice-president of the United States in Polk's administration and who also viewed the Mormons in a friendly light. This letter, together with two others by the same authors, and including additional material detailing earlier persecution of the Mormons, was published in pamphlet form and widely distributed. Copies were sent to President Fillmore, accompanied by a letter to the president that summed up the case for the Mormons. Their basic statements were three. In terms of some eloquence they claimed the rights of:

> 1. Religious liberty, including the right of individuals to establish and maintain, as well as to bestow ecclesiastical titles upon, a church hierarchy, as far as themselves judge proper. . . .
> 2. Political liberty, admitting the largest possible power of self-government in the community, and the entire independence of its domestic institutions. . . .
> 3. And for all beyond this, we contradict every single statement of the delinquent officers, and by wage of law or battle will equally rejoice to be brought to prove their falsehood. We call for the examination under oath. Of this we put ourselves upon the country. Our last cry is, *trial!*[7]

In the elided text above the writers compared the claims of the Mormons with, respectively, those of (1) the Roman Catholics and (2) the southern states.

The Mormons were not without friends in high places in Washington, and here we may mention, in addition to George Dallas, presumed coauthor of the letters noted above, Senator Stephen A. Douglas and Secretary of State Daniel Webster. The powerful Webster wrote to the runaways demanding that they return forthwith to their duties, or resign. They resigned.

In the meantime, in September 1851, the territorial legislature petitioned President Fillmore to fill the vacancies with people who were resident among them. After the disconcerting experience with his first appointees, Fillmore did nominate Orson Hyde for one of the two judicial vacancies but that nomination was not sustained by the Senate on the grounds that Hyde was not a professionally trained lawyer. Again, then, "foreigners" were dispatched to the valley to govern the Territory. Benjamin G. Ferris accepted appointment as secretary, because, he said, he had long been curious to visit the region. He left after six months, having been there long enough to gather material for a book, *Utah and the Mormons,* which appeared two years after his departure.

The judicial appointees were Lazarus H. Reid, chief justice, and Leonidas Shaver, associate. Judge Reid, after a year in the Territory, returned home on a visit, during which he died, at the age of 40. Judge Shaver remained on the job for three years, until his sudden and untimely death from "a disease in the head."[8] It should be noted that Shaver's appointment demonstrated well enough that the Mormons could get along and function in good spirit with Gentile appointees if those selected were of caliber adequate to the position. George A. Smith said of Judge Shaver that he was "a worthy man and profound jurist, who by his upright course has honored his profession. His studious attention to his duty, his fine intellect, polished education and gentlemanly bearing won for him the universal admiration and respect of this community."[9]

While the business of transforming the State of Deseret into the Territory of Utah was proceeding, albeit awkwardly, what other problems were facing the Mormons? The bounty of the gold rush was over, and the flood of seekers dwindled into a trickle. The situation was, in that sense, settling down. Many problems required solution, but three were of major importance: (1) There were many Saints far from the Great Basin, including a great number in England, who had to be gathered into the valley. Thousands were in need of transport to Utah. (2) The Territory must be made self-sufficient to all possible extent. Dependence on the rest of the nation and the world must be diminished if not done away with altogether. (3) The sparsely occupied territory beyond the boundaries of Great Salt Lake City must be colonized—with Mormons.

The Perpetual Emigrating Fund

At the beginning of the gold rush there were about 6,000 Mormons in the valley of the Great Salt Lake. The majority of American Saints were still living near the Missouri. They had to be "gathered," for that was an important aspect of church doctrine. The Saints must be assembled in Zion to await the last days and the eventual establishment of the Kingdom of Jesus Christ on earth. The gathering was a problem because many of those that had to be gathered were poor, unable to buy wagons, horses, cows, oxen, and the other necessary means of travel and survival. As the influx of gold seekers slowed down in the fall of 1849, Brigham established the Perpetual Emigrating Fund (PEF). A year later, in September 1850, the Perpetual Emigrating Fund Company was formed and formally incorporated. Brigham was the president of this operation and continued to serve in that capacity throughout his life. Other members of the company were high church officials and authorities.

The basic plan was that funds and materials would be given to those who needed them to make the journey. They would be given as a *loan*, not as a gift. Upon reaching the valley the emigrants were expected to repay that loan by whatever means at their disposal. When such repayment was made (it wasn't always), it was usually by various public works for the church, such as working on roads or building the Tabernacle. Contributions to the fund were solicited from those already in the valley, and these were made in considerable volume, mostly in the form of livestock and produce.

As already noted, much of the bounty harvested from the gold-seekers found its way into the PEF, and this was of great help in gathering the Saints from the Missouri into the valley. The skill with which this complex operation was organized and administered commands generous admiration. Bushels of wheat grown in the valley by a resident farmer were turned in to a local tithing office, in exchange for which the Fund would transport his wife and children from the Missouri, from Liverpool, or wherever they lived. Church members in Missouri who had liquid assets were asked to deposit them in exchange for drafts that could be exchanged in the valley for horses, oxen, grain—the things they had to have to start new lives. Missouri funds were held in a bank in St. Louis; monies contributed by European emigrants were held in Liverpool. There were also church offices in New York and New Orleans. Funds were shifted from one location to another according to need. The PEF worked.[10]

By the end of 1852 most of the Missouri Mormons had been gathered into the valley, and it was time to bring those in from England, Scandinavia, and other countries. The largest concentration was in Liverpool. Until 1854 the European converts traveled to Salt Lake primarily via New Orleans, then upriver to Missouri, then across the plains and mountains. After 1854 their point of arrival in the United States was almost always New York.

There were about 30,000 Mormons in Europe in 1852. As already noted, self-sufficiency of the kingdom was of great importance, and preference was given to converts who had the most of what was needed in the valley: carpenters, weavers, machinists, potters, masons, iron-workers, artisans, and craftsmen of all kinds. Initially three plans were established for the European Mormons: (1) Those who could pay their way did so. (2) Those without resources were carried by the PEF. (3) Those in between, who could pay, say, ten pounds to the fund, did that. About 2,400 were brought over in 1853; of these, about a thousand paid their own way, and another thousand were in the ten-pound plan, leaving about 400 to be carried entirely by the PEF.

Usually the Mormon agent in Liverpool chartered an entire ship. When that was not possible it was arranged that the Mormon part of the vessel be partitioned off from the rest. The Mormons soon developed such a reputation that ships' captains were pleased to have them as passengers. For each crossing, the Liverpool agent would choose a president for the voyage, and together they would choose two counselors, thus creating a small analogue of the group that governed the church. The president and his counselors were usually missionaries, returning to the valley after their labors. The ship would be divided into wards, presided over by bishops. Each ward was responsible for taking care of their part of the ship, and discipline was strict. Services were held regularly, as were classes of instruction. Many non-British passengers learned English during the ocean crossing.

The presence of thousands of Mormons in England aroused the curiosity and interest of many Britons, including Charles Dickens and Sir Arthur Conan Doyle. Dickens visited the London docks to witness the boarding of a company of some 800 Mormons on a chartered ship, the *Amazon*. He recorded his impressions in a journalistic essay, "Bound for the Great

Salt Lake." He boarded the ship and found himself surrounded by a great bustle of people moving about in all directions, carrying cabbages, loaves, cheese, butter, milk, beer, tin cans, boxes, bundles, and beds. "But nobody is in an ill-temper, nobody is the worse for drink, nobody swears an oath or uses a coarse word, nobody appears depressed, nobody is weeping," he wrote. A great many of them, he noted, were quietly writing letters. Dickens was much impressed by their general "exemption from hurry."

He spoke to the captain, who informed him that most of the passengers had come aboard the evening before:

> They came from various parts of England in small parties that had never seen one another before. Yet they had not been a couple of hours on board, when they established their own police, made their own regulations, and set their own watches at all the hatchways. Before nine o'clock the ship was as orderly and as quiet as a man-of-war.

Dickens was impressed not just by the discipline, calmness, and order but also by the people. Speaking to the Mormon agent, he said he thought it would be difficult to gather 800 people together anywhere else, and find such beauty, strength, and capacity for work among them. He closed his essay with an admission that he had gone on board prepared to bear testimony against them if the Mormons deserved it, as he believed they would:

> . . . To my great astonishment they did not . . . and my predispositions and tendencies must not affect me as an honest witness. I went over the *Amazon's* side, feeling it impossible to deny that, so far, some remarkable influence had produced a remarkable result, which better known influences have often missed.[11]

As for Arthur Conan Doyle, he vented a considerable anti-Mormon bias in his *A Study in Scarlet,* a melodramatic tale of thwarted romance, kidnapping, and murder in Utah and (to bring Holmes in) London. In a perhaps not entirely irrelevant aside, I mention that although Doyle had apparently conceived an animus against the Mormon movement, in his later years, he was most enthusiastic about spiritualism and medium-istic phenomena. Many thought he made a questionable figure of himself by carrying about photographs of alleged spirits, which he was happy to show to all who would look.

In Search of Self-Sufficiency

When Brigham first entered the valley of the Great Salt Lake he proclaimed his intention to have as little trade and commerce with the Gentile world as possible. The influx of gold seekers in 1849 and, to a diminishing extent, in following years changed that. That the change was to the monetary benefit of the Mormons did not alter Brigham's underlying drive toward economic separatism. And this was not just a matter of economics; church doctrine was involved as well. With respect to clothing, for example, the divine command was to wear what you made yourself. This word had been proclaimed by Joseph Smith, in Kirtland, Ohio, on 9 February 1831; "let all thy garments be plain, and their beauty the beauty of the work of thine own hands."[12]

Further, the non-Mormon world, frequently referred to as "Babylon," could not be depended upon to supply the needs of the Kingdom of Zion, since Babylon was headed toward calamity and destruction—a view supported to no small extent by the growing and acrimonious national discord over the slavery question. So, the means needed for self-sufficiency must be gathered to the valley, together with the Saints themselves. Food, clothing, and shelter were three basic material needs.

It soon became apparent that food could be grown abundantly in the valley. There would be plagues of grasshoppers and crickets, and there would be drought, but crops could be raised. Sugar, however, was a problem. It was expensive to transport it to the valley from the States. In 1852 sugar was selling in Salt Lake for 40 cents a pound, with at least one traveler reporting $1 a pound. If all the sugar consumed in the valley during a year had to be brought in from the outside it would drain the Mormon economy by more than a quarter of a million dollars.[13]

Apostle John Taylor, on a mission, was in France in 1851. Included among his other responsibilities were Brigham's instructions to find ideas and machinery to further the planned industrial buildup in the Great Basin. Among Taylor's many interests in this respect was the manufacture of sugar. Since the days of its founding the church had relied on missionary work for the church's continuing existence and growth. A happy result of this activity was that in France in 1851 Apostle Taylor had immediately on hand a skilled technical assistant in the person of Phillip De La Mare.[14]

Taylor had met De La Mare on the Channel Island of Jersey. De La Mare was of French descent, his ancestors having fled to Jersey to escape religious and political unrest in France. His father was a successful contractor and builder, who had given his son considerable responsibility, and Phillip was technologically knowledgeable. He had been converted some years earlier and was now in Paris on a mission with Taylor. Together they visited a flourishing factory in the historic town of Arras, capital of Pas-de-Calais, about 80 miles north of Paris. The town was noted for the tapestries created there, and it also had a sugar factory that was producing two or three million tons of sugar a year from sugar beets. (France had turned to the manufacture of sugar from beets in consequence of the British blockade during the Napoleonic wars, which cut off the cane sugar supply from the West Indies.) Taylor was enthusiastic, and in August he and De La Mare organized the Deseret Manufacturing Company. De La Mare agreed to put the equivalent of a thousand British pounds into the project.

They bought 1,200 pounds of sugar beet seed in France, and started it on its way back to Salt Lake. They then went to Liverpool to order the necessary machinery and to raise more money to fund the company.[15] Taylor was a successful fundraiser; he found three other converts of substance who put 11,000 British pounds into the enterprise. Thus they began with a capitalization of about $60,000.

The machinery arrived in New Orleans in March 1852, but Deseret Manufacturing was jolted by the first of many unexpected turns of fortune, this one in the form of a customs bill of over $4,000—a heavy charge of 40% ad valorem. The church absorbed this expense, and the heavy load went up the Mississippi, thence to Ft. Leavenworth. Wagons and cattle were needed to transport the machinery, and De La Mare assembled them at considerable cost. He also bought a quantity of flour, which was found not only to be full of worms but also adulterated with plaster of paris. He had to buy more—on credit. The wagons acquired were found to be too small to carry the heavy loads; those not broken were distributed to poor families of Mormons, who had gathered at Ft. Leavenworth to join the "Sugar Train." Deseret Manufacturing then bought, on credit, 40 strong wagons—the famous Santa Fe prairie schooners. The equipment was loaded, and the Sugar Train set off across the plains on 4 July 1852.

Troubles continued as the train crossed the plains; they ran short of food and had to slaughter some of the cattle, and they ran into heavy snow, but, with some assistance sent out from the valley by Taylor, they eventually arrived in Salt Lake in November. The machinery was then taken southward to Provo.

Before building the factory, some exploratory attempts at manufacture showed the entrepreneurs that formidable problems—chemical, mechanical, and financial—had to be solved. The Deseret Manufacturing Company was out of funds and in debt. Brigham now thought that the only organization with sufficient resources to help the company out was the Public Works Department in Salt Lake. Accordingly, the machinery was returned to that city in December and temporarily set up on a corner of Temple Square.

By February 1853 the company was able to produce only a small quantity of inedible molasses, and Taylor and De La Mare were ready to throw in the towel. A valiant attempt to establish a new industry, not only in the Great Basin but also in the United States, had failed. The Public Works Department, under the direction of Orson Hyde, took over the operation. Construction on a factory started in April, on the Church Farm, about four miles south of Temple Square, in the area now known as Sugar House. Problems continued, despite the importation of expert advisors, and the foundation of the factory was not completed until September 1854.

Putting all the machinery together was another problem; parts were apparently not labeled or numbered, and the plans furnished were not sufficiently detailed. When the plant was fired up, in February 1855, it produced some molasses but no sugar. An imported expert, one Mollenhauer, noting the darkness of the beet juice produced, looked for the retorts used to produce animal charcoal with which to purify the product, but found that there were none. (Retorts are cast-iron ovens in which bones are burned to make charcoal.) They had never been ordered in Liverpool; the plans provided in Arras had not included them. Humiliation—and defeat.

But the indominatable De La Mare didn't altogether give up. He and Mollenhauer gathered some bones and burned them to charcoal. They passed black beet juice through the charcoal a few times and produced a fluid "clear as crystal." He had satisfied himself that sugar could be produced from sugar beets in the valley. And so it could, but the first successful factory did not go into operation until the 1890s, in Lehi.[16]

Brigham Young did not take too literally Joseph's 1831 revelation instructing the brethren to make their own clothes, and in 1851 the legislature of the State of Deseret appropriated $2,000 to help establish the manufacture of wool and cotton in the valley. The territorial legislature also appropriated the same amount toward the establishment of a wool factory on the Jordan River. Church officials abroad were under instruction to form a company for the purpose of obtaining machinery and personnel to establish these industries in Salt Lake. Taylor formed such a company in Paris in 1851, but the machinery did not arrive in the valley until 1862. In 1863 a woolen factory was set up on Big Canyon Creek.

These enterprises were not particularly successful, in part because of the difficulty in obtaining, and keeping alive, sufficient numbers of sheep to support a large-scale, wool-producing operation. Wolves were a problem, as were the severe winters. Furthermore, much clothing *was* made at home. Spinning wheels stood in many parlors and quilting bees were frequent.

Clearly, in the 1850s a major difficulty in building up industrial self-sufficiency was the enormous task of transporting the necessary machinery from Europe or the States. The golden spike that marked the completion of the transcontinental railroad would not be driven until 1869. The industrialization of the kingdom would be facilitated if iron could be produced there—and vigorous attempts were made in this direction.

Beginning in 1849 many exploratory and colonizing expeditions were sent off in all directions from Salt Lake. Parley Pratt led one of these expeditions, a large one, into the southern reaches of what is now Utah. Near Parowan this expedition located deposits of both iron ore and coal. In November 1851 Brigham enlisted a cadre of 35 men—the Pioneer Iron Mission—to go there and begin the work of producing iron. Their efforts at first met with reasonable success, and on 28 September 1852, at Cedar City, a short distance south of Parowan, a small quantity of workable iron was produced, from which were made some horseshoe nails and one pair of andirons. As Apostle Taylor had been pressed into work on the sugar project in France and England, so were the church mission presidents in Scandinavia and England, Erastus Snow and Franklin Richards, assigned the task of raising money and buying machinery to further the progress of making iron in the

Great Basin. The Deseret Iron Company was formed in 1852, and Apostles Snow and Richards were instructed to establish an iron works in southern Utah. The company went into operation with enthusiasm, but, as with the sugar enterprise, unforeseen difficulties dogged the project. The distressing chronology may be briefly summarized:

1853: A road was constructed to facilitate hauling coal to the works, and a blast furnace was built. Then news of the "Indian War" reached them, and all iron-producing activity was suspended as the men built fortifications and tried to gather what they would need to get through the winter. Severe flooding in September inundated the works and caused much destruction.

1854: The furnace was fired up but was found to be ineffective. Most of this year was spent building a new one.

1855: The furnace was put into operation and some iron was produced, but the power supply ended when the stream froze.

1856: The blast pipes burned out and had to be replaced. The water power failed again, this time because of drought. A great plague of grasshoppers afflicted most of the territory and kept the men busy trying to gather enough food to get through the winter.

1857: Drought was followed by great flood danger, forcing the men to move the entire works to higher ground. The threat of the Utah War occupied the iron missionaries for most of the year.

1858: They built another furnace, but the lining proved to be defective, and they had little fuel to fire it with. They gave up.

Again, as with the sugar, they had shown that it could be done, that iron could be produced—but not efficiently or consistently, not by a small group of "volunteers," some of whom were working on the project against their will, and had earlier asked Brigham to be released from the program.

Another urgent need of the early settlers was pottery, particularly earthenware crocks for the storage of food, and Brigham had directed the apostles abroad to make a special effort to recruit potters. This was done both in England and Scandinavia, and Mormon convert potters were brought to the valley, particularly from Denmark and from Staffordshire, England. Under church auspices, the Deseret Pottery was established in Salt Lake, and here a group of men from Staffordshire tried to achieve a successful operation, modeled upon English methods, but the enterprise was abandoned in 1853. The major cause of the failure was, apparently, an insufficient supply of wood—quaking asp and balsam—to fire the ware.

Whereas English potteries were generally large-scale operations, Danish potters usually worked in small shops scattered about the country. A group of Danish potters arrived in Salt Lake in 1852. Using simpler methods and sagebrush for fuel, they succeeded, within 18 months, in producing useful hand-thrown ware, but large-scale production of pottery in the valley was not achieved until 1856.[17]

The kingdom also stood in need of paper and lead, but those manufacturing operations were also unsuccessful. The question arises: why? The Mormons were generally industrious, conscientious, and hardworking. Granting that some of the missionaries were unwilling workers, specifically in the case of the iron missionaries, who wanted to be back home with their families, that seems insufficient cause for so many disappointments. It seems to this writer that the drive for industrial self-sufficiency was premature. The kingdom of the Saints, establishing themselves in what was an essentially unpopulated wilderness, was somewhat analogous to a third-world nation of today. As Arrington has suggested, it might have been better had they put less of their resources into the press for immediate industrialization and more into improving their agriculture.[18] They could have improved their irrigation systems and acquired agricultural machinery.

Further, one of the consequences of the intertwining of the church and the industrial enterprises was a paucity of technical expertise. They probably should have called in skilled engineers who had nothing to do with the church and given them a fairly free hand. Taylor and De La Mare, for example, returned to the Great Basin with an incomplete set of plans for setting up a sugar refinery; a knowledgeable consultant would have pointed out that the necessary retorts were not included in the plans.

The Walker Indian War of 1853-54

We have seen that among the obstacles to iron production in the territory was trouble with the Indians. Brigham's policy was, in general, one of pacification and forbearance. It was, as he often said, cheaper to put up with them, treat them kindly, and feed them, than to fight them. But Brigham couldn't always control his followers, nor could Chief Walker his Ute warriors. In mid-June 1853, in Springville, a small settlement south of Provo, a Mormon named Ivey became involved in an Indian family row when he objected to a brave beating his squaw. Ivey struck the Ute with such force that the Indian soon died. The Indians didn't take kindly to this and began a series of assaults upon Mormons.

Though the Ivey incident was the apparent precipitating cause of the war, there was a deeper underlying problem that led to the hostilities, namely, Mormon interference with the Indian custom of selling children, as slaves, to traders from New Mexico and Mexico. Brigham's opposition to slavery, both Indian and African, was strong, and he did what he could to stop the practice. (The Indians didn't necessarily sell their *own* children, though they did do that at times; mostly they stole from other Indians and sold *theirs*.)

Brigham directed that the Mormon settlements be converted into forts by the construction of protective walls. Isolated houses and even a few entire settlements were dismantled and moved by wagon to larger, walled settlements. The construction of protective walls further enraged Chief Walker, who was unpersuaded by Brigham's suggestion that the same walls could be seen as protection against *his* enemies. The series of Indian raids and attacks that followed took at least 12 Mormon lives, and hundreds of cattle were killed or stolen.

The relationship between Brigham and Chief Walker was on and off, with Walker manifesting anger and fear, followed by protestations of friendship. Let us read a letter that Brigham addressed to Walker on 25 July 1853:

> I send you some tobacco for you to smoke in the mountains when you get lonesome. You are a fool for fighting your best friends, for we are the best friends, and the only friends that you have in the world. Everybody else would kill you if they could get a chance. If you get hungry send some friendly Indians down to the settlements and we will give you some beef-cattle and flour. If you are afraid of the tobacco which I send you, you can let some of your prisoners try it first, and then you will know that it is good. When you get good-natured again, I would like to see you. Don't you think you should be ashamed? You know that I have always been your best friend.[19]

The Indians tired of the "war" as winter approached, and in late November of 1853 one of Walker's brothers, Amwon, entered Parowan, in southern Utah, to discuss ending the war. This led to a meeting the following May at which Brigham and Walker, together with other Indian chiefs, reached a peaceful settlement.

Notes

1. Roberts, *CHC,* vol. 3, p. 510.
2. Brooks, ed., *On the Mormon Frontier,* vol. 2, p. 403.
3. Roberts, *CHC,* p. 524.
4. *Journal of Discourses,* 1:86-87, 19 June 1853, cited in Arrington, *American Moses,* p. 227.
5. Furniss, *The Mormon Conflict,* p. 23.
6. Hosea Stout's account of this trial is in Brooks, ed., *On the Mormon Frontier,* vol. 2, pp. 404, 407. The quotations in the text are from the *Deseret News,* 15 Nov. 1851, cited in Roberts, *CHC,* vol. 4, pp. 135-136. The Egan-Monroe case touches upon the doctrine of "blood atonement," and Roberts's reference to this murder is in a footnote to his discussion of blood atonement. (See Glossary.)
7. Roberts, *CHC,* vol. 3, p. 528.
8. So sudden and unexpected was Shaver's death that it was rumored that he had been poisoned. No evidence to that effect was ever adduced. There was testimony at the inquest that Shaver had been a user of opium.
9. *Deseret News,* 18 July 1855, in Roberts, *CHC,* vol. 3, pp. 518-519. At the time of Shaver's death the chief justice of the territory was John F. Kinney. With respect to Judge Shaver's qualifications and ability, see also, in this reference, the remarks of Judge Kinney, at Shaver's funeral. It is important to understand the relationship between Judge Shaver and the Mormons because of the clear statement made about that relationship to the effect that the Mormons could work comfortably and with mutual respect with "outside" appointees who merited that respect.
10. See Arrington, *Great Basin Kingdom,* chap. 4, esp. pp. 97-108.
11. Charles Dickens, "Bound for the Great Salt Lake," chap. 33, pp. 220-32, in Dickens, *The Uncommercial Traveller,* a collection of journalistic articles.
12. *Doctrine and Covenants,* 42:40.
13. This datum is from Arrington, *Great Basin Kingdom,* p. 116. The figure stated is $240,000 per year. In 1852 the population in the valley was about 20,000. At two pounds of sugar per dollar, this represents 480,000 pounds of sugar—or about 24 pounds per person per year. (Sugar consumption in the United States from 1940 to 1974 averaged about 100 pounds per person per year.)
14. De La Mare's name is spelled differently by different historians. Here I follow Roberts.
15. The French manufactured their machinery of cast iron. Taylor went to Liverpool where wrought iron was used, to take advantage of its relative lightness.
16. The problems of sugar manufacture in Utah are discussed in more detail in Roberts, *CHC,* vol. 3, pp. 395-402, and Arrington, *Great Basin Kingdom,* pp. 116-120. My account draws largely upon these two sources.
17. For a detailed account of the early pottery industry in Utah, see Henrichsen's

"Pioneer Pottery of Utah . . . ," pp. 360-95.
18. Arrington, *Great Basin Kingdom,* pp. 129-32.
19. Roberts, *CHC,* vol. 4, p. 49.

8

Zion the Hard Way—1856

Let the saints, therefore, who intend to immigrate the ensuing year, understand that they are expected to walk and draw their luggage across the plains, and that they will be assisted by the fund in no other way.

The Perpetual Emigrating Fund (PEF) was, as we have seen, at the heart of a complex and efficient operation that contributed very greatly to the transport of thousands of Mormons to the Great Basin. Its resources were not, however, unlimited. As early as September 1851 Brigham and his counselors were chiding the "saints scattered throughout the earth" for expecting too much in the way of assistance for the gathering in Zion. If they wished to cross the plains in good wagons and fine carriages, attended by all the comforts of life, they were, wrote the First Presidency, wishing in vain. They noted that some men, worshipping another god—gold—had crossed to the gold fields with nothing but a pack on their back. They painted a marvelously optimistic picture. "Families might start from the Missouri river, with cows, handcarts, wheel-barrows, with little flour, and no unnecessaries, and come to this place quicker, and with less fatigue, than by following the heavy trains, with their cumbrous herds, which they are often obliged to drive miles to feed."[1]

That was in 1851, but no handcart or wheelbarrow trains were organized; emigration continued with wagon trains, and, on the whole, with considerable success through 1855. During that year crisis came to the valley as crops were destroyed by a combination of drought and another plague of grasshoppers. The food supply of those already in Zion was threatened; times were hard, funds were low. Faced with many difficult problems, in September 1855 Brigham wrote an overly optimistic letter to Franklin D. Richards, president of the European mission of the church:

We cannot afford to purchase wagons and teams as in times past. I am consequently thrown back upon my old plan—to make hand-carts, and let the emigration foot it, and draw upon them the necessary supplies, having a cow or two for every ten. They can come just as quick, if not quicker, and much cheaper. . . . A great majority of them walk now, even with the teams which are provided, and have a great deal more care and perplexity than they would have if they came without them.[2]

In marvelously optimistic terms Brigham went on to note that if they walked but 15 miles a day they could make the trip in 70 days. But, he noted, as they got used to it they could walk as many as 30 miles a day, "with all ease, and no danger of giving out, but will continue to get stronger and stronger."

Emigration of Saints from England was unsually heavy in 1856. Eight ships carried 4,326 church members to the United States. The usual procedure was to travel by train from New York or Boston to Iowa City, then the westernmost terminus of the railroad. Here, 1,300 miles from Salt Lake City, the overlanders were initially fitted with provisions and handcarts. They would travel across Iowa to old Winter Quarters, now a settlement called Florence, in the Nebraska Territory. Here they could enjoy some days of rest while the handcarts were checked and repaired before they finally headed for the valley. From here they would strike out on the Mormon Trail toward Salt Lake. Personal possessions, which were primarily bedding, clothing, and utensils, were limited to 17 pounds per person. These possessions were carried on the carts, together with some provisions, principally flour. One cart provided for five emigrants. Teams and wagons were provided to carry provisions and tents. Tents accommodated 18 to 20 people. A few cows were driven along for milk, a few beef cattle for slaughter. Buffalo would be shot en route.

In June 1856 the first three handcart companies departed from Iowa City. These were led by Edmund Ellsworth, Daniel D. McArthur, and Edward Bunker, all Mormon missionaries returning home after their labors. These companies left, respectively, on 9, 11, and 23 June.[3] And, remarkably enough, the companies traveled better than might have been expected. McArthur's group caught up with Ellsworth's on 11 September, and they continued together, arriving at Salt Lake on 26 September. When Brigham heard that the handcart emigrants were near the city, he went out to meet them with a military escort and the Nauvoo Band, playing gayly. The 486 emigrants were cheered and given enthusiastic welcome, homes were found for them, and they became part of the community. They had averaged about 12 miles a day. They could have traveled faster, they said, but for having to wait frequently for the slower oxen. The *Deseret News* reported that the new arrivals, "though somewhat fatigued, stepped out with alacrity to the last, and appeared buoyant and cheerful."[4]

Hosea Stout was impressed:

> Today the handcart company of saints arrived. . . . They were escorted in by Prest. Young and a large concourse of Saints who met them in Emigration Canyon with a treat of melons, fruits, vegetables. They marched in good order and fine spirits and seemed to be happy and in excellent health. They have drawn their carts from Iowa City, a distance of 1300 miles. Thus men, women and children, young and old, have been their own teams and performed this long journey far out-traveling ox trains without incurring the expense for an outfit which would have taken them years of harder labor to procure than thus coming in carts. This is a new and improved method of crossing the plains.[5]

There is indeed an air of optimism in the contemporary accounts of the arrival of the first handcart emigrants, but there is a darker side as well. Although 486 mostly happy Mormons marched down Emigration Canyon at the end of their travel, 497 had started. Here are some diarist's entries:

"June 15th. [Six days out.] Got up about 4 o'clock to make a coffin for my brother John Lee's son named William Lee, aged 12 years . . . and at the same time had to make another coffin for Sister Prattor's child."

"June 26th. Traveled about 1 mile. Very faint from lack of food."

"July 26th. . . . The lightning struck a brother and he fell to rise no more."

These entries are from the diary of Archer Walters, English carpenter, maker of coffins, repairer of handcarts. Walters himself made it to Zion, but died two weeks later.

"August 3rd. . . . I was so weak from thirst and hunger and being exhausted with the pain of the boils that I was obliged to lie down several times, and many others had to do the same. . . . I thought my heart would burst . . . and poor Kate . . . crawling on her hands and knees, and the children crying with hunger and fatigue." This from the diary of Patrick Bermingham.

In the Second Company were two women who walked together, Mary Bathgate and Isabella Park. Both were over 60 years old. On 16 August Mary was bitten just above the ankle by a large rattlesnake. She and Isabella were walking about a half-mile ahead of the main company. Mary had the presence of mind to apply her garter tightly above the wound, impeding the circulation. They sent a little girl back to the main company for help. Captain McArthur, Truman Leonard, and Spencer Crandall went forward with all haste. They enlarged the wound with a pocket knife and squeezed out all the "bad blood" they could. "We then took and anointed her leg and head, and laid our hands on her in the name of Jesus and felt to rebuke the influence of the poison, and she felt full of faith."[6]

Mary, a determined women, then consented to be carried in a wagon but not before asking others to bear witness that she rode only when compelled to do so by the "cursed snake." The company stopped shortly for water, then prepared to move onward. Isabella, hurrying to see how her friend was doing, passed in front of a wagon just as the driver shouted his team onward. She was knocked down and a front wheel of the heavy wagon rolled over her hips. Truman Leonard quickly pulled her away, but not before a rear wheel ran over both her ankles. Amazingly enough, not a bone was broken.

The two ladies continued on, and both were walking as before by the time they reached Salt Lake. As a pleasing afterword, we note that Mary Bathgate later found a husband in the valley.

From the first company seven families—37 men, women, and children—had dropped out along the way, finding the going too hard. Among those in the first two companies to continue, there had been 20 deaths—13 in the first company, 7 in the second. Men, women and children had died. The mortality rate for these two companies was comparable with those of the ox trains. Babies had been born, couples had married. Captain Ellsworth, one month after arrival in Salt Lake married two of the young girls he had shepherded to the valley.[7]

The third handcart company to leave Iowa City in 1856 was, as noted, under the direction of returning missionary Edward Bunker, a man who knew something about walking; in 1846 he had marched from Fort

Leavenworth to San Diego with the Mormon Battalion. This company, composed almost entirely of converts from Wales, left Iowa City in late June. The travel across Iowa was relatively easy. One of the participants, Priscilla Evans put it so: "The weather was fine and the roads were excellent and although . . . we were very tired at night, still we thought it was a glorious way to go to Zion." It became more difficult later. "The flour was self-rising, and we took water and baked a little cake. After the first few weeks of traveling this little cake was all we had to eat . . . I was expecting my first baby and it was very hard to be contented on so little food."[8]

The third company reached Salt Lake on 2 October. The travel had not been easy, although at least one of the participants had described the beginning as glorious, and there had been deaths; the exact number is not known but it was fewer than seven. As historian Roberts later noted, had the handcart operation ended with the arrival of the third company in the valley, handcart travel might have been acceptable, "without very serious objections, beyond a protest against the hardship of excessive toil involved in it." But it didn't end there; two more companies would cross the plains that year.

The first to leave Iowa City was led by James E. Willie, the second by Edward Martin. Willie's company left Iowa City on 15 July. It consisted of 500 Saints, 120 handcarts, 45 beef cattle and cows, 24 oxen, and 5 wagons. Martin's company was larger, including 576 Mormons, 146 handcarts, 50 cows and beef cattle, 30 oxen, and 7 wagons.[9] It left Iowa City on 28 July. The significance of these dates would soon become apparent: it was too late in the year. The two companies left Florence on 16 and 24 August.

As we follow these two bands of hopeful converts, enduring privation and hardship as they travel toward the place of salvation, it is useful to see, briefly, how they were treated by Gentiles along the way. Iowa, by this time, was a relatively settled region, and as the Mormons moved westward they encountered local populations. They met, on the one hand, good-natured jeering, hooting, and badinage—but also, from time to time, threats of violence. Willie's company was greeted at one point by a sheriff's posse armed with a warrant to search the wagons for young women alleged to be tied down in one of them. On the other hand—a happier comment on human nature—the appropriately named Charles Good *gave* Willie fifteen pairs of childrens' boots as the company passed through Des Moines.

Here we have specific instances of how relations were at the time between Mormons and Gentiles. Seen here on a small screen, we see a reflection of a larger picture. The interaction between the Mormons and the Gentiles ranges from hostility and threat of violence, through relative indifference, to a benovelent wish to help a struggling company of overlanders—in short, a cross-section of the way humans in general relate to each other.

Willie's company arrived in Florence on 11 August. This was thought by many to be too late in the summer to start out across the plains. Many converts, not really understanding the nature of the dangers lying ahead, were consumed with zeal and wished to go forward. A large meeting was held at which the alternatives of proceeding westward or going into winter quarters were discussed.

Of Willie's handcart company only four men had been to the valley before; these were Willie himself, Levi Savage, Millen Atwood, and William Woodward. These four were all subcaptains, in charge of groups of about 100 each. Also in Florence were George D. Grant and William H. Kimball, church members of prominence who were overseeing matters. At the meeting to debate the question, all of these men, save one, spoke in favor of going on. Only Levi Savage, a missionary returning from Ceylon and Siam, spoke against that position. He argued vigorously that they should go into winter quarters in Florence. The Willie company contained both small children and aged adults, and Savage predicted suffering and death if they continued the trek now. The day was carried, however, by those who wanted to go on. Savage is reported to have said, "What I have said I know to be true; but seeing you are to go forward, I will go with you; will help you all I can; will work with you, will rest with you, will suffer with you, and if necessary, will die with you. May God in mercy bless and preserve us."[11]

This company left Florence on 18 or 19 August. In the early days of the journey they "moved gaily forward full of hope and faith. At our camp each evening could be heard songs of joy, merry peals of laughter, and bon mots on our condition and prospects. Brother Savage's warning was forgotten in the mirthful ease of the hour."[12] A major problem appeared soon enough as the hastily constructed carts broke down. The carts were made almost entirely of wood; the axles broke easily, and repair took time. The trail was dusty, and grit got into the bearing boxes, increasing wear and adding friction. Since they had no proper lubricant, they improvised with bacon, which they could ill afford to spend that way, and with soap, which was also in short supply.

When the company came to Wood River, near Grand Island, their cattle were stampeded by buffalo. The men rounded them up as best they could, but next morning, when they began yoking the animals to the wagons they discovered that 30 head were missing. They spent three days looking for them, but the missing beasts were not found. Three valuable days were lost. They now had oxen enough to provide only one yoke for each wagon. The wagons were heavily loaded with flour, and the oxen couldn't move them. The men put beef cattle, cows, even heifers to the yoke, but the animals didn't take kindly to this unaccustomed procedure and drew poorly. The wagons had to be lightened, so a sack of flour was loaded onto each handcart, and that didn't help either. They were now only about 170 miles from Florence, 860 miles from Salt Lake.

A few days later, on 12 September, Willie's group, the fourth company, was overtaken by a party that included Franklin D. Richards, George Grant, and William Kimball. Richards was returning to Salt Lake from England, where he had been president of the British Mission. He had arrived in Florence in time to help oversee the departure of the last of the emigrants, including the fifth company of handcarts. It becomes important to remember now that Grant and Kimball had been among those opposing Levi Savage's plea that the handcart companies go into winter quarters and resume the trek in the spring.

Richards and company reached Salt Lake on 4 October and surprised Brigham with the news that two more handcart companies were on the trail. Richards and Daniel Spencer later wrote a formal report, not printed in the *Deseret News* until 22 October. In this document they wrote that although they had found Willie's company considerably weakened by the loss of many of their oxen, they were in good spirits. Describing their crossing to the south bank of the Platte, Richards and Spencer said, "Never was there a more soul-stirring sight than the happy passage of this company over that river. Several of the carts were drawn entirely by women, and every heart was glad and full of hope."[13] Be it noted that Richards and party, traveling in carriages and with light wagons drawn by horses and mules, had been nine days on the trail from Florence; Willie's company had taken about 25 days to travel the same distance. On the evening of the 4th Richards and Brigham conferred with other church officials and discussed the handcart companies. Brigham became acquainted with their general locations and the extent of their supplies.

The next day, Sunday, the semi-annual conference of the church convened, and Brigham lost no time in setting its agenda. A pragmatist, he considered the situation of the handcart companies as nothing less than critical.

> I will now give this people the subject and the text for the Elders who may speak today. . . . It is this. On the 5th day of October, 1856, many of our brethren and sisters are on the plains with handcarts, and probably many are now seven hundred miles from this place, and they must be brought here, we must send assistance to them. The text will be, "to get them here." . . . And the subject matter for this community is to send for them and bring them in before winter sets in.[14]

He called upon the bishops to get to work today, not tomorrow. He wanted good horses and mules, he said, not oxen, and he wanted 40 good young men. He was going to send two tons of flour. The men could rise right now and give their names. The women, the sisters, could fetch blankets, skirts, stockings, shoes, hoods, almost any description of clothing.

Franklin Richards, by contrast, had his head in the clouds. He said that the emigrants out there with their handcarts expected to get cold fingers and toes. "But they have this faith and confidence towards God, that he will overrule the storms that may come in the season thereof, and turn them away, that their path may be freed from suffering more than they can bear. They have confidence to believe that this will be an open fall."

But Brigham's religion called for action. "That is my religion . . . to save the people . . . our brethren that would be apt to perish, or suffer extremely, if we do not send them assistance." Brigham wanted action now, and he got it. The first rescue train left Salt Lake on Tuesday the 7th with 27 young men, 16 teams and wagons. Before the end of the month 250 wagons would be on the road. This first group was led by George D. Grant and included William H. Kimball, both of whom had been in Salt Lake only two days before turning back to help the handcart emigrants. It is reasonable to suppose that they felt some degree of responsibility for the plight of the emigrants, their voices having been raised, in Florence, in support of the companies going on that year rather than waiting for spring.

Willie's company, still far from Salt Lake, was beginning the long ascent to South Pass. Assessing their supplies, it became apparent that their consumption of flour would have to be reduced, and rations were cut to three-quarters a pound per day for adults. And now came a welcome letter from Apostle Richards saying they might expect supplies from the valley to meet them by the time they reached South Pass.[15] They could see that at the present rate of use they would be out of flour before they got to the Pass; the ration was cut even further, to ten ounces per day.

The difficulty of travel along the trail was exacerbated on 19 October when an early, driving snowstorm fell upon the entire area. It caught Willie's company ill prepared to cope with the terrible consequences. They were forced to stop and make camp in the most deplorable conditions. Behind them, the fifth company had just made their last crossing of the Platte, a crossing that had been extremely difficult. Just as it had been completed, the wind and snow blasted into them and they had to make camp. Their plight was made worse by the fact that two days earlier, finding the going very heavy, they had discarded both clothing and bedding to make their loads lighter. They now needed these desperately. And ahead of Willie's camp Grant's relief train was assaulted by the same storm and camped to wait it out—only a few miles short of Willie's destitute company.

On 18 October Captain Willie, all too aware of the danger his company was in, took Joseph Elder with him and continued west searching for the relief train. He found it, camped at Willow Creek, on the 20th. Willie told Grant, Kimball, and the others that his people were freezing, starving, and dying, that they would all be dead if help didn't reach them soon. They broke camp early the next morning and traveled through deep snow with all possible speed, reaching the forlorn company that evening.

> When the people of the camp sighted us approaching, they set up such a shout as to echo through the hills. Arrriving within the confines of this emigrant camp a most thrilling and touching scene was enacted, melting to tears the stoutest hearts. Young maidens and feeble old ladies, threw

off all restraint and freely embraced their deliverers expressing in a flow
of kisses the gratitude which their tongues failed to utter. This was certainly the most timely arrival of a relief party recorded in history for the
salvation of a people.[16]

All possible aid was given—food, clothing, bedding, transportation.
Relief had come in time to save many lives; but many others had perished during recent days. Grant's party now divided into two. Grant
went further back along the trail to find and assist the fifth company,
while Kimball led Willie's company westward. Progress at first was slow,
though Kimball's men, teams, and wagons had improved the situation.
Those who couldn't walk, rode in the wagons. Those who could still
pull carts did so. They reached Fort Bridger, where more help awaited
them, on 4 November. From this point on Willie's people rode the
rest of the way. They reached Salt Lake on 9 November. They had
been on the road three months and three and a half weeks; 67 had
died en route.

Back on the trail an advance company of three men on horseback,
Joseph A. Young (son of Brigham), Daniel Jones, and Abel Garr, had
been sent on ahead of Grant's rescue train to find Martin's company.
They reached them on 28 October, not far from Independence Rock,
and found them in truly terrible shape, provisions almost gone, clothing
almost worn out. Fifty-six had died in the nine days since they had
crossed the Platte. The advance party gave such aid as they could, and
told them of Grant's rescue train just ahead, at Devil's Gate, and urged
them to go forward as best they might. The advance team continued
east to locate the last wagon trains of the season, Hunt's and Hodg-
ett's, which they urged westward. They then rode back to Devil's Gate,
arriving there on the 30th. They told Grant of the condition of the
fifth company, and Grant went out to meet them the next day. Grant
provided the emigrants with flour and clothing, and they all moved
westward, camping at Devil's Gate on 2 November. From here, that
same day, Grant sent a dispatch to Brigham:

It is not of much use for me to attempt to give a description of the situation
of these people . . . but you can imagine between five and six hundred
men, women and children, worn down by drawing hand carts through
snow and mud; fainting by the wayside; falling, chilled by the cold; children
crying, their limbs stiffened by cold, their feet bleeding and some of them

bare to snow and frost. The sight is almost too much for the stoutest
of us . . . I think that not over one-third of Dr. Martin's company is able
to walk.[17]

There wasn't much protection at Devil's Gate; people and cattle
were dying, and it was not known when more help might arrive. On
3 November the handcart company moved forward two and one-half
miles toward a somewhat sheltered bend against the granite mountains.
But it was on the other side of the Sweetwater, down which ice was
floating. Strong men wept. A few crossed the chilling shallow stream,
but most were unable even to attempt it. In the rescue party were three
18-year-old men. They saved the day by carrying across all of the emigrants who couldn't make it on their own, a feat of enormous cour-
age, for which they would later pay a high price.[18]

The shelter in what became known as Martin's Cove was meager.
They had to move forward, but many couldn't walk, let alone pull
a handcart. The last two wagon trains of this disastrous emigration
year had arrived at Devil's Gate, and it was decided to empty the wagons
there, storing their contents over the winter, in the charge of three
volunteers who would remain there until the spring.[19] The wagons would
then be used to carry the fifth company toward Salt Lake. Handcarts
were now left behind, and the fifth company, together with the last
two wagon companies, left Martin's Cove on 9 November—the same
day, as it happened, that the fourth company, 325 miles ahead of them,
arrived in Salt Lake.

More rescue wagons had reached the vicinity of South Pass, where
some of them, convinced that the handcart company had either gone
into winter quarters or had perished, turned back toward Salt Lake.
A Mormon scout of some renown, Ephraim Hanks, refused to turn
back, and here he enters the book of Mormon history as a great hero.
Leaving his wagon behind, he went ahead on horseback, leading a pack
horse. He met a buffalo, killed, skinned, and dressed it, and carried
it forward on his horses. He met the company just as they were camping for the night, very short of provisions. "When they saw me coming
they hailed me with joy inexpressible, and when they further beheld
the supply of fresh meat . . . their gratitude knew no bounds."[20] While
the emigrants cooked and ate the meat, Hanks went through the camp,
bathing hands and feet until the frozen flesh fell off, after which he

used scissors to remove remaining shreds of flesh. He sent an express to the wagons that hadn't turned back from South Pass. They moved down the Sweetwater immediately, and reached the company on 12 November. Other rescue wagons reached them as they continued and, finally, the stricken company reached Salt Lake on Sunday, 30 November.

The exact number of deaths that occurred in Martin's company cannot be determined, but Le Roy R. Hafen and Ann W. Hafen put it between 135 and 150. The fifth company had originally consisted of 576. Pain and suffering had been almost beyond description. Nor did all the pain end when they arrived in the valley. There would be amputations, and there would be more deaths. They were, of course, given all possible comfort upon arrival. It was Sunday, and the Saints were assembled in the Tabernacle. When Brigham heard of the imminent arrival of the emigrants he told his congregation that he didn't want them put into houses by themselves; they were to be taken in among families that had good and comfortable houses. Brigham said: "The afternoon meeting will be omitted, for I wish the sisters to go home and prepare to give those who have just arrived a mouthful of something to eat, and to wash them and nurse them up." Here we see Brigham at his best. "Prayer is good, but when baked potatoes and pudding and milk are needed, prayer will not supply their place. . . . Give every duty its proper time and place. . . . We want you to receive them as your own children, and to have the same feeling for them."[21] And taken in they were, together with a lot of scar tissue.

Many of the Saints safely in the valley had friends and relatives coming in the fourth and fifth Companies. When word of their presence on the trail so late in the year became known in Salt Lake it caused fear, apprehension, anxiety. And there was talk of responsibility, of blame. On 2 November, one week before the arrival of the fourth company, Heber C. Kimball, speaking in the Tabernacle, noted that there was unrest in the community and that blame was being attributed to President Young. He then tried to get Brigham off the hook, noting that if things had gone according to Brigham's general instructions—that is, had they not left unseasonably late—all would have gone well. After all, had not three handcart companies already arrived with less sickness and death than was usually the case with wagon companies? Brigham,

ZION THE HARD WAY—1856   143

who had already addressed the congregation, rose again and leapt with vigor into a sharp defense of himself.

It had never occurred to him, he said, that *he* (together with his counselors) was being blamed for the plight of the emigrants. "There is not a person, who knows anything about the counsel of the First Presidency concerning the immigration, but what knows that we have recommended it to start in season." If blame were to be levied, let it not be on his shoulders. He didn't know, he said, if he would attach blame to Franklin Richards and Daniel Spencer. That said, he lashed out:

> But if, while at the Missouri river, they had received a hint from any person on this earth, or if even a bird had chirped it in the ears of brothers Richards and Spencer, they would have known better than to rush men, women, and children on to the prairie in the autumn months, on the 3rd of September, to travel over a thousand miles. I repeat that if a bird had chirped the inconsistency of such a course in their ears, they would have thought and considered for one moment, and would have stopped those men, women and children there until another year. If any man, or woman, complains of me or of my Counselors, in regard to the lateness of some of this season's immigration, let the curse of God be on them and blast their substance with mildew and destruction, until their names are forgotten from the earth.[22]

No, sir. Brigham Young could not be accused of mismanagement. Didn't gold, silver, houses, and land multiply under his management? Wasn't he the equal of any financier they ever knew? His skirts, he said, were clear of the emigrants' blood.

And it was true that no one in the valley had urged the handcart companies on in late August. But at the meeting in Florence only one voice had been raised against it, that of Levi Savage. With tragic consequences his words had been unheeded.

Five other handcart companies would cross the plains—two in 1857, one in 1859, and two in 1860. They all left Florence in June or July; the latest departure date was 7 July. They all arrived in Salt Lake in August or September; the latest arrival date was that of the last handcart company to reach Salt Lake, 24 September. These crossings were relatively easy. Deaths were few, probably not more than 15 in all five companies. From this time on, transport of emigrants to the valley was by wagon train, drawn by oxen, round trip, from Salt Lake to the

Missouri and back in the same season. The coming of the railroad in 1869 brought the end of the wagon trains. As noted earlier, the descendants of the handcart pioneers share a particular and understandable pride.

Notes

The principal work upon which I have largely drawn in preparing this chapter is *Handcarts to Zion* by Hafen and Hafen. This work covers the handcart operation in great detail, and includes many entries from handcart diarists. All such diaries of participants cited in this chapter are from the Hafens' book. The Hafens also provide complete rosters of each of the handcart companies. It is of some interest to note the dedication of *Handcarts to Zion:*

To Mother
Mary Ann Hafen
Who, as a child of six years,
trailed a Handcart to Utah in 1860

The descendants of the handcart pioneers share, quite understandably, a particular pride.

    1. General Epistle from the Presidency, 22 September 1851. Cited in Roberts, *CHC,* vol. 4, pp. 83–84. Also in *Millennial Star,* vol. 14 (1852), pp. 17–25.
    2. Hafen and Hafen, *Handcarts to Zion,* pp. 29–30.
    3. Roberts gives 23 June as the date upon which the Bunker company left Iowa City. Bunker, in a brief autobiography written later, cited by Hafen and Hafen, gives the date as 28 June.
    4. The *Deseret News* quotation is cited in *CHC,* vol. 4, p. 87.
    5. Brooks, ed., *On the Mormon Frontier,* vol. 2, p. 601.
    6. McArthur's report on the second handcart company; appendix B in Hafen and Hafen, pp. 214–17.
    7. Ellsworth had earlier married two other wives, one of which was Brigham Young's oldest daughter, Elizabeth.
    8. Hafen and Hafen, pp. 82, 85.
    9. The fast-moving company of President Richards, who was returning to Salt Lake from the European mission, overtook these two companies in September, Martin's on the 7th, Willie's on the 12th. According to his later report to Brigham, Willie's company now consisted of 404 persons (down from 500), 87 handcarts (down from 120), 32 cows (down from 45), and only 6 yoke of oxen (down from 12). The figures he reported for Martin's company were essentially the same as those given in the text as the starting figures.
    10. I have found no other reference to the good Charles Good in Mormon history. I, for one, would like to know more about him.
    11. *Chislett's Narrative,* cited in Stenhouse's *Rocky Mountain Saints,* p. 316. John Chislett was another subcaptain of the Willie company, as was Jacob Ahmensen, these two in addition to those named in the text.
    12. Ibid., p. 318.

13. Hafen and Hafen, pp. 218–21.

14. This quote and the two following are from Hafen and Hafen, pp. 120–21.

15. In the early days of the opening of the West, though there was no formal governmental postal service, a lot of mail moved freely in both directions—letters and "expresses." These would be carried as a courtesy to one party from another, a system that had advantages all around. Therefore, it is not surprising that out on the trail, in the middle of nowhere, Willie's party received a letter from Richards.

16. This is from the journal of Harvey H. Cluff, cited in Hafen and Hafen, pp. 232–38. Cluff played another part in Mormon history 12 years later. In 1868, the last year of ox trains across the prairie, Cluff shepherded the last large part of Mormon emigrants to sail the Atlantic; after that travel was by steam packet.

17. Grant's dispatch is cited in full in Hafen and Hafen, Appendix E, pp. 227–29.

18. The three boys who showed so much manhood that day were C. Allen Huntington, George W. Grant, and David P. Kimball. Hafen and Hafen report (p. 133) that "in later years" these three men all died from the effects of their exertion and exposure during this rescue.

19. The man designated to stay the winter with the goods was Daniel W. Jones. He chose as his companions Thomas Alexander and Ben Hampton.

20. Hafen and Hafen, p. 135.

21. Ibid., p. 139.

22. Kimball's and Young's addresses were reported in the *Deseret News* for 12 November 1856, cited in Hafen and Hafen, Appendix H, pp. 293–47.

9

A Plurality of Wives

... If any man espouse a virgin, and desire to espouse another ... and if he espouse the second, and they are virgins, and have vowed to no other man, then he is justified.

The doctrine of plural marriage, or "celestial marriage," though it had been practiced by a select and privileged group of Joseph Smith's friends since about 1840—and by Joseph since 1835—was not officially and formally announced to the public until 29 August 1852. On that date, at a church conference in Salt Lake City, the doctrine was set forth before the assembly by Orson Pratt. As noted by historian Roberts, though this public announcement would lead to difficulties, the action was timely. It was high time that all Mormons, as well as the Gentile world, had the issue set squarely before them.

We begin a brief historical survey of the Mormon practice of plural marriage by noting that the term usually used to describe it, polygamy, is inaccurate. The correct word is *polygyny*—one husband, a plurality of wives; *polyandry,* a multiplicity of husbands, was not (with a few exceptions) part of the package.

As the founder of the church freely admitted, Joseph was attracted to pretty girls and women. Let it be stated as an oversimplification that plural marriage became church doctrine as an accommodation to Joseph's physical and emotional needs. The essential statement is in Section 132 of *Doctrine and Covenants,* from which is taken this chapter's epigraph. This is a revelation given to Joseph in Nauvoo, recorded on 12 July 1843. The text specifically demands that Joseph's wife, Emma, not make a fuss about it. "I command my handmaid, Emma Smith, to abide and cleave unto my servant Joseph, and to none else. . . . If she will not abide this commandment she shall be destroyed." Harsh words. When Emma was first shown the text, she tore it up. To the end of her life she denied that Joseph had other wives.[1]

Prior to the 1852 public announcement a relatively small group of Joseph's close friends and associates were granted the privilege of having more than one wife. It is commonly held that Joseph's first plural marriage was solemnized on 5 April 1841, when he married Louisa Beeman, but the evidence suggests that he may have married five women before that (or had sexual relations with them), beginning with Fannie Alger in 1835. Brodie lists four other wives between Fannie Alger and Louisa Beeman. Her complete list names 48 wives of Joseph.[2] Brigham was initiated into the practice early on; he married Lucy Ann Decker Seeley in June 1842. Other intimates and friends of Joseph, including William Clayton, entered into plural marriage at this time, but the practice was generally kept hidden from the rank and file of the church. The word inevitably spread, however. Indeed, whispers of polygamous practice had been contributory to Gentile hostility toward the Mormons in Ohio and Missouri, as they were in the early '40s in Nauvoo. The Gentiles tended to view plural marriage not as a religious practice but as sexual license pure and simple.

When Elder Pratt made the public announcement of the doctrine in Salt Lake, he specifically noted that this practice had nothing to do with gratification of carnal lust. It was, rather, the way in which to fulfill the divine command to be fruitful and multiply. Thus there is here an implicit rationalization of multiple wives, but not of multiple husbands; a man with many wives can father a theoretically unlimited number of children, but a woman can bear but one man's child at a time.

Pratt also addressed the constitutionality of the practice, concluding that it would be unconstitutional for the federal government to forbid it:

> I think, if I am not mistaken, that the Constitution gives the privilege to all the inhabitants of this country, of the free exercise of their religious notions, and the freedom of their faith, and the practice of it. Then, if it can be proven to a demonstration that the Latter-day Saints have actually embraced, as a part and portion of their religion, the doctrine of a plurality of wives, *it is constitutional.*[3] (Emphasis added.)

On the afternoon of 29 August the actual text of the 1843 revelation was read to the assembled multitude. Hosea Stout wrote in his journal that this was a time of great joy for the Saints; now they could publicly declare the true principles of their holy religion:

> I feel that the work of the Lord will rule forth with a renewed impetus. The nations of the earth will be wakened up to an investigation of the truth of the gospel, and the nation that has driven us out of their midst so unjustly and unlawfully will have to again investigate our principals and thousands among them will yet be brought to an understanding of the truth by virtue of this revelation.[4]

There was a considerable reaction, worldwide, to this public avowal of plural marriage, but not of the kind envisaged by Stout. In due course Mormon missions scattered abroad reported increased hostility and persecution as news of the proclamation spread, and the reaction of the United States press was adverse. There was a considerable apostasy in the church in 1852 and 1853 and anti-Mormon writers, including Linn and Stenhouse, made much of these data, citing them as indicative of widespread dissatisfaction within the church, particularly in England, over the plural-marriage question. The data, however, do not support this interpretation.

In the six-month period ending 31 December 1852 the number of excommunicants was 2,164. (The number of excommunicants is essentially equivalent to the number of apostates. When a member left the church for whatever reason, he was excommunicated, or "disfellowshipped.") We can but guess as to the exact date when the news of the public avowal of the doctrine reached the British Saints, but it could scarcely have been before mid-December; thus the figure given above probably doesn't provide any meaningful reflection of the effect of the doctrine's publication. In the two following six-month periods the numbers of members excommunicated were 1,776 and 1,413, and it seems safe to say that among the general church membership the proclamation of the plural-marriage doctrine didn't have much effect. Some members left the church, and new ones came in. Nothing new about that, it had been that way since 1830.

It is interesting to note the membership figures for the English branch of the church before and after the proclamation:

Six-months ending	Members	Newly Baptized	Emigrated
30 June 1852	32,340	3,265	496
31 Dec 1852	32,339	3,400	85
30 June 1853	30,690	2,601	1,722
31 Dec 1853	30,827	1,976	58
30 June 1854	29,797	2,213	1,380

The hostile reaction of the Eastern press was such that church leaders were sent east to establish Mormon publications in defense of Mormon doctrines and beliefs. Orson Pratt went to Washington, where he published *The Seer* for a year and a half, beginning in January 1853. John Taylor went to New York and audaciously set up shop between the offices of the *New York Herald* and the *Tribune;* here he published *The Mormon* for two and a half years. There were many heated exchanges and challenges between the Mormon and Gentile presses, usually reflective of Gentile hostility toward plural marriage.

Such was the animus of the Eastern press that when the Mormons were threatened with famine in 1855, because of the plague of grasshoppers, Eastern papers hinted that if a serious famine resulted, that might solve the "Utah question." An article decrying this attitude appeared in another Mormon paper, *The Women's Advocate,* and Taylor reprinted it in *The Mormon.* A piece in the *New York Sun* noted that the Mormons had not asked for help. "If an appeal were made in the name of humanity, the degrading and disgusting doctrines of Brigham Young, and others of the priesthood, promulgated as articles of faith, would not hinder the American people from responding to it."

To this, Taylor, in *The Mormon,* made a fiery reply:

And shall they now ask charity for those that robbed and despoiled them of their goods and murdered their best men? . . . Talk to us with your hypocritical cant about charity! Pshaw! It's nauseating to everyone not eaten up with your corrupt humbuggery and pharisaical egotism. . . . The "Mormons" neither need your sympathy nor your cankered gold. Your malicious slanders only excite contempt for those base enough to utter them. Your contemptible falsehoods fail to ruffle a feather in our caps.

Historian Roberts, not without cause, compared Taylor's tone to that of Tertullian's defense of the early Christians.[5]

The Gentile interest—comprised of curiosity, fascination, and revulsion—in Mormon polygamy did not fade away after the furor initially aroused by the 1852 disclosure. Kimball Young noted that in "the half-century from 1870 to 1920 Mormonism and polygamy rivaled with prostitution and prohibition as the main interest of American reformers."[6] A vast literature was published, most of it by anti-Mormon Gentiles who considered Mormon polygamy to be a barbaric outrage, not to be tolerated.

A number of accounts appeared, written by plural wives who had not found that way of life to their liking; notable among these was one by one of Brigham's wives, Ann Eliza, who had her say in *Wife Number 19.* Brigham at age 66 had married the fiery Ann Eliza Webb, age 24. Ann Eliza divorced Brigham after seven years of marriage, wrote her book, and spent much time lecturing about her evil experiences in Brigham's menage. To balance these accounts, a number of Mormon women, notably Eliza Snow and Helen Mar Kimball Whitney, wrote of the glories of the polygamous life. We shall now sample some of these writings.

Fanny Stenhouse, a native of the island of Jersey, was converted to the Mormon faith, in England, by missionary Thomas Stenhouse. At the time of her conversion she was, she later wrote, entirely unaware of any practice of polygamy by any Mormons anywhere. Elder Stenhouse and Fanny were married, in February 1850, a few months after she joined the church. When Stenhouse's mission was complete the couple returned to New York, and later went to Salt Lake, where Stenhouse became an important member of the community, and a Seventy of the church. (See Glossary.) In due course, because of church pressure, he took a second wife. The household became unhappy, and the second marriage ended in divorce. Later, in 1869, Stenhouse joined a group of church members in rebellion against what they saw as the tyranny of the church, and the Stenhouses were excommunicated. (See pp. 239-40.)

Both Fanny and Thomas were thoughtful and articulate about their experiences within the church, and they each produced a book about them—Fanny's *Tell It All,* and Thomas's *The Rocky Mountain Saints.* A preface to Fanny's book was contributed by no less a personage than Harriet Beecher Stowe. Referring to the abolition (at least officially) of slavery, she spoke of that "glorious breaking of fetters . . . the songs of emancipated millions are heard through our land." It was now time to turn to that other relic of barbarism, polygamy. "Shall we not then hope that the hour is come to loose the bonds of a cruel slavery whose chains have cut into the very hearts of thousands of our sisters—a slavery which debases and degrades womanhood, motherhood, and the family?"[7]

Mrs. Stenhouse's book is lengthy and detailed. She may not tell it all, but she tells a great deal. She omits only, for the sake of decency, she writes, impure statements and disgusting atrocities uttered and committed by the church leadership. She has been motivated by a need to alert the Congress of the United States to the true state of affairs in Utah. And, she declares, she writes in the cause of freedom for all women.

> I earnestly desired to stir up my Mormon sisters to a just sense of their own position. I longed to make them feel, as I do, the cruel degradation, the humiliating tyranny, which polygamy inflicts. I wanted to arouse them to a sense of their own Womanhood, and a just appreciation of those Rights and Duties which, as women, God has conferred upon them . . . that they might learn to hate and loathe the falsely-named "Celestial" system of marriage.[8]

Jennie Froiseth's book, *The Women of Mormonism,* is a collection of antipolygamy documents, including many accounts of polygamous family life told by first wives, whose identities are generally protected. Mrs. Froiseth was the editor of the *Anti-Polygamy Standard,* published in Salt Lake, beginning in 1881. The Preface to her volume is contributed by Frances E. Willard, ardent reformer and temperance crusader of the time. After referring to Turkey as the most debased country on earth, she sounds the alarm:

> Turkey is in our midst. Modern Mohammedanism has its Mecca at Salt Lake, where Prophet Heber C. Kimball (successor to Brigham Young) speaks of his women as "cows." Clearly the Koran was Joseph Smith's model, so closely followed as to exclude even the poor pretension of originality in his foul "revelations."[9]

Included in Froiseth's collection is a letter from Wife Number 19, Ann Eliza Young. She speaks of her escape from the dark prison of polygamous slavery, with but one thought uppermost in her mind. "If

I could only show to every woman the contrast between the lives of women in Utah and those in all other parts of this great land . . . then it seems to me they would make every effort, run almost any risk, to break their chains and find true liberty."[10]

Most of the accounts of polygamous life in Froiseth's book are horrific; none display anything approaching a harmonious family life. One of Froiseth's accounts provides, however, a touch of Mack Sennett humor. Here Mrs. Froiseth quotes from a story in the local morning paper—no doubt the *Salt Lake Tribune*. The story describes what happened when the ward bishop called upon an erring member to suggest it was time he adhered to the Principle (of multiple celestial marriage) and take upon himself another wife. His chances of exaltation, the bishop warned, were slim indeed unless he set about looking for another spouse at once. The lady of the house, hearing this, seized a broom immediately and turned to the offending bishop.

> "Get out of here, you villain; I'll teach you to come into an honest woman's house and advise her husband to take another wife. Take that, and that"—laying the broom-handle vigorously about his head and shoulders. The wretched bishop grabbed his hat and made for the door; but before he could reach it, the blows fell thick and fast on his defenseless head. Once outside, he thought himself safe, but he soon discovered his mistake. Nemesis was behind him in the shape of that broom, and his flight through the gate and down the street was accelerated every few steps.[11]

Counting his bruises at home, the bishop decided that future such admonitions to reluctant men would be given out of the hearing of potentially indignant wives. This perhaps frivolous anecdote does underscore an important point: Mormon men were not just offered the privilege of a plurality of wives; it was more like a duty, and the "counseling" to get on with it was more like coercion.

And there was, of course, the other, the *pro,* side of polygamy, though its advocates were less numerous in print. One who spoke for it was Helen Mar Kimball Whitney, who expressed her view with some force:

> As for its being degrading, it has proven to be the very opposite. It was exalting in its tendency and calculated to raise mankind from the degraded condition into which they had fallen under the practice of a corrupt and hypocritical system of enforced monogamy.[12]

Orson Pratt put it this way:

> Instead of a plurality of wives being a cause of sorrow to females, it
> is one of the greatest blessings . . . it gives them the great privilege of
> being united to a righteous man, and of rearing a family according to
> the order of heaven. Instead of being compelled to remain single, or marry
> a wicked man . . . she can enter a family where peace and salvation reign
> . . . where the head of the family stands forth as a patriarch, a prince,
> and a savior to his whole household; where blessings unspeakable and
> eternal are sealed upon them and their generations after them . . . Rejoice,
> then, ye daughters of Zion, that ye live in this glorious era![13]

There can be no doubt but that the "truth" about plural marriage
lay somewhere between those who reviled it and those who told of
its virtues. It was a practice that obviously worked well for some families,
disastrously in others. Kimball Young, after studying the histories of
175 polygamous families, concluded that 110 of these accounts provided
sufficient data to permit him to attempt an evaluation, admittedly
subjective, with respect to how the families fared under the Principle.
He summarized his findings as follows:

	Families (N = 110)
Rating	%
1. Highly successful, unusually harmonious 2. Reasonably successful	53
3. Moderately successful, some conflict	25
4. Marital difficulty, considerable conflict 5. Severe conflict, leading in some cases to separation or divorce	23

Let us consider briefly, then, some of the factors that determined
which were the harmonious houses and which were riddled with conflict.
As an example of a successful house Young cites the case of the Olsons,
a Swedish Mormon family. Hans Olson, one of the first Swedish converts
to the church, came to Salt Lake with his wife in 1853. Olson and
his wife believed in the Principle, and by 1861 he had married three
additional wives. The four of them bore Olson a total of 32 children.

The family at first lived in cramped quarters, but as Olson's resources grew he established different quarters for each wife. The wives got along well together, possibly in part because they were all Swedish. Further, they were all about the same age—and thus so were the children. The family was formed during a relatively short period of time, and they all grew older together. The three later wives liked and respected Emma, the first wife, who was easy to get along with and who avoided any domination of the others. As for Olson, he treated his ladies with scrupulous fairness; if one got a new dress, so did the others. No doubt about it, this was a successful, happy, and harmonious family. Note also that Olson was a relatively well-to-do man.

By contrast, consider the case of the Mormon husband who, after many years of monogamous marriage, brings home a new wife younger, perhaps, than his daughters. This is a different matter entirely with respect to everyone, including the children. Surely it would take a saintly woman indeed not to feel jealousy and rage, Principle or no. One aspect of the Principle was that the first wife must give her consent to additional marriages, but pressure was applied, by the church, to the wife as well as to the husband to fall in line. Young tells of a family in which the husband wanted another wife but was afraid to ask for his wife's consent. He attempted to solve the problem by announcing that he had had a revelation that he was to marry a certain woman. His first wife, then, in the face of such divine directive, must give her consent. "The next morning she announced that she, too, had received a revelation 'to shoot any woman who became his plural wife.' Being the more drastic, her revelation ended the matter once and for all."[14]

Another problem with the plurality system was that there was scant room therein for romantic love, love in the traditional sense of what a man feels when he falls in love with a woman. Many men took on additional wives because they firmly believed in the Principle; they were doing what their church required of them. But neither the church nor any other power could enforce the love presumed to exist in a monogamous marriage. As we have seen with Hans Olson, the husbands in polygamous households generally made a real effort to be fair to all— and certainly many first wives did all they could to treat additional wives as equals and to try to get along with them. That may have made for a degree of compatibility, congeniality even, but where was romantic love?

Until the day of her death, Esther (the first wife) would not allow him to favor her. She was all for me and so I was the same with her. We were the shining example of a happy polygamous family. She did everything she could to make me happy. I think she told him ways in which he slighted me, for when he did he came to beg my pardon. As time went on such slights grew less, but he never came to fully love me—to love me as he did her. I don't think it possible for a man to love two women · at once, not in ways that are the same.[15]

Quite so. Here was a household in which every effort was made for all to go well, but there is an aura of wistful sadness in the second wife's account.

Before turning to the conflicts and struggles that eventually led to the abandonment of polygamy, let us first examine in a more quantitative way how popular it was within the church membership. To what extent did the dutiful Mormons participate in this social experiment? As the Gentiles of the United States saw it, certainly, the average Mormon male presided over a multiplicity of wives. In point of fact, that was far from the case. One of the founding fathers of American sociology, Lester Frank Ward, addressed himself to this question in 1875, when he was in Utah for field explorations; he was at this time a paleontologist, working for the Smithsonian Institution. (He would later be professor of sociology at Brown University.) His observations led him to conclude that only one man in seven practiced polygamy.

From the acquaintances which I have formed here, from my observation of the people with whom I have come in contact, and from careful inquiries in all quarters and fair and unbiased estimates that I have solicited from candid and disinterested citizens I derive the general conclusion that for the entire Mormon population the proportion of monogamous to polygamous men is about 6 to 1. . . . The greatest check upon the institution is the jealousy of the women. They do not resist it so much by refusing to marry as by refusing to live under the same roof with other wives . . . all is cold calculation. . . . That heroic attachment that welds one soul to another for life and defies the storms of both the outer and the inner world . . . is swept down like a gossamer by the poisonous breath of polygamy.[16]

Ward went on to note that the practice of polygamy was largely limited to the wealthier classes of the Mormon population.

So much, then, for the report of an interested and competent observer on the scene at the time. An interesting study addressing the same subject in quantitative terms was made much later by Stanley S. Ivins, who found that, throughout the period when polygamy was practiced—from the early 1840s, say, until the official end in 1904—the vast majority of Mormons were derelict in their adherence to the Principle. Participation waxed and waned according to a number of factors, which we shall shortly examine, but Ivins's finding was that *maximum* participation of Mormon families in polygamous relationships comprised about 15 to—at the outside—20 percent of families.

Mormon plural marriages were never a matter of *public* record, so statistical studies must be approached with caution; still the data are there in any number of contemporary records, such as letters and diaries, though troublesome to assemble and analyze. Ivins discovered clear evidence that the degree of participation in polygamy had several ups and downs between its beginning and end.

The first spurt in the number of plural marriages can be traced to the completion of the Temple, before the Saints evacuated Nauvoo. There was an understandable decline thereafter; they were busy enough crossing the plains and establishing Zion. The next jump in activity followed Orson Pratt's public announcement of the doctrine in the Tabernacle in 1852, and again, after the initial rush, the rate subsided. Then, in late 1856 and most of 1857 came a "reformation," in which religious fervor was rearoused. (See Chapter 10.) This produced many plural marriages, but the following decline was striking; the number of such in 1859 was less than one-fifth of those in 1857!

In 1862 the U.S. Congress passed the Morrill Anti-Bigamy Act, signed by President Lincoln in July. The act was widely thought to be unconstitutional, and serious attempts to enforce it were not successfully made. The Mormon response was to revive polygamous marriages. There was another short-lived spurt in 1868 and 1869, in response to Gentile agitation in the Territory, after which the rate of plural ceremonies declined to a very low rate by 1881. In 1882 Congress enacted the Edmunds Act. This legislation was provided with sharp teeth, and again the Mormons defiantly responded with a large increase in plural marriages. The Saints, yearning for statehood, formally capitulated in 1890, although official abandonment of plural marriage was held back until a church conference in 1904—after statehood had been achieved.

Some of Ivins's findings are surprising. He speculates, for example, that to the extent that the Mormons entered into plural marriage to follow the divine admonition to be fruitful and multiply, they might have done better on a monogamous basis. Plural wives, he found, bore an average of 5.9 children to their husbands, while monogamous wives came forth with no fewer than eight.

How many wives did the typical man of polygamy have? By no means as many as in the popular Gentile view. Granted there were three champion marriers—Joseph, Brigham, and Heber Kimball—but no other Mormon came close to approaching their numbers. A typical polygamist, Ivins found, married first at age 23, to a woman of 20. He would not marry again until he was 36; his bride would be 22, and the chances were now two to one that he had had enough. If not, four years later, at age 40, he would marry his third wife, who would be a woman of 22. The odds were now three to one that he would marry no more; if he did it would be four years later, when he would marry a bride of, again, 22 years. The average age of drawing the line against further marriage was 40. Of Mormon men who had plural wives, 66.3 percent had married but two.

It is apparent that they did marry young women. In the group studied by Ivins, 38 percent of the young brides were in their teens, and two-thirds of them were less than 25. There were marriages of women over 50, but these were generally for theological, not connubial, purposes.[17] Jessie Embry, in her study of polygamous families, reported the age of marriage of 376 polygamous wives.[18]

	1st Wife	2nd Wife	3rd Wife	4th Wife
No. of wives	152	145	56	23
Age at marriage	%	%	%	%
15-20	74.3	56.5	58.9	65.2
21-25	25.0	28.3	25.0	17.4
26-30	0.7	7.6	3.6	4.4
31-35	0.0	4.1	10.7	8.7
36-40	0.0	2.1	0.0	8.7
41-45	0.0	1.4	1.8	0.0

It is an interesting fact that there was a noticeable tendency for men to marry their wives' sisters—which is not, perhaps, surprising.

A woman faced with the fact that another wife was coming into the family might well ask that her husband marry her sister, since things might reasonably be expected to go better that way.

During the Civil War the Eastern states were occupied with other than Mormon problems, but when that struggle ended the "Mormon Question" again became prominent in the national arena. In 1869 Congressman Shelley N. Cullom introduced his Cullom Bill in the House. This was a *drastic* piece of proposed anti-polygamy, anti-Mormon legislation; among other provisions, it withdrew trial by jury from Utah, and it more or less dismantled self-government in the Territory. Nevertheless, the bill passed in the House by a resounding 94 to 32. So far-reaching was the bill that it led to reactions of alarm that were not confined to the Territory. The Eastern press, generally not profusive in support of Mormon causes, considered the bill altogether too punitive. In addition, the enactment of legislation was not the way to attack the problem.

The *New York World,* for example, editorialized that the federal government should not interfere with polygamy forcibly, and suggested that pacific forces were already afoot that would make it impossible for polygamy to exist much longer. The *New York Times* stated the view that since neither force nor legislation could possibly be successful in destroying Mormonism, neither should be attempted.[19] Such was the outcry that the bill was defeated. The Cullom bill, however, had the very positive effect of focusing attention upon the polygamy problem throughout the nation, including Washington. President Grant, in a message to Congress in December 1871, declared that there was in the Territory of Utah a repugnant remnant of barbarism that could no longer be permitted.

The last twenty years of Mormon life observing polygamy were characterized by a virulent persecution that measured up in all essentials to the trials the Saints had endured at other stations on their way to Zion. There wasn't as much murderous shedding of blood— though there was indeed some of that—but the degree of danger and discomfort, hardship and confinement, particularly of the plural wives and their children, was enormous.

Though there were prosecutions of polygamous Mormons under

the Morrill Act of 1862, there was extensive Gentile pressure for
sterner measures, and in 1882 the more punitive Edmunds Act became law. That act defined polygamy and "unlawful cohabitation"
as crimes, and stipulated that those guilty of such were excluded
from voting and from holding any public office. Nor could they serve
on juries. These crimes were punishable by fines of up to $300 and/
or imprisonment for up to six months. If a polygamous husband
went to the penitentiary, served his time, and came out and went
back to his plural family he was guilty of the same crime again.
Thus, with rigorous enforcement, he either had to give up some part
of his family or spend most of his time in prison.

Some polygamous families fled to Canada or Mexico, but many
stayed in the Territory and went into hiding, "in the underground,"
as it was referred to. Many Mormons used the device of leaving
the country on a church mission. Some husbands scattered their
families widely, hoping to escape detection. The deputy marshals—
"deps"—were everywhere, looking for the "cohabs." Some of those
who went into hiding found it very tough going indeed.

> We had to be secret. When my children come the first wife was the
> only one I had. She was no midwife, but she was my only doctor for
> fear people would find out. . . . It was a miracle that I lived and that
> the children lived, though all my life I'm suffering from not having
> proper care. When my babies was young I couldn't live like a normal
> human being. I had to hide in the granary out there all day long . . .
> at night I had to lie in that little bedroom and stifle my baby's cries . . .
> there was no one you could trust in them days.[20]

At least one plural wife was in hiding for a full ten years. The
president of the church in the mid 1870s was John Taylor; he conducted
the affairs of the church hidden from the deps in a relatively secure
farmhouse a few miles northwest of Salt Lake. Taylor hid out there
until his death in 1887, during which year Congress mounted an even
more virulent attack upon the church by passing the Edmunds-Tucker
act, whose provisions included the actual disincorporation of the
church. One of the consequences of this disincorporation was that
the church was required to forfeit to the federal government all of
its property of value exceeding $50,000, excepting only buildings and
grounds used for the worship of God, parsonages, and burial grounds.

D. WELLS.

HUNTER.

F. D. RICHARDS.

J. TAYLOR.

C. C. RICH.

L. SNOW.

G. A. SMITH.

O. HYDE.

BRIGHAM YOUNG.

W. WOODRUFF.

E. SNOW.

O. PRATT.

A. LYMAN.

E. T. BENSON.

H. C. KIMBALL.

G. Q. CANNON.

J. YOUNG.

BRIGHAM YOUNG AND THE TWELVE APOSTLES OF THE MORMON CHURCH.

Utah State Historical Society

A later reenactment of a Pioneer wagon train emerging into Salt Lake Valley from a canyon.

Harper's Weekly, 9 October 1858

Brigham Young's compound in Provo during "Mormon War."

Mormon polygamists in prison stripes. Bearded figure in center is George Q. Cannon. Cocky figure next to jailer is great-granduncle of the author.

Harper's Weekly, 27 January 1872

MAIN STREET, LOOKING NORTH.

MAIN STREET, WEST SIDE.

Two views of Main Street, Salt Lake City.

Residences of Brigham Young (*left*) and Daniel H. Wells (*right*) on South Temple Street.

Panoramic view of Salt Lake City, looking north.

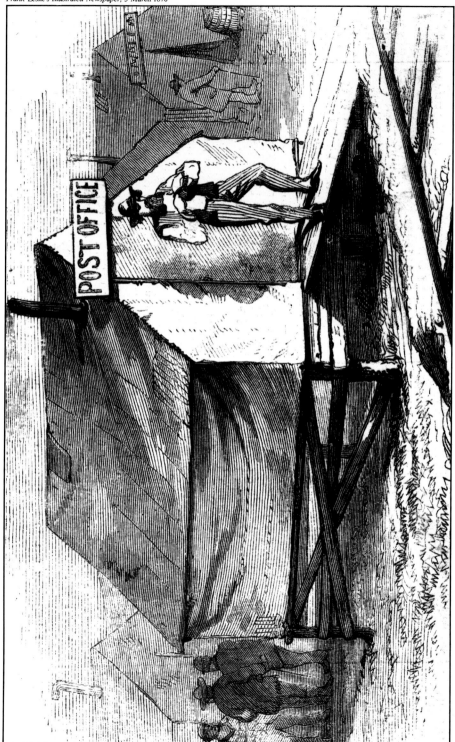

Promontory Point post office—probably the only known rendition thereof.

Frank Leslie's Illustrated Newspaper, 5 March 1870

Railroad at entrance to Echo Canyon.

Brigham Young cemetery park, city buildings to the south beyond. (Photo by the author.)

A receiver, Frank H. Dyer—the U.S. marshal of the territory—was appointed to take over the escheated property, the value of which was claimed by the government to be in excess of $3 million.[21] Life was becoming difficult indeed for the Saints, be they polygamous or monogamous. And hanging over the complex conflict was a black cloud of hostility on the part of many Gentiles, both in the territory and in the United States. The Mormons' response to these times was also varied and complex, involving political, theological, and practical considerations. and many of these were in conflict with each other.

The polygamists, generally, believed in the Principle, an essential part of their religious system. But they also were, generally, law-abiding citizens, and the law had declared a part of their belief to be illegal, *and* that law had been declared constitutional. Since another of their religious beliefs was that the U.S. Constitution was of divine inspiration, this presented a troublesome set of circumstances. The overriding political datum was the need for statehood, and with that in mind it may be noted that many Mormons were beginning to wonder if the Principle was really necessary. Couldn't one at least wonder if it wasn't so much a demand performance as a privilege to be made use of according to circumstance? Indeed, hadn't it been true all along that the vast majority of Mormon families were monogamous? The Mormons were tiring of the conflict, and the number of plural marriages was declining. In the late 1890s, the leaders of the church could no longer look away from the futility of continuing the Principle in the face of the federal forces confronting them. What manner of church was this, with hundreds of its elders in prison, other hundreds in exile? Theological considerations weakened as political necessity demanded surrender.

The result—predictable enough in hindsight—was the Woodruff Manifesto, issued on 24 September 1890. (Wilford Woodruff was then president of the church.) The important part of this document, this bow to the inevitable, was in the last two paragraphs:

> Inasmuch as laws have been enacted by Congress forbidding plural marriages, which laws have been pronounced constitutional by the court of last resort, I hereby declare my intention to submit to those laws and to use my influence with the members of the Church over which I preside to have them do likewise. . . .

There is nothing in my teachings to the Church or in those of my associates during the time specified, which can be reasonably construed to inculcate or encourage polygamy; and when any Elder of the Church has used language which appeared to convey any such teaching, he has been promptly reproved. And I now publicly declare that my advice to the Latter-day Saints is to refrain from contracting any marriage forbidden by the law of the land.[22]

The reference to "the time specified" in the quotation is to an allegation in a report during this year, 1890, by the Utah Commission that Mormon officials were continuing to perform plural marriage ceremonies, and that 40 or more had been solemnized during the past year.

There is no reference in the complete text to suggest that the Manifesto had come to Woodruff by revelation, and in this respect it is a matter of no small interest to read his journal entry for 25 September:

I have arrived at a point in the history of my life as the president of the Church . . . where I am under the necessity of acting for (its) temporal salvation. . . . The United States government has taken a stand and passed laws to destroy the Latter-day Saints on the subject of polygamy, or patriarchal order of marriage; and after praying to the Lord and feeling inspired, I have issued the following proclamation which is sustained by my counselors and the twelve apostles.[23]

We have seen, then, that the text of the Manifesto makes no mention of revelation, though Woodruff's journal notes that his prayers with respect to the matter were followed by a "feeling" of inspiration. The church membership, however, tended to view the Manifesto as a revelation, a belief that must have made them feel better about abandoning the Principle.

After the Manifesto was issued, it became important that its scope and interpretation be made a matter of record—among other reasons, to support the church's efforts to regain property that had been taken from it in consequence of anti-polygamy legislation. Thus, in testimony given under oath, the First Presidency, together with the president of the Quorum of the Twelve Apostles, Lorenzo Snow, stated that "all regarded the Manifesto as the result of the inspiration of God upon the mind of President Wilford Woodruff; that *in effect* it was the word of the Lord to the church forbidding the practice of plural marriage."[24] (Emphasis added.) Further, at the dedication of the Salt Lake Temple on 6 April 1893, Woodruff said that he had been shown a vision of what would happen to the church unless plural marriage was disavowed. "The Lord," he said, "had commanded him to do what he did."[25]

If no more plural marriages were to be entered into, what was the status of the polygamous families already existing? Different individuals interpreted the Manifesto in different ways but the church view was, in general, that the husband should honor and take care of his families as before, but if he lived with more than one of them he was at risk.

Divorce was sanctioned by the church, and Brigham had allowed it, though he hadn't liked it. In the zeal of the Reformation, for example, many polygamous marriages were entered into without much thought, and many of these turned out badly. Brigham counseled unhappy wives to stay with their husbands as long as they could, but, if things got too tough, to leave the husband and get a divorce.

The long conflict was officially and formally ended, and the coveted statehood would follow in due course. Before returning to the (more or less) chronological train of our narrative, it may be added that the Principle remains, to this day, a matter for thought and consideration. There is, for example, the question of what happens when the plural wives—and plural husbands—ascend into Heaven? Do twentieth-century Mormons live in the expectation of continued existence, continued growth and development in a hereafter where polygamy is the order of the day? That is an important question, is it not, in view of the fact that the Woodruff Manifesto did not deny either the rightfulness or the divinity of the Principle. Do Mormons of today look forward with relish to a plurality of wives after death—or do they anticipate that future with foreboding? One Mormon who has given long and careful thought to such questions is Eugene England, some of whose speculations we shall briefly examine.

England, writing in 1987, begins with the thesis that marital fidelity is central both to mortal joy and eternal life thereafter. Many of the problems in our world today are caused, England speculates, by widespread neglect of that concept—both by society in general and by many Mormon families as well. A great danger to the ideal of marital fidelity is posed, he suggests, by "the expectation, shared [he fears] by many Mormons, that the highest form of marriage in the celestial realm is what is technically called polygyny, plural wives for a single husband."[26] Many Mormons, that is to say, now believe that when they reach the celestial kingdom they will find it polygynous. (And, to a much lesser degree, polyandrous.) Indeed, England supposes that this belief causes some Mormons, here and now, to prepare for that day by practicing for it now—by diverting their affections and loyalties from what they see as the tough job of, in effect, getting it all together with *one* spouse exclusively, in spiritual and physical unity.

If true grace in human relationships is to be found only in faithful monogamous relationships, what is a good Mormon to do when faced with the concept of a polygynous afterlife? England provides a solution. Though the divinity of plural marriage is not questioned, he proposes that it doesn't follow that the celestial kingdom is polygynous. The implication is that the practice was instituted as an exception— commanded to meet the needs of a specific historical circumstance. For one thing, England notes, polygamy is not firmly grounded in either the Bible *or* the Book of Mormon. Further, if polygyny is the most exalted form of marriage, the church would permit its practice wherever it could. In actuality, it also prohibits such marriage of its members in countries where the practice is commonplace. After adducing other arguments, England concludes that Heaven will be occupied by monogamous couples.

What, then, of all those marriages sealed for eternity? Good question, but England is ready: for each person, man or woman, all but one of those sealings will be invalidated, and the unsealed partners will be free to seek relationships elsewhere. Nor will that be difficult, for, in England's view, the numbers of males and females in the celestial kingdom is precisely equal.

Polygamy, that unique social experiment in the United States, has come and gone—gone except for an isolated community here and there.[27] During the period in which it was practiced it aroused no end of interest and no end of controversy among Gentiles and among Mormons. Its history continues to be examined as a matter of not inconsiderable interest. And its future, to a good number of Mormons, is no less something about which to speculate.

Notes

1. See Taves, *Trouble Enough*, chap. 18.
2. Fawn Brodie, *No Man Knows My History*, pp. 457-88.
3. Roberts, *CHC*, vol. 4, p. 56.
4. Stout's diary entry for 29 August 1852, in Brooks, ed., *On the Mormon Frontier*, pp. 449-50. On the preceding day, the first day of this church conference, 80 or 90 elders had been selected to carry the message of the kingdom to the corners of the world. Stout had been chosen to go to China. He would leave Salt Lake, on what turned out to be an abortive mission, on 20 October.
5. The quotations from the *Sun* and *The Mormon* are cited by Roberts in *CHC*, vol. 4, p. 65. The comparison of Taylor with Tertullian is apt. As had Taylor, Tertullian had converted to a new religion, having embraced Christianity near the end of the second century.
6. Kimball Young, *Isn't One Wife Enough?* p. 1.
7. Mrs. Thomas B. H. Stenhouse, *Tell It All*, Harriet Beecher Stowe's Preface, p. vi.
8. Ibid., pp. 618-19.
9. Froiseth, *The Women of Mormonism*, Frances Willard's Preface, p. xvi.
10. Ibid., pp. 169-70.
11. Ibid., pp. 325-26.
12. Helen Mar Kimball Whitney, in *Why We Practice Plural Marriage*, cited in Young, *Isn't One Wife Enough?* p. 29.
13. Ibid., p. 44.
14. Ibid., p. 123.
15. Ibid., p. 182.
16. Ibid., pp. 79-80. The text is from Ward's letter to the *New York Tribune*, 5 Sept. 1875.
17. These quantitative data are from Ivins, *Notes on Mormon Polygamy*, pp. 229-39. Ivins was a teacher of animal husbandry at the University of Nebraska, whose avocation became the study of Utah and Mormon history.
18. Jennie Embry, *Mormon Polygamous Families*, p. 35. Other interesting tabular data are on pp. 35-37.
19. Roberts, *CHC*, vol. 5, pp. 315-16.
20. Young, p. 390.
21. Letter of U.S. Attorney General to Senate, 12 December 1888, Senate Executive Document No. 21. In this document (p. 4) the government claims values of $2 million for real estate and $1 million for personal property. Also provided is a detailed inventory of these properties.
22. The complete text of the Manifesto is in Roberts, *CHC*, vol. 6, pp. 220-21. It is also found immediately following Section 136, *Doctrine and Covenants*, in all editions published from 1922.
23. Ibid., p. 220.
24. Ibid., pp. 224-25.
25. Young, p. 377.
26. England, "On Fidelity, Polygamy, and Celestial Marriage," pp. 139-40.
27. Small splinter groups of excommunicated Mormons continue to practice polygamy openly, particularly in the twin towns of Hildale, Utah, and Colorado City, Arizona. Though polygamy is a third-degree felony in Utah, there are no prosecutions. See Casey, "An American Harem."

10

The Reformation

This is loving our neighbor as ourselves; if he needs help, help him; if he wants salvation and it is necessary to spill his blood on earth in order that he may be saved, spill it. . . . That is the way to love mankind.

Our focus now turns to 1856 and to the extraordinary phenomenon known as the Reformation that began on 13 September of that year. We focus upon that date and upon the person of Jedediah M. Grant, church member since 1833, participant in just about everything that happened to and within the church after that, first mayor of Salt Lake City, member of the First Presidency from 1854 until his death. Grant was a major general in the Nauvoo Legion, speaker of the House in the Territorial Legislature, and a man of many parts, endowed with more than adequate zeal, and—as some saw it—an impressive bigotry.

On the morning of 13 September he traveled to Kaysville, a small community in Davis County, about midway between Salt Lake City and Ogden, there to participate in a local church conference. He invited other elders—"home missionaries"—to meet him there, and loaned one of them his mule for transport. He greeted the elders as they arrived and noted the condition of the horses and of his mule. He didn't like what he saw; the animals were jaded and sweating. Nothing was said about that then, however, and they went in for the conference. Jedediah let the others speak first. That done, he rose to address the gathering— and here we mark the beginning of the Reformation.

He began by bitterly denouncing the elders who had ridden the animals to Kaysville, laying the scourge upon them for their harsh treatment of the beasts. He then lashed the preceding speakers for the differences between their preaching and their practice, calling them hypocrites. Addressing the bishop of that ward, he charged him and his counselors with negligence and carelessness. As for the gathering generally, one and all were accused of "all manner of wickedness," and told that they must "do their first works over again"—they must confess, repent, go back to the beginning, and be rebaptized. In short, they'd best mend their wild and wicked ways instantly, else God's judgment and retribution would be upon them.[1] The evidence upon which Grant's charges rested is not stated.

The conference continued the next day, Sunday, with more exhortations to keep the faith, repent, and be rebaptized. And there was much talk of cleanliness, a concept with which Jedediah appears to have been obsessed. The conference carried over into Monday morning, when rebaptisms were performed.

Though this Kaysville conference is generally cited as marking the beginning of the Reformation, its inauguration had been extensively foreshadowed by repeated expressions, by church leaders, of dissatisfaction with the behavior of the brothers and sisters. Here, for one example, is Jedediah addressing the brethren in Provo, 14 months before the Kaysville gathering:

> The Church needs trimming up, and if you will search, you will find in your wards certain branches that had better be cut off. The Kingdom will progress much faster and so will you individually than it will with those branches on, for they are only dead weights to the great wheel. . . . I would like to see the works of reformation commence and continue until every man had to walk the line. Purify yourselves, your houses, lots, farms and everything around you on the right and on the left and then the spirit of the Lord can dwell with you.[2]

Similar complaints had been made repeatedly by other leaders.

Eight days after the Kaysville conference, on 21 September, Brigham spoke in the Tabernacle with some violence. The souls of the Saints, he said, were clearly in need of redemption, salvation, and the harshest of measures might be required. He set forth a throat-cutting, blood-spilling doctrine to the general effect that if the sin of a man or woman was of sufficient magnitude, the only way to save that soul was to kill the man—or woman. Here was blood atonement made frighteningly clear.

> As it was in ancient days, so it is in our day. . . . There are sins that the blood of a lamb, of a calf, or of turtle doves cannot remit, but they

must be atoned for by the blood of the man. That is the reason why men talk to you as they do from this stand; they understand the doctrine, and throw out a few words about it. You have been taught that doctrine, but you do not understand it.[3]

An evangelical zeal now swept over the territory, reminding one of the not dissimilar passions that had, decades earlier, swept the "burnt over" area of New York State before Joseph had there established his church. Accusation, punishment, confession, and rebaptism comprised the order of the days, some of which were tragic, while some provided a measure of comic relief. With Brigham's authority a catechism was distributed to elders, missionaries, teachers, and bishops, and throughout the settlements Mormon men, women, and children were asked the most searching questions about their private activities, including their thoughts.

If the Saint refused to answer, he was reported forthwith, denounced, and considered as a candidate for disfellowship. If sins and evil deeds were admitted to, these were reported to the bishops as well, and the perpetrator became an object of abuse and attack. High on the list of reportable departures from discretion was *adultery,* and here we have what seems to this reporter, at least, a moment of light-hearted relief.

In one meeting in the Social Hall, attended by the First Presidency and many male members, Brigham asked all those present who had been guilty of the sin of adultery to rise. To his and his counselors' surprise and consternation, more than three fourths of those present rose to their feet. A prominent Salt Lake bishop later reported to Stenhouse that at this point Brigham was as appalled as Macbeth had been when he beheld Birnam Wood advancing on Dunsinane. Thinking— and no doubt hoping—that there had been a misunderstanding, the question was rephrased. Had they committed the sin *since embracing the church?* They stood again, to a man.

Interesting. Were the men confessing to sins they hadn't committed, to escape blame for failing to confess enough sin? Were they carried away in the religious fervor of the moment? Outdoing each other in the magnitude of the confession produced? Brigham saw that things were getting out of hand, and the rules were changed on the spot. "There are some brothers here," he said, "who have confessed sins they have not done."[4] He proceeded to offer one and all a relatively easy way out, a way that avoided the disgrace and embarrassment of public confession. "Repent of your sins, and be baptized for the remission of sins, and, as they are washed away by the ordinance of baptism, you can say truly that you are not guilty of the sins inquired of by the catechism, though you may have committed them."[5] If they sinned after this repentance they were back to square one and would have to start over again. Many of the Saints did so repent and were duly rebaptized.

Nevertheless, the use of the catechism continued, one version containing as many as 26 questions, including one that inquired into frequency of bathing. Jedediah Grant was not alone in his interest in cleanliness. Here is Brigham addressing a church conference in October 1856:

> When you go home tonight, we want every man and woman and every child . . . to wash themselves with pure water inside and out. . . . As soon as you are released from this meeting, go home and wash yourselves, and already many of you would do well to have a tub and soak overnight and perhaps by morning you would get the scale off. . . . I believe that is all I have to say to this congregation.[6]

He addressed the subject again in a ward meeting in the same month:

> It is your duty to keep clean. I've given the teachers a new set of questions to ask the people. I say to them, "Ask the people if they keep clean. Do you wash your bodies once a week. . . . Do you keep your dwellings and outhouses and dooryards clean? The first work of the reformation with some should be the cleaning of filth away about their premises. How would you like President Young to visit them and go through their buildings and examine their rooms, etc.?" Many houses stink so bad that a clean man cannot live in them nor hardly breathe in them. Some men were raised in stink and so were their fathers before them. I would not attempt to bless anybody in such places.[7]

Were the Saints in 1856 really that filthy, that sinful, in such desperate need of redemption? Probably not, according to most other accounts, but it is understandable that they might have become somewhat lax. They had gone into the wilderness to establish their kingdom, and circumstances weren't exactly normal. It might be more important to fight grasshoppers or to irrigate than to observe the Sabbath. Historian Roberts makes note of the emphasis on sexual sins during the Reformation:

The unsettled life . . . was crowded with circumstances that lent themselves
to continous temptations in this kind of evil. There were the long weeks
of ocean travel by mixed companies . . . followed by long journeys of the
same mixed companies up the American rivers. . . . Then there was the
longer overland journeying by handcart or ox train means of travel, all
classes being thrown into constant and closest contact, which not all the
care of the organized camp, nor the watchfulness of faithful pastors could
rob of insidious and sometimes ruinous temptations.[8]

Indeed. Still, there can be no doubt but that the Reformation was
executed to a fanatic excess. With respect to sex, for example, one
young man from San Pete was castrated for his offenses. Hear how
Bishop Blackburn of Provo addressed his flock after that event: "I want
the people of Provo to understand that the boys in Provo can use
the knife as well as the boys in San Pete. Boys, get your knives ready,
there is work for you! We must not be behind San Pete in *good works.*"

Throughout the Reformation the Saints were admonished, "Live
your religion!" One of the aspects of that religion was the doctrine of
plural marriage, and a renewed emphasis was now brought to that
institution. The brethren were directed to marry more wives, and young
girls were pressured into marriage with older men. According to
Campbell's account, competition for unwed girls and women became
intense, to such an extent that men volunteered to be sent on missions
in order to find wives outside the valley.

Some of the men found the pressure to take on more wives oppressive,
but some—including my great-granduncle Philo T. Farnsworth—
welcomed the opportunity. I was more than a little bemused to come
across that familiar name in Campbell's analysis. He quotes from a
letter from Farnsworth to Brigham Young from Beaver, where the
Farnsworth family was then living: "Is it my privilege to take a couple
more wives if I can find some free girls? If so, I thought I'd come
up this summer when you get home from your trip north."[9]

Such fanaticism as the Reformation fostered obviously could not long
endure, and it did not. Jedediah Grant began the movement on 13
September 1856. He died some 11 weeks later, on 1 December, most
likely of pneumonia, thought by many to have been contracted because
of his zeal in rebaptizing many Saints in cold weather. Unsustained
by Grant's vehemence, the Reformation faded shortly after his death,

particularly in Salt Lake City and its vicinity. It did spread beyond, mostly southward, for a time, but without Grant to provide the fire it died a natural death. How does this brief movement stand, then, in Mormon history? Did it have long-term effects? If so, for better or worse?

These questions are not easily answered. Campbell, in his analysis, found it difficult to respond to such queries. Beyond question the balance sheet lists many debits. The emphasis on blood atonement gave anti-Mormons lots of ammunition to use against the Saints. (Stenhouse thought that the use of Jesus' words in promoting the doctrine was a frightful perversion.) A number of very young girls, younger than child-bearing age, were coerced into marriage with older men. (Brigham wrote to one prospective applicant, "Go ahead and marry them, but leave them to grow."[10]) There were crimes of violence, of which the instance of castration was but one. Many of the faith were embarrassed, humiliated, and subjected to public abuse.

And what about the credit side? Were their bodies and houses cleaner? Were the rebaptized better people? These questions are generally unanswerable. Not much can be placed on the credit side. Stenhouse's informant summed it up thus:

> When the excitement of fanaticism had died away, and calm reflection enlightened the minds of those in authority; when they had seen and learned the evil effects of the movement, they deeply regretted the part they had taken in it, and Brigham Young himself has frequently said in public that he was "ashamed of the Reformation."[11]

Nor was historian Roberts hesitant to note that there had been, in connection with the Reformation, "things to be regretted." A fair statement. The Reformation remains an interesting, albeit brief, passage in the history of Zion.

Notes

1. This account is from Thomas B. H. Stenhouse, *The Rocky Mountain Saints,* pp. 292-93. Stenhouse was not in Salt Lake at this time, and here cites "a graphic sketch—never before published—from the pen of an eye-witness, then and now a resident of Salt Lake City."

2. Grant's sermon delivered in Provo on 13 July 1855, cited in Campbell, *Establishing Zion,* p. 183.

3. From Brigham Young's discourse delivered in the Tabernacle, 21 September 1856, cited in Stenhouse, p. 305.

4. Quotation from account of participant John Powell, in Campbell, p. 192.

5. Quotation from Stenhouse's eyewitness, p. 296.

6. Brigham Young manuscript history, cited in Campbell, p. 189.

7. Ibid., pp. 196-97.

8. Roberts, *CHC,* vol. 4, p. 121.

9. Campbell, p. 197. Philo T. Farnsworth had four wives, who bore him a total of 30 children. The letter to Brigham cited in the text was written on 26 March 1857. In August of that year, when Philo was 31, he married a woman of 17; in December 1858 he married a girl of 14; finally in June 1860 he married a woman of 29. (A grandson of his, bearing the same name, is given credit in the United States as the inventor of television. Farnsworth received that recognition after winning a lengthy legal battle over patent infringement with RCA. It should be added that television was also invented independently a few years earlier, by a Scottish engineer.)

10. Ibid., p. 198.

11. Stenhouse, p. 301.

11

The Mountain Meadows Massacre

Here . . . may as well be considered that event which is the most lamentable episode in Utah history, in the history of the church.

The tenth anniversary of the arrival of the Pioneers in the Great Basin was 24 July 1857, a date that called for celebration. A three-day outing in Big Cottonwood Canyon was laid on, beginning on the 22nd, and the brethren converged here from all parts of the territory.[1] Three open-air stands had been made ready, and no fewer than six bands were on hand to provide music for dancing and entertainment. As the festivities neared their culmination on the third day, the 24th, Orrin Porter Rockwell and three others rode into camp bearing what had every appearance of being alarming tidings. Moses Farnsworth described their arrival thus:

> I saw the messengers when they rode into our camp. They had ridden or driven 500 miles in five days in order to get the word to Governor Brigham Young. They were tired, travel stained, and dirty. I hastened to the gathering at the bowery there, for I knew these men: A. O. Smoot, Judson Stoddard, and Orrin P. Rockwell, and I felt anxious to know what was up. . . . Their arrival was as startling as a bolt of thunder out of the clear sky above.[2]

As the music and dancing went on, they told Brigham and his counselors in private that troops from the United States Army were on the way to Utah. How much they knew of the army's intent and how they expressed it to Brigham and the others we can only guess, but as it was announced to the gathering later, the army was on the march to put down the "Mormon rebellion." That there *was* a Mormon rebellion was news to many of the participants, over whose celebratory outing the United States flag was flying. We must now examine the context in which that news reached Salt Lake.

As already noted, Utah had been a Territory since late 1851, and from the beginning there had been great problems between Brigham and his followers on the one hand and federal officers sent into the territory to do federal work on the other. Particularly troublesome were non-Mormon judges sitting in federal courts. Brigham was governor of the Territory, with the total allegiance of the church behind him, and the federal officers had soon seen that there wasn't much they could do. These "runaway" officials had returned to President Fillmore with that information. Now, the U.S. Army was marching toward the Territory, and there is no question but that this was perceived by Brigham and other leaders of the church as a dire threat.

Two days after the Big Cottonwood celebration ended, Heber Kimball delivered a fiery—and arguably treasonous—diatribe in the Tabernacle. In the course of his dithyramb he noted the quantity of provisions that such an army must have with it and said, "Suppose the troops don't get here, but all these goods and cattle come; well, they would be a mighty help to us."[3] In rough translation: Let's do away with the troops and bring home the spoils. There can be no doubt but that Kimball was suggesting that the Mormons prepare to fight for their independence from the government of the United States. Just one week after Kimball's exhortation, Brigham announced that the time was coming when the Mormon kingdom would have to cut away from all others. The time for this would be signaled by an army coming to the Territory to, as he put it, chastise him.

With the leadership of the church speaking in such a manner, the stage was being set for what would, within a few weeks, be written up as the blackest, most lawless page in Mormon history. Historian B. H. Roberts, as suggested in the epigraph to this chapter, approached the subject reluctantly. This page would not be directly related to the threat of forthcoming conflict between the army and the Mormons, but if that confrontation were to come shortly (in actual fact, the army wintered that year in Fort Bridger—beyond the boundaries of the Territory—but the Mormons did not know that would happen), Brigham had the perspicacity to see that the excitable Indians would become active on one side or the other, and he wanted them on his side. On 4 August he wrote to Jacob Hamblin, newly appointed president to the Santa Clara (Utah, not California) mission to the Indians, giving him the crucial instruction to be conciliatory in his dealings with the Indians, and to convince him that if they didn't side with the Mormons, then the United States would kill people from both sides.

On the same day that Brigham wrote to Hamblin, the Mormon George A. Smith began a tour of the southern settlements, instructing all militia leaders to be fully prepared for action, and to be ready to march to anyplace in the Territory on a moment's notice.[4] He spared no pains to arouse fiery warlike emotions as he passed through town after town, like an arsonist lighting fuses. (Each Mormon town had a military organization, and now, in the late summer of 1857, all able-bodied men were on call.) Let us listen briefly to one example of Apostle Smith's message. In the village of Parowan he learned that some of the local boys had gotten into trouble by stealing fruit. Smith listened to both sides in dispute and advised the community to plant fruit trees in their public square so the lads could have all they wanted. He pointed out that bones were good fertilizer for such trees, and then referred to the army supposed to be approaching: "As for the cursed mobocrats, I can think of nothing better that they could do than to feed a fruit tree in Zion."[5] Another fuse lit: kill the troops and use their bones for fertilizer.

The addition of three more names completes the cast of characters who would play the leading roles in the drama about to be enacted. Isaac C. Haight was Stake President of the Iron County Mormons; Colonel William H. Dame was the commanding officer of the Iron County militia, Haight's immediate superior; and John D. Lee, an adopted son of Brigham Young and a devoted Mormon, a man of immense valor, honor, and integrity, was fated to play the fall guy, the only man to take the rap for the crime in which many had participated.

At the same time that federal troops were thought to be approaching, numerous emigrant trains were passing through Utah Territory, many of them traveling toward California. Most of these, earlier in the summer, took the northern route from Salt Lake; there were two such routes, both of which got the emigrants out of Utah with relative dispatch. One went north of Great Salt Lake, then turned southwestward to follow the Humboldt River. The other went south of the lake and turned sharply westward on the Hastings Cutoff. These trails joined in what is now central Nevada, and continued, after again diverging into a number of trails, toward Sacramento, California. In the late summer the northern routes became dangerous because of the bad weather they were likely to find in the Sierra Nevada before reaching their destination.

Those taking the southern route spent more time among the Mormons and passed through many Mormon towns before they left the territory. One group, the Fancher train (after Charles Fancher, the apparent leader), had passed through Salt Lake in early August and had reached Cedar City in the south by 5 September. Two groups of emigrants had earlier combined to form this train: one group was composed of families from four counties in Arkansas; the other was primarily a group of horsemen from Missouri—in all a company of about 140 men, women, and children. The behavior of the Missourians, as they encountered Mormons along the way, was rebarbitive in the extreme. One man, brandishing a firearm, claimed that this was the very weapon that had killed Joseph Smith! They threatened to gather an army together in California, to return and do a proper job of exterminating the Mormons once and for all. They named their oxen after Mormon leaders and addressed them harshly in the presence of Mormons. They claimed to have participated in the infamous Haun's Mill Massacre.[6] In short, they made enemies everywhere they went.

Part of their hostility (though only a part) was aroused by the refusal of the Mormons to trade or barter for provisions of any kind —this, in turn, a reflection of the Saints' wish to hold onto everything they could, in the face of possible war with the U.S. Army. The Missourians had been particularly obnoxious and infuriating passing through Cedar City, and on 6 September, the day following their passage, events took an ominous turn.

The leading authority in the area was Haight. After the regular church service on this day he called an "indignation" meeting, at which was discussed the question of what to do about the lawless Missourians in the Fancher party. Opinion was divided. Some thought the party should be attacked and eliminated; others firmly opposed such violence. It was decided to send an express to Brigham, describing the situation and asking for advice. It was also decided to send for John D. Lee. Lee was the appointed "Farmer to the Piedes Indians." These Indians had been trailing the Fancher train for some distance, and it was thought to bring Lee in to control them. A messenger was sent to his home in nearby Harmony to summon him to Cedar City forthwith.

Haight and Lee conferred privately that Sunday night, taking blankets to the old iron works and spending the night there. What emerged from their meeting was the decision to stir up the Indians to attack the emigrants and rob them of their wagons and cattle. There was, apparently, no outright talk of extermination. In any case, the idea was to wreak a measure of vengeance upon the emigrants if they could get the Indians to do it.

The Indians attacked the encamped Fancher group, prematurely and without adequate preparation, on Tuesday.[7] The emigrants entrenched themselves behind their wagons and returned the Indians' fire, killing one or two and injuring others. The siege continued until Friday. It will be remembered that Haight had sent an express to Brigham Young asking for instructions. That express had arrived in Salt Lake on Thursday, and a reply was on its way back, but would not arrive until too late, on Sunday, the 13th. Lee wrote later that he had not been told about the messenger sent to Brigham; it is easy to believe that had he been, he might not have been induced to follow Haight's orders. Indeed, perhaps Haight also would have been more hesitant to go ahead had it not been for a crucial incident.

The besieged group knew they had acted badly toward the Mormons, and they also knew that the Mormons harbored vast ill will toward them. Still, would not these white brothers band together against this onslaught by "savages"? The emigrants sent three men back to Cedar City on Wednesday night to ask for help. One of these, William Aiden, was ambushed by a Mormon and shot to death. The other two, wounded, escaped but were followed by Indians and also killed. This heightened the tension enormously. If word got out that a murder— the *first* murder of one of this party of emigrants—had been committed by a Mormon, then indeed there would be additional cause for an army to be sent from California to deal with them.

Messages passed swiftly between Lee, Haight, and Colonel Dame, the result being that Dame ordered that the emigrants "be done away with"—in ignorance of the fact that even as he was giving that order Brigham's instructions were probably on the way. When Lee was handed his orders by Haight he read them, dropped them on the ground, and said he couldn't do it. He was beseeched. He went off to pray by himself, weeping bitterly. (He was ever after called Yauguts by the Indians, meaning "crying man.") In the end, in the belief that he was doing what was required, he went along with the plan.

Lee and Charles Hopkins went out to the besieged emigrants, who welcomed them as their deliverers. The Fancher party were desperate by now, probably short of ammunition. Even so, it is not easy to understand why they went along with what was proposed. They would be led out, accompanied by guards of the Mormon militia, leaving their wagons and cattle to the Indians, who would be thus satisfied. They agreed to this cockamamie scheme and were led away. At the given command each armed "guard" was to kill the emigrant he was escorting, while the Indians took care of the women and children. (Thus the Mormons would not, in their view, themselves shed *innocent* blood.) The command was given and the shots rang out. Some men ran, but all were pursued and shot. The party was wiped out except for the children too young to talk about it later. Seventeen such children were taken to Hamblin's ranch. The massacre was over.

The next day Colonel Dame visited the site, together with Isaac Haight and John D. Lee. He had already been shocked by the sight of the crying and frightened children at Hamblin's house. Now, at the scene of the carnage, he was further shaken. Bodies had been hastily—and shallowly—buried, and would soon be (if they hadn't already been) dug up by hungry wild animals. "I didn't know there were so many," said Dame. He and Haight then got into an argument about whether, and how, the massacre should be reported. Dame said he would report it as it had happened. Haight replied, "Yes, I suppose so, and implicate yourself with the rest?"

Dame said he would not implicate himself, as he had had nothing to do with it. Haight pointed out that he had *ordered* the carnage. The argument became violent. Lee intervened, asking what the problem was. Haight replied:

> The trouble is just this. Colonel Dame *counseled* and *ordered* me to do this thing, and now he wants to back out, and go back on me, and by God he shall not do it. He shall not lay it *all* on me. He cannot do it. . . . I will *blow him to hell* before he shall lay it all on me. He has got to stand up to what he did like a little man. He knows he ordered it done, and I dare him to deny it.[8]

THE SCENE OF THE MOUNTAIN MEADOWS MASSACRE, UTAH TERRITORY.—[FROM A RECENT SKETCH.]
Harper's Weekly, 13 August 1859)

No hint here that the one—the only one—who would eventually pay the penalty for the massacre would be Lee. What followed was a massive cover-up. An act of this magnitude couldn't be concealed, but the participation of the Mormons could be, and the blame was placed entirely upon the Indians. The Mormons who had participated were immediately sickened as they recognized the horror and dimension of what they had done, and they resolved, to a man, to keep their own actions secret. (It should be pointed out, parenthetically, that it appears that some of the Mormons on the scene did *not* participate; when the order to fire came, they shot into the ground, or the air, unable to shoot the assigned target—leaving others to do the killing.)

Colonel Dame's distress was not lessened when he returned home to find Brigham's message replying to Haight's urgent inquiry for advice. Brigham's letter ordered the Mormons not to meddle with the emigrant trains passing through. But it also said, "The Indians we expect will do as they please but you should try and preserve good feelings with them."[9] Thus there can be no doubt that Brigham did not order Mormon participation in the massacre—but is there a suggestion that he might have tolerated the Mormons' allowing the Indians to do the job?

An act of the magnitude of the Mountain Meadows Massacre could not be kept hidden, and various versions of it were reported in the Eastern press. *Harper's Weekly* devoted its front page to the story in its issue for 13 August 1859, which included a grisly engraving of the scene. (See illustration.) The unnamed correspondent began his story thus:

> The story of so horrible a human butchery as that which occurred at the Mountain Meadows, Utah Territory, in the autumn of 1857, has by this time, no doubt, reached the States; but as no account which I have yet seen can in the slightest degree approximate to a description of the hideous truth, being myself now on the ground, and having an opportunity of communicating with some who were no doubt present on the occasion, I deem it proper to send you a plain and unvarnished statement of the affair as it actually occurred.[10]

The correspondent wrote that he had spoken with some of the Indians who had participated in the attack, who said they were but following the orders of Brigham Young, sent by letter. They told the writer that the Mormons had instigated and led the attack and had taken possession of the spoils. No Mormon other than Brigham is named in the article—and that accusation was, of course, false. The writer stated that he had found the bleached remains of many bodies at the site and that he had buried 30 of these. Sixteen children, he wrote, had been recovered from the Mormons and had described what had happened. The article ended with the statement that the time was fast approaching when "justice shall be laid to the line, and righteousness to the plummet."

Such justice as was done was a long time coming. Lee did not come to trial until July 1875. The jury could not agree; three Gentiles voted for conviction; the others, eight Mormons and one Jack-Mormon, found Lee not guilty. Lee was tried again in September 1876 before an all-Mormon jury. The evidence was convincing, no defense was offered, and he was found guilty. He had the option of choosing death by hanging or by shooting. He chose to be shot. He was executed at the site of the crime in March 1877. (See illustration.)

(For a pleasing postscript to this tragedy, see note 11 on page 185.)

John D. Lee (Courtesy Merrill Library, Utah State University).

John D. Lee sitting on his coffin before his execution at site of Mountain Meadows massacre. (Courtesy Merrill Library, Utah State University.)

Notes

1. I append here the wording of an invitation to this celebration received by my great-grandfather, Moses Franklin Farnsworth:

Pic Nic Party
at the Head Waters
of Big Cottonwood

Pres. Brigham Young respectfully invites M. F. Farnsworth and family to attend the Pic Nic Party at the Lake in Big Cottonwood Canyon on Friday, 24th of July.

Regulations

You will be required to start so as to pass the first mill about 4 miles up the canyon before 12 o'clock on Thursday 23rd as no person will be allowed to pass that point after 2 o'clock P.M. of that day. All persons are forbidden to smoke cigars, or pipes, or kindle fires at any place in the canyon except on camp ground.

The Bishops are requested to accompany those invited from their respective wards and see that each person is well fitted for the trip, with good substantial steady teams, wagons, harness, holdbacks, and locks; capable of completing the journey without repair and a good driver so as not to endanger the life of any individual. Bishops will before passing the first mill, furnish a full and complete list of all persons accompanying them from their respective wards, and hand the same to the guard at the gate.

Great Salt Lake City, July 18, 1857.

From Forsgren and Rasmussen, *The Descendants of Moses Franklin Farnsworth,* p. 104.

2. Ibid., pp. 104–05. Rockwell had been a particular friend of Joseph Smith's, his sometime bodyguard, a man of many talents and little fear. Some of his exploits are described in Taves, *Trouble Enough.* In addition to the companions mentioned by Farnsworth, there was also Nicholas Grosbeck.

3. *Deseret News,* 12 August 1857, cited in Brooks, *The Mountain Meadows Massacre,* p. 12.

4. George Albert Smith was Joseph Smith's cousin. He had been the youngest member of Zion's Camp, marching proudly at his cousin's side. At the time here referred to he was an apostle of the church. He was thought of by some as "the father of the southern settlements," since he had been active in their establishment.

5. Brooks, p. 23.

6. Seventeen Mormon men and boys were killed, and 15 more injured, by a mob at Haun's Mill in Missouri on 30 October 1838, a few days after Governor Lilburn W. Boggs issued his order that the Mormons be exterminated. The Mormons had not forgotten that massacre, and now here, in southern Utah, were men riding through claiming to have taken part in it—an open invitation to revenge. See *Trouble Enough,* pp. 131–32.

7. The initial attack is also reported to have been made on Monday. Lee gives the day as Tuesday, and I follow his account here. His account is, in general, the most honest and the least self-serving of the many versions that have been recorded.

8. Lee, *Mormonism Unveiled,* pp. 245-47.

9. This letter is in Church Letter Book #3, pp. 827-28, cited in Brooks, pp. 44-45.

10. Anonymous. "The Massacre at Mountain Meadows, Utah Territory." The anonymous writer is listed as a "correspondent."

11. As this book was going to press a most extraordinary gathering took place in St. George and Cedar City, Utah, on the weekend of 15-16 September 1990. After two years of planning for the occasion, descendants of the victims and of the perpetrators of the massacre met together in a spirit of forgiveness. Events and ceremonies included bus tours to the site of the tragedy, where a new plaque had been placed. The text uses the word *massacre,* but does not mention John D. Lee. One of the participants was Karl Brooks, son of Juanita Brooks, author of *The Mountain Meadows Massacre,* whose grandfather had been present on the meadows the day of the massacre. Brooks said, "Now it feels like a cemetery, more like Arlington. . . . Until now it's been a massacre site, but beginning today it's a memorial site." Gordon Hinckley, First Counselor of the church, called the day "a miracle, a benediction, a bridge across a chasm of bitterness." (*Washington Post,* 17 September 1990, pp. B1 and B3.)

12

The "Mormon War"—1857-58

By 1857 the Church had become so defiant that to President James Buchanan's thinking only a display of force could bring order in Utah. . . . Not much blood was spilled during this war, and to Capt. Jesse Gove and other men of Johnston's army the whole affair was a farce from beginning to end. Certainly it was not a military engagement of glorious report.

The quotation marks in the title of this chapter are meant to suggest that this conflict was not a war in the ordinary meaning of that word. True, federal troops were dispatched to deal with a hostile opposition and the lives of a considerable population were inconvenienced, but no side achieved brilliant victory and neither suffered ignominious defeat. Despite the destruction of property and the disruption of many everyday lives, farce is not a bad word to describe the enterprise.

When the Saints made their first settlements in the Great Basin, they were putting down roots in essentially virgin territory, not part of the United States. There they proposed to be self-sufficient, as we have seen, having as little traffic with the Gentile world as they could. That situation was changed drastically by the outcome of the Mexican War and by the discovery of gold at Sutter's Mill. With the signing of the Treaty of Guadalupe Hidalgo in 1848, the Mormons again came under the protection and control of the United States—not to say that that hadn't been foreseen by them from the beginning. The discovery of gold and the ensuing gold rush brought Gentile traffic and commerce aplenty into the basin. The causes leading to the Mormon War were many; but even if there were no consideration of polygamy, these two events made a generous contribution to the later conflict.

In the first place, when the federal government inserted its hand into the local affairs of the Mormon settlements, it too often did so with officials poorly equipped to discharge the responsibilities associated with their posts. Frictions were created that grew and festered. Secondly, with respect to the excitement over gold, many emigrants passed through the valley and many of them reported their experiences and impressions to the world outside. These expressions of opinion and descriptions of the Mormon kingdom were in the form of books, pamphlets, letters, diaries, press reports, and word of mouth, and many of these were anti-Mormon. Thus Gentile–Mormon hostility, which had dogged the Mormons since 1830, continued after the establishment of Zion.

There was, in addition, the vexing question of the relationship between the Mormons and the Indians. In general, the Mormons cultivated the friendship of the Indians, and they tried to teach them and to live in harmony with them. After all, their doctrine required them to bring them into the fold, that they might in the end become (again) "a white and delightsome people." This was interpreted by some Gentiles as an indication that the Saints were turning the Indians against Americans, as distinct from Mormons. Though this notion may not have represented the reality of Mormon–Indian relationships, there can be no doubt but that this was, as will be seen shortly, a frequently observable effect.

Further, the workings of the territorial judiciary tended to favor the Mormons, and often enough it worked genuine hardship upon the Gentiles that came within its jurisdiction. This was because Brigham had, through the territorial legislature, which was responsive to his bidding, established a system of probate courts that effectively allowed the Mormons to bypass the territorial courts presided over by federally appointed officers.

So there were grievances aplenty between the Mormons and the Gentile population generally, plus the federal bureaucracy in Washington. The precipitating causes leading to President Buchanan's decision to send troops to bring order to the unruly territory were transmissions to Washington of accounts of how things were within the Great Basin, directed to Washington through many sources, but particularly by federal appointees. We shall briefly consider the works of five of these disgruntled reporters.

David H. Burr arrived in the Territory as Surveyor General, his assigned task designated by his title. His arrival was immediately viewed as a grave threat, though it must be noted that there may have been at first—as with many other appointees—an initial period of friendly assessment, as evidenced by his possession of a place of honor in the

Independence Day parade, in Salt Lake, in 1856.[1]

Why was Burr's arrival seen as threatening? Because there had been no federal enactments, nor had any treaty or document been signed by the Indians and the Mormons giving the Saints possession of the lands they occupied. Thus the entire Mormon population were, by one interpretation, squatters. Here was threat indeed, the Mormons perceiving Burr's assignment as preliminary to an attempt at federal eviction, and they set to work to impede his efforts and to intimidate him. Part of this activity lends credence to the claim of Gentiles that the Mormons were setting the Indians against them; one Indian chief, Arapeen, told one of Burr's coworkers that the Mormons had warned his people against the surveyors, claiming that their work was part of a scheme to deprive them of their land.[2]

Burr was denounced from the Mormon pulpit, and one of his men was beaten almost to death. Surveyors' corner posts were removed, and a house in Fillmore, within which Burr and his men spent a night, was stoned. One of his clerks escaped through a window to flee to California, as intruders banged on his door at midnight. It was too much, and Burr departed the scene in April 1857, thinking with ample cause that his life was in danger if he remained. In due time his descriptions and reports reached the bureaucracy in Washington.

Dr. Garland Hurt, our next purveyor of intelligence to the nation's capital, was a federally appointed Indian Agent. Hurt was an educated man, a doctor from Kentucky, and he got along better with the Indians than with the Mormons. Among other activities, he established Indian farms with a view to giving them the experience of a more settled existence, hoping to lead them away from their nomadic life. In his reports to Washington he set forth his view that, as he saw it, the Mormons were trying to ingratiate themselves with the Indians, attempting to turn them against the Gentiles in their midst. With the threat of federal invasion hanging over them, the Mormons didn't want influential government officers in positions to do them harm, so they inquired into the situation in Spanish Fork, where Hurt had established one of his Indian farms. They discovered what seemed to them a dangerous situation.

The Indians liked Garland Hurt, and they distrusted the Saints. This could not be tolerated, and a band of Mormon men was assembled to march on the farm with the intent to harm Hurt. The Indians warned their friend and helped him elude the band of Mormons. The Utah

Expedition was now (September 1857) in winter quarters in the vicinity of South Pass, far to the north, and toward this refuge Dr. Hurt made his way—accompanied by two or three hundred friendly braves.[3]

Another source of reportage about matters in the territory was W. M. F. Magraw. In view of the isolation of Salt Lake the transport of mail between the Territory and the United States was a matter of great importance. The practice of the government was to give the contract for carrying the mail to the lowest bidder, and for some time this had been Magraw. He was given a new four-year contract in 1854, but the service was so poor that the Mormons made loud and bitter complaint, particularly in their press. Magraw's service became so unsatisfactory that his contract was canceled, whereupon the Saints seized the opportunity to get the contract for themselves.

Hiram Kimball submitted a bid, whether for himself or on behalf of the church, of just over half of that of Magraw's contract. He was awarded the contract, which was shortly taken over by Brigham and expanded into a much larger operation designed to carry goods as well as mail—the Brigham Young Express and Carrying Company, which soon became known as the Y. X. Carrying Company. Elaborate plans were made, and way stations and forts were constructed along the route, the work continuing during the severe winter weather of 1856–57. When the clouds of the Mormon War began to gather, however, the contract was canceled, in June 1857. A lot of money, well over $100,000, had been put into it, and now the enterprise had crashed in disarray.

The point here is that the disgruntled Magraw sought to take his spite out upon the Mormons; having lost his contract he made virulent representation to Washington. In October 1856 he wrote to "The President" (Franklin Pierce), saying he wrote as a personal and political friend. Territorial laws, he wrote, were really conspiracies, enforced at midnight by organized bands of "bravos and assassins." The only available courts (Brigham's probate courts) had become "engines and instruments of injustice." Magraw continued:

> There is no disguising the fact that there is left no vestige of law and order, no protection for life or property; the civil laws of the territory are overshadowed and neutralized by a so-styled ecclesiastical organization, as despotic, dangerous, and damnable, as has ever been known to exist in any country, and which is ruining, not only those who do not subscribe

to their religious code, but is driving the moderate and more orderly of the Mormon community to desperation.

Magraw warned the president that conflagration lay ahead. The elements were rapidly combining, he wrote, "to bring about a state of affairs which will result in indiscriminate bloodshed, robbery and rapine, and which in a brief space of time will reduce that country to the condition of a howling wilderness."[4]

That this letter was considered thoughtfully in Washington may be open to question, since it was addressed to an outgoing president. It surfaced in January 1858, when Buchanan was assembling papers, at the request of the House of Representatives, to provide documentary evidence that would throw light on the decision to send troops to Utah, and to provide information about the Mormons' state of rebellion against the U.S. Government. Magraw's letter was the only relevant document Secretary of State Lewis Cass could find in his files. But, as Furniss noted, to rationalize or justify the sending of troops, this letter served the purpose.

Next on the scene was Judge W. W. Drummond, probably as incomprehensible an appointment as Washington has ever made. Historian H. H. Bancroft believed that Drummond was the one man "who did more than any other, and perhaps more than all others, to bring about the Mormon War." Bancroft's descriptions of the judge are, to say the least, colorful. According to Bancroft, Drummond abandoned his wife and family in Illinois and took with him to the territory a woman picked up on the streets of Washington. Not only that, but he now and then had this woman at his side on the judicial bench. The Saints were affronted by seeing the law represented by, as Bancroft put it, "a gamester with a strumpet by his side."[5]

The Mormons made some inquiries of their own into Drummond's history and found that he had been convicted of fraud, indicted for perjury, and sentenced to a house of correction, in New York, for stealing stamps from a mail box to get enough money to buy a drink![6] He was, however, a federal judge, and his principal attack upon the Saints was directed at their judicial system. Their probate courts, presided over by territorial appointees, were effectively putting the federal courts out of business. There wasn't much Drummond could do in the Territory of Utah, apart from offending the Saints. He had ample opportunity to write anti-Mormon letters, which he did with enthusiasm.

Before Buchanan's administration took office in 1857, Drummond had written to President Pierce proclaiming the evils of the church, and he was ready to resign soon after Buchanan gained the White House. On 30 March 1857, 26 days after Buchanan's inaugural address, Drummond wrote his letter of resignation to Attorney General Jeremiah S. Black. When this letter came to Buchanan's attention it may have been the final persuasion that, added to all that had been written earlier by others, decided the commander-in-chief to dispatch his troops. This letter also contributed to the arousal of the populace when it was widely printed in the Eastern press.

Drummond wrote of Brigham's despotic government, all the more intolerable because of the claim that it was sanctioned from on high. He made accusations of Mormon crimes, including involvement in at least three murders, including that of Leonidas Shaver, whose death created the vacancy that President Pierce filled with the appointment of Drummond.[7] The situation was dark indeed, he wrote, with federal officials being most vilely maligned and abused with all manner of wickedness. The Mormons, he continued, look to Brigham Young for their law, and they consider no law of Congress as binding upon them in any manner. He accused them of burning court records stolen from Judge Stiles's office (see p. 193). Moreover he proposed a solution, one that may have contained a hope for his own advancement. "I do believe that, if there was a man put in office as governor of that Territory, who is not a member of the church [Mormon], and he was supported with a *sufficient* military aid, much good would result from such a course; but as the Territory is now governed . . . it is noonday madness and folly to attempt to administer the law in that Territory."[8] Drummond's hopes to get the job, if indeed he harbored them, were in vain; when that appointment was made, Drummond was not the man chosen.

The deputy clerk of the U.S. Supreme Court for Utah, Curtis E. Bolton, countered Drummond's charges with a reasoned response to Attorney General Black, dated 27 June 1857. He specifically denied that court records had been burned and stated categorically that all were still safe in his possession. He addressed other of Drummond's accusations briefly and to the point, and closed as follows:

I could . . . go on and refute all that [Drummond] has stated in his aforesaid letter of resignation, by records, dates, and facts; but believing the foregoing is sufficient to show you what reliance is to be placed upon the assertions or word of W. W. Drummond, I shall leave the subject.[9]

The *Millennial Star,* the Mormon journal published in Liverpool, England, made a less restrained response. It published a rousing editorial beginning: "This infamous scoundrel and dastardly wretch, having escaped from the just penalty of the law, is still running at large, endeavouring to hide his own filthy, and most heart-sickening crimes, by abusing and slandering the 'Mormons.' " Other terms applied to the judge in a six-page screamer: Lying, adulterous, murderous fiend . . . a loathsome specimen of humanity . . . infernal liar . . . horrible monster . . . beastly criminal.[10]

Finally, there was George P. Stiles, Drummond's colleague as associate justice in the Territory. With his name we complete our short roster of federal appointees driven from Zion, who carried reports to Washington of what had happened to them in the valley. Judge Stiles was no stranger to the Mormons or their church; he had been one of Joseph Smith's advisors who counseled him to destroy the *Expositor* in Nauvoo, a precipitating event that led to Joseph's assassination. He had later left the church, so here was not just a Gentile, but an apostate, come among them to administer justice. Obviously his choice was not a wise one.

The territorial legislature, in its efforts to fend off federal intervention, had established the post of territorial marshal to be the executive officer in the handling of territorial cases at law. From the federal bench, Stiles declared that the U.S. marshal, normally a Gentile, would have jurisdiction over territorial as well as federal cases. Stiles's act was legal but no doubt ill-considered. It aroused massive Mormon hostility, to such extent that Stiles was physically threatened, as well as being crudely abused by Mormon lawyers who appeared before him. Stiles asked Brigham for protection and was told he'd better close his court if he couldn't enforce the law!

Further, on 29 December 1856, a band of Mormons raided his offices and burned books and records in the yard behind. (It *appeared* that they had burned the court records, but it later transpired that they had removed them and hidden them away.) Stiles fled Utah in early

1857. In Washington, together with Drummond and others, he vigorously complained about the situation that had driven him from the Territory, as well he might. In his own view, his words carried considerable weight, as evidenced by his language in later applying for a federal appointment in Carson Valley: "And it does appear to me that I have a righteous claim to an official position there, seeing that I was one of the Fathers of the Military Expedition."[11]

The U.S. military expedition got off to a slow and shaky start. Precisely when President Buchanan decided to send troops into Utah Territory is not disclosed by available documentary evidence, but certainly he had reached that conclusion before the end of May. The top general of the U.S. Army, the General-in-Chief, as this office was then designated, was Brevet Lieutenant General Winfield Scott, "Old Fuss and Feathers," who had served his country long and well in many capacities. Brevet Brigadier General William S. Harney was to be the leader of the expedition.

Having decided to dispatch the troops, the administration was unaccountably lethargic in getting things under way. When Scott got news of the plan he took a dim view of it because of the lateness of the season. The army would have to cross the Rockies, and it was dangerously late to set the machinery in motion. Scott's opposition did not carry the day, however, and may not even have been communicated to the president. Buchanan's secretary of war was John Buchanan Floyd, who had been given that post because of his assistance in Buchanan's election campaign, and Floyd supported the dispatch of the expedition. He would later leave his post under a considerable cloud of incompetence and suspected fraud, but now he was in favor and had the president's ear. (Floyd would later become a general in the Confederate army, a post from which he would be dismissed because of incompetence.)

The decision to proceed having been made, Harney was informed on 29 June 1857, by letter from General Scott's aide-de-camp, George W. Lay, that "the community and, in part, the civil government of Utah Territory are in a state of substantial rebellion against the laws and authority of the United States."[12] On this same day he was ordered to proceed forthwith to Fort Leavenworth with his Fifth Infantry. Those troops, as it happened, were at that time tired and in need of rest and recuperation; they had been down in the Everglades, in Big Cypress Swamp, fighting mosquitoes, mud, fatigue, and Seminoles. Two hundred of them deserted when they learned of their new assignment.

To Harney's Fifth Infantry would be added eight additional companies from the Tenth Infantry. Cavalry would be provided by the Second Dragoons, and artillery companies would be brought down from Minneapolis. Many of the troops assembling in Fort Leavenworth in July were raw recruits, insufficiently trained, and certainly ill-equipped to undertake a formidable expedition over the distant Rockies, with late summer just around the corner. The troops that would comprise the Utah Expedition gathered in Fort Leavenworth, Territory of Kansas, and on 18 July they began their march westward, thus marking the formal beginning of the Mormon War.

They left, however, without their commanding general, Harney. There was trouble in Kansas Territory at this time, caused by warfare between proslavery and free-state factions, and Governer Robert J. Walker needed help. General Harney obligingly detached seven companies of dragoons and remained in Kansas with them. His command was assumed by Colonel Edmund Alexander of the Tenth Infantry. So the army went marching off without its intended commanding officer, and that would have consequences later. Also traveling with the army was the newly appointed governor of the Territory of Utah, Alfred Cumming, and his wife. By this time President Buchanan had committed two errors.

First, he was sending an army of considerable size to the west at a dangerous time of the year to deal with "a state of substantial rebellion," so designated in official correspondence to Harney dated 29 July 1857. He was doing this on the basis principally, it appears, of allegations by Judge Drummond and Magraw, beginning this considerable undertaking before sending in advance an investigative team to ascertain at first hand what the situation in Utah was. This error might have been obviated had Buchanan had the opportunity to read an editorial published in the *Deseret News* on 1 July, while the army was still shaping up in Fort Leavenworth. "Advice to President Buchanan and the cabinet" ran the headline. "Demand for a commission of investigation." The advice offered in the editorial was certainly sound:

> . . . We most respectfully suggest . . . that he select one or more civilians unbound by any 'ism' or 'isms,' if such can be found, also intelligent, strictly honorable, upright and gentlemanly, in the true sense of those terms, and send them to Utah on a short visit to look around and see what they can see, and return and report.

Should this be done, the editorial concluded, "we will guarantee that Governor Young and the people of Utah will treat them with more true courtesy and kindness than they have ever met with."[13]

Buchanan's second error (among others)—and this seems altogether indefensible—was to send the new governor to Utah without giving official notice to Brigham Young that he was being replaced and that his replacement was on the way.

It must be noted now that in Lay's letter to Harney, the mission of the expedition is stated with reasonable clarity—and with one unmistakable directive:

> If the governor of the Territory, finding the ordinary course of judicial proceedings of the power vested in the United States' marshals and other proper officers inadequate for the preservation of the public peace and the due execution of the laws, should make requisition upon you for a military force to aid him as a *posse comitatus* in the performance of that official duty, you are hereby directed to employ for that purpose the whole or such part of your command as may be required. . . . And in no case will you, your officers or men, attack any body of citizens whatever, except on such requisition or summons, or in sheer self-defense.

Clearly enough this army was not intended for invasion and conquest; it was to uphold civil authority. A *posse comitatus* is a body of men that civil officers may call upon to assist in preserving the peace and upholding the law, not an avenging army to exterminate people or put down a religion. It is too bad that Harney didn't pass these instructions on to Colonel Alexander when he sent the expedition on without him, and also unfortunate that a copy wasn't sent to the Mormons in the valley.

In early July the mayor of Salt Lake City, Abraham O. Smoot, was headed eastward, carrying the June mail from Salt Lake to Independence. Before reaching Independence, Smoot met both U.S. troops and heavy supply trains traveling west; they were secretive about their destination. In Independence Smoot discovered that they were on their way to Salt Lake, and this was disconcerting news. Also unwelcome was the discovery that the Y. X. Company's contract had been canceled, and they were no longer in the mail-carrying business. Smoot began to break up the company at Independence and to move that operation west. On this move west, accompanied by Judson Stoddard and others, he met Orrin Rockwell going east with more mail. After exchanging news and information at Fort Laramie, some 500 miles from Salt Lake, these three decided to proceed with all speed to Salt Lake with their news of the advancing troops. They left Fort Laramie on 18 July, the day that marked the Utah Expedition's departure from Fort Leavenworth. As noted in Chapter 11, they found the Mormon hierarchy and many of the brothers and sisters celebrating Pioneer Day in Big Cottonwood, where they told them the news. So, the federal troops were on the way, but who in the valley knew their intent?

The basic function of the expedition, as stated in Harney's orders, was to escort Governor Cumming there and—if need be—serve as his *posse comitatus* to see that the law was upheld. The new governor and Mrs. Cumming would travel with the army. Other federal appointees would be required to man the new regime; some of these would accompany the army, some would arrive later. The appointment of Alfred Cumming was a happy one, but we can see in most of the others that President James Buchanan—King James, as he would at times be referred to in the valley—had learned little from recent history in the Territory of Utah. The chief justice was Delany R. Eckels, a man known for his bitter anti-Mormon sentiments. He would arrive in Salt Lake with the army. Associate Justice John Cradlebaugh was another outspoken anti-Mormon, but he wouldn't get there until November 1858. To complete the federal bench was Charles E. Sinclair. Mormon historian Roberts would later describe his entire course in the valley in one word—despicable. He arrived in his new jurisdiction on 31 July.

The army, now under the command of Colonel Alexander, followed the usual route from Independence—Big Blue, Little Blue, then the Platte and North Platte to Fort Laramie and beyond, up the Sweetwater, and over the Continental Divide at South Pass. It would descend then along Big Sandy and Little Sandy to Fort Bridger, onward through canyons in the Wasatches, and finally down into the valley. The expedition would not go according to plan, however, because (Winfield Scott was right) they had started too late. The expedition didn't reach Fort Laramie until 3 September—two days before the doomed Fancher party passed through Cedar City.

As the troops moved westward they were passed by a soldier with a mission, Captain Stewart Van Vliet. He was a quartermaster, and was under orders to precede the army into Salt Lake to determine conditions there, particularly with reference to the availability of lumber, forage, and other supplies that might be needed by the army. He left Fort Leavenworth on 28 July with a small train of six mule wagons. Leaving his escort behind at Ham's Fork he traveled on alone to Salt Lake, arriving there on 8 September. Though he had been warned by some mountain men he met at the Green River that he would not be permitted to enter the valley, he encountered no difficulty with the Mormons, and was received cordially by Brigham Young.

Van Vliet was no stranger to the Mormons; at Winter Quarters he had employed many of them in government service, and he had had good relations with them. He remained in Salt Lake for six days and had several meetings with Brigham and other church leaders. He discovered that though there were adequate supplies in the valley to meet the army's requirements, the Mormons would sell none of these to them. Brigham and the others were convinced that the mission of the expedition was religious persecution. Van Vliet was back at Ham's Fork on 16 September. From there he sent a detailed report back to Fort Leavenworth. It brought no cheer to General Harney.

> During my stay in the city I visited several families, and all with whom I was thrown looked upon the present movement of the troops towards their Territory as the commencement of another religious persecution, and expressed a fixed determination to sustain Governor Young in any measures he might adopt. From all these facts I am forced to the conclusion that Governor Young and the people of Utah will prevent, if possible, the army for Utah from entering their Territory this season. This, in my opinion, will not be a difficult task, owing to the lateness of the season, the smallness of our force, and the defenses that nature has thrown around the valley of the Great Salt Lake.[14]

On 15 September Brigham issued a proclamation to the citizens of the Territory. It began: "We are invaded by a hostile force who are evidently assailing us to accomplish our overthrow and destruction." It went on to forbid the entry of any armed force into the Territory and to declare martial law. Be it noted that the opening statement of the proclamation is in total contradiction to Harney's orders, in which the mission of the expedition is clearly stated. One can only wonder at the magnitude of the trouble that might easily have been avoided by even a minimal communication between James Buchanan and Brigham Young. Or between General Harney and Brigham.

(Interestingly enough, as has been discovered only recently, Brigham's proclamation had been prepared more than a month earlier. The earlier publication, which was neither proclaimed nor distributed, bears the date of 5 August.)

The first engagement between the Nauvoo Legion and the Army of Utah erupted in the early morning hours of 24 September. Colonel Alexander's troops were camped at Pacific Springs, on a forced march to Ham's Fork. The troops didn't know it, but a body of 70 legionnaires under the command of Colonel Robert T. Burton was nearby, keeping tabs on them. He sent a small group of six men, including the intrepid Orrin Porter Rockwell, to stampede the federal mules. Something of a comedy of errors began at 2:00 A.M., when Rockwell fired a signal shot over the camp. He and his men drove their horses through the camp and sent the mules scattering. Consternation and confusion!

By the time the camp had been roused, Rockwell and friends and the mules had disappeared. The troops went back to sleep. Later that morning, about a mile from the camp, Rockwell and one of his men had dismounted when the last mule passed and were preparing a rear-guard action in case the troops began a pursuit. The four other stampeders were at the head of the mule herd, and they also dismounted, waiting for Rockwell to arrive. They had gone no further because the lead mule, the "bell mule," had gotten its rope caught in a clump of sagebrush, and the rest of the herd stopped with it. Now, from the camp, the bugler blasted forth with Stable Call. The mules knew that meant oats, and the herd stampeded back to the camp—joined by the riderless horses of the legionnaires! Rockwell stood there, a mile off, unable to believe what had happened. Round one to the feds.

Ten days later, on 4 October, the Mormons struck again. A group of men under the command of Major Lot Smith bypassed Alexander's troops and burned two of the army's supply trains at the Green River. The next day they burned a third. They had destroyed 300,000 pounds of food, together with other supplies. Round two to the Nauvoo legionnaires.

The teamsters driving the trains were not harmed and were allowed to salvage clothing and food for their own use. But the army's supplies had been drastically diminished. The season was getting on; winter came early here. Note that no men were harmed. General Daniel H. Wells had earlier ordered his men to take no life, but to harass the army at every opportunity—destroying supplies, stampeding animals. The basic objective was to delay the army's advance to such extent that they would have to go into winter quarters before arriving at the valley. Perhaps things would somehow be settled by then.

Meanwhile, Colonel Alexander was beleaguered, had no superior officer to turn to, and was unaware of his mission! He knew Colonel Johnston was coming to command his troops, but he didn't know where he was. On 8 October he sent a rather desperate communication to "The Officers of the United States Army, Commanding forces en route to Utah." He began by noting that the season was very late, that the time available for any military operations was very limited. "No information of the position or intentions of the commanding officer has reached me, and I am in utter ignorance of the object of the government in sending troops here, or the instructions given for their conduct after reaching here."[15]

In the absence of instructions, he conceived the idea of moving north along Ham's Fork, thinking to cross over to the Bear River and go down into the valley by that route. His troops set out with that aim in view but made scant progress before they were stopped by a snowstorm on 17 October. Fortunately for Alexander, his rescue, in the person of Colonel Albert S. Johnston, was catching up with him. Johnston established contact with Alexander by express and ordered him back to Camp Winfield, where he would meet him.

Johnston finally arrived at Ham's Fork in early November. The season was now far advanced, and there could be no question of proceeding into the valley. Johnston, a forceful and capable commander, saw at once that there was no way to establish winter quarters at Ham's Fork. Therefore, he began a race to Fort Bridger to spend the winter. Many animals dropped dead along the way, but the various units of the army did assemble at Fort Bridger, and at that site and in the general area they established Camp Scott, named for their commander-in-chief, General Scott.

The Mormons had torched Fort Bridger before abandoning it to the federal troops, but the adobe walls remained, and the location was a reasonable one in which to establish winter quarters. Governor and Mrs. Cumming, traveling with Lieutenant Colonel Philip St. George Cooke and his Dragoons, arrived at the camp on 20 November. Cooke's units had had a terrible time coming from Fort Laramie, with many men frostbitten and most of their horses dead. Cooke had lost but one man, however, a fatality caused by tetanus.

The various units of the army took up quarters both within the walls of the burned Fort Bridger and along the streams in the nearby area. The population of the encampment was more than 2,000, including troops, federal appointees, and teamsters from the supply trains. Having nothing else to do during the winter, no place to go to, many of these wagon drivers, a ragged lot on the whole, enlisted in the army.

The camp consisted mostly of tents of a new design; these were heated easily, and life was supportable.[16] Governor and Mrs. Cumming lived in a suite of no fewer than five connected tents. Johnston took a careful inventory of his food supplies and knew that rations would have to be cut, which they were, gradually, as the winter wore on. There was a three-month supply of food at Fort Laramie, 350 miles to the east, but its accessibility would have to wait until spring. Also the army was desperately short of horses and mules. On 24 November Captain Randolph B. Marcy, a soldier of distinction and quality, who would later rise to the rank of brigadier general and the position of Inspector General of the Army, was ordered south with a company of more than 30 men, including two Indian guides, to Fort Union, near Taos, New Mexico. He completed this hair-raising wintertime trek over the Uintah Mountains with the loss of only one man and, under escort by infantry and mounted riflemen, returned to Camp Scott the following June with 1,500 head of horses and mules.

The Eastern press exhibited considerable concern about the situation of the Utah Expedition. As early as 12 November the *New York Herald* editorialized that the troops were in a needlessly desperate situation, possibly leading to a "disgraceful catastrophe." On 14 January the *New York Tribune* expressed alarm: "Should Colonel Johnston and his 2,000 men come to any harm, their blood will rest upon the heads of those who placed them in their present position." No need to worry about bloodshed now. As the army settled down in winter quarters, obviously without any possibility of marching into the valley until spring, the Nauvoo Legion returned to Salt Lake, leaving behind only small patrols to guard against the unlikely event of some kind of surprise attack.

There were, no doubt, uneasy thoughts in many quarters about what would happen when the arrival of spring opened the routes into the valley. Enter now into the picture, again, the seemingly tireless Thomas

L. Kane, faithful non-Mormon friend of the Mormons. Traveling incognito as "Dr. Osborne," he arrived in Salt Lake on 25 February 1858, via the isthmus of Panama, California, and the southern overland route to the valley.[17]

Though he carried a letter from President Buchanan, Kane's mission was strictly his own with no official backing, and was undertaken at his own expense. He met with the church hierarchy—who knew him as Kane, of course, from much past experience—but, and most particularly, he had a private half-hour interview with Brigham. The substance of this meeting was not made a matter of specific record, but apparently Kane suggested that Brigham welcome the troops when they approached in the spring—a suggestion that Brigham repudiated. But Brigham *did* urge Kane to go to Camp Scott, there to "do as the Spirit of the Lord led him, and all would be right."[18]

It is arguable that Kane's self-appointed role of negotiator or peacemaker proved of crucial importance in determining the eventual outcome of the Mormon War. He stayed in Salt Lake until 8 March, when he began his trip to Camp Scott, possibly bearing a letter from Brigham authorizing him to act as negotiator. (Roberts found no mention of such a letter in church annals, but such a document was mentioned in an 1859 article in the *Atlantic Monthly*.)[19]

Kane arrived at Camp Scott on 12 March. He conferred at length with Governor Cumming, with whom he got along well, but he rubbed the military the wrong way and had trouble communicating with Colonel Johnston, who was, in any case, much enraged by Brigham's offer of food to the army, also carried by Kane. Kane's most important achievement was to convince Cumming to proceed to Salt Lake in advance of the army. Cumming announced his intention to do just that to Colonel Johnston on 13 April, and two days later Cumming and Kane left Camp Scott for Salt Lake.

Meanwhile, back in the valley, Brigham's plans had changed from fight to flight. He unveiled his proposal in an extraordinary gathering in the Tabernacle on 21 March. He would lead the church south. They would evacuate the city. The federal troops, when they arrived, would find Salt Lake City empty. (He had earlier thought of executing a scorched earth policy, burning the city to the ground, but that plan had been abandoned.) The Mormons would evacuate their homes—yet again— going first to Provo, then later on to a great unexplored area to the south where they would establish a new Zion. He was their earthly shepherd, and the Saints must follow him. "A great many parents follow off their children, and men follow their women. For a man to follow a woman is, in the sight of Heaven, disgraceful to the name of a man."

> Where are you going? To the deserts and the mountains. There is a desert region in this Territory larger than any of the Eastern States, that no white man knows anything about. Can you realize that? What is the reason you do not know anything about that region? It is a desert country with long distances from water to water. . . . Probably there is room in that region for 500,000 persons to live scattered about where there is good grass and water. I am going there, where we should have gone six or seven years ago. Now we are going to see whether the sheep will follow the shepherd. I do not care whether they follow me or not.[20]

Brigham did not specify the area they would trek to, but there is no doubt that he had in mind a region to the southwest of Fillmore, the White Mountain area in the Wah Wah mountains, dominated by Frisco Peak. The immediate move was to Provo, and the evacuation of the city commenced forthwith. Most of the Mormons moved to Provo, where many of them lived in difficult and uncomfortable hovels. Brigham established a substantial compound for his household. Exploratory teams were sent to the White Mountains.[21]

News of Cumming's approach to the valley preceded him, and on Sunday, 11 April, he and Kane were met by a military band playing "The Star-Spangled Banner" and other patriotic airs! Brigham and other church leaders returned to Salt Lake, where Cumming and Kane arrived the next day, and a number of meetings followed. Governor Cumming found, possibly to his surprise, that he *liked* Brigham Young and the two other members of the First Presidency, and he did his best to convince them that it was not his intention or wish to destroy the Mormons. Cumming wished, indeed, to prevent a shooting war at almost any cost, and such was his comportment that he was favorably received.

On 15 April he wrote to General Johnston of his good reception, and assured Johnston that he, Cumming, was accepted by the church hierarchy as the governor of the Territory. Ten days later he was introduced to thousands of Mormons in the Tabernacle, and was invited to address them. He did so, explaining that he was in their midst to uphold the law and that he had nothing to do with their social and religious concerns. The army would not, he said, be quartered within their community, but would stay apart; it was there to be called upon as a *posse comitatus* only in case of necessity. The new governor was listened to attentively, but when he asked for questions the meeting became boisterous. It seemed that many of the Mormons thought Cumming was a Missourian, hence beyond the pale. Some even thought he had been a member of the Jackson County mob of detested memory, which mob had indeed included a man named Cumming or Cummings. Cumming assured them that he was a Georgian. That statement, together with Brigham's exhortation, quieted the gathering.

Now, back east on this same day, 25 April, President Buchanan's Peace Commission left Fort Leavenworth on its way to the valley, carrying his *Proclamation of Pardon* to the Mormons. Buchanan, in response to public pressure, had issued this pardon on 6 April, and had appointed Ben McCulloch and Lazarus W. Powell as peace commissioners. McCulloch was a legislator from Texas; Powell had been governor of Kentucky and was now senator from that state. Buchanan hoped that this action would end the war; he was, after all, offering a free pardon for all past seditions and treasons, provided only that those who had been guilty of such would now submit to federal authority. Cumming wanted to end the war also, and on 2 May he wrote to Secretary of State Lewis Cass to contradict the earlier report that the Mormons had destroyed court records. Cumming wrote that the records were in perfect shape, as was the territorial library. Two days after Cumming wrote to Cass, the Congress provided the necessary appropriations to keep the army going. At this same time Cumming was trying to persuade the Saints who had gone south to return to Salt Lake. In this he was not successful. The exodus to the south was still continuing.

On 13 May Cumming and Kane began their trip back to Camp Scott. The Governor would fetch Mrs. Cumming and take her back to Salt Lake; Kane would continue on to Washington. They arrived in camp three days later. Cumming now wanted to persuade Johnston that no organized armed forces would oppose him in the valley, and that the army might best remain where it was for the present. Unaccountably, he didn't communicate with Johnston until 21 May, and then only by letter. Johnston—and his men, many of whom wanted to do battle with Mormons—wanted to proceed to the valley forthwith.

Cumming wanted no such movement until he had replies from his communications to Washington. Buchanan's peace commissioners arrived in camp on 29 May, and the next day the impatient Johnston pledged not to move the army until he had word from Salt Lake.

The Commissioners left camp for Salt Lake on 2 June, and Governor and Mrs. Cumming, accompanied by Jacob Forney, Superintendent of Indian Affairs, left the next day. The travelers found Salt Lake almost deserted, but word of their arrival was sent to Provo, and a number of church leaders returned to Salt Lake. The commissioners and the church leaders met on 11 June. After lengthy discussion Brigham put the matter squarely to the commissioners. "What do you want of us?" Commissioner Powell's response was direct: "We only want you to let the government send in the troops, and that you submit to the laws—let the army come in, go through and locate lands—protect the inhabitants"[22]

The meeting continued the next day, and that day, 12 June 1858, marks the end of the Mormon War. The Mormons capitulated, putting upon the day the best interpretation they could. George Albert Smith spoke at considerable length, and to good effect. He noted that though Buchanan's proclamation contained no less than 42 false charges, he would accept it. "I am a man of peace, and not of war. I accept the pardon." He said that if the Saints fell upon the federal troops and crushed them, thousands more would be sent to exterminate them.

He spoke in glowing terms of Governor Cumming, who had come to them, bravely and nobly, without supporting troops. He came, Smith said, not to govern as a military despot, but as a fellow citizen. He ended with a plea not to reject the overture presented by Buchanan's proclamation.[23] Brigham Young's concluding remarks do not, apparently, survive, but clearly he was with Smith. The war was over. That evening, from the cramped quarters the Saints had uncharacteristically provided them, the commissioners wrote to the Secretary of War.

> We have settled the unfortunate difficulties existing between the government of the United States and the people of Utah. . . . They will cheerfully yield obedience to the Constitution and laws of the United States. They consent that the civil officers shall enter upon the discharge of their respective duties. . . . No resistance will be made to the officers, civil or military, of the United States in the exercise of their various functions in the Territory of Utah.

Thus ended a murky chapter in territorial and Mormon history, with neither side having much to boast about. General Johnston had violated his pledge not to move the army toward the valley until he had word from Governor Cumming, but in view of the result of the meetings of 11 and 12 June that didn't make much difference. He broke camp on 13 June and the army, marching in three columns, headed for Salt Lake City, with the advance guard in the lead, followed by infantry and artillery batteries, mounted riflemen, supply trains, and the rear guard of weapons gleaming in the sun, the caissons rumbling— here was a fine spectacle for the Indians who, half naked, raced to and fro on their horses, thrilled by the parade put on by the white men.

Johnston had earlier stated his clear intention not to camp his troops in or near Salt Lake City, and so timed his movements that he passed through the (largely deserted) city early on 26 June. The Saints who had deserted their homes to move south had been alarmed by the thought that the army might cause damage as it marched through the streets, but those fears proved groundless; there was no pillage or looting. The army made camp that night beyond the city limits, and some days later established the permanent Camp Floyd in Cedar Valley, about 36 miles south of Salt Lake City.

The Mormons returned to their homes and businesses. The situation in the valley didn't exactly return to "normal." There began, rather, a slow adaptation to a new situation. Federal troops were camped within the territory, but they were distant from the city. The threat of military struggle was past, as was that of fleeing to the inhospitable desert. And a good thing too, because as Roberts noted, based on later knowledge of how barren that desert is, such a flight would have resulted in overwhelming disaster. Finally, it is arguable that the reasonably satisfactory outcome of the Utah expedition can be attributed to the tireless intervention of Thomas L. Kane.

Notes

1. Roberts, *CHC,* vol. 4, p. 227. It should be noted, as does Roberts on this page, that the Gentile view that the Mormons celebrated their Pioneer Day (July 24) but not the nation's Independence Day was not justified. Roberts shows that there were elaborate Independence Day celebrations in the years preceding and following the Mormon War.

2. Furniss, *The Mormon Conflict, 1850–1859*, pp. 45-46. This work, relying largely on government documents, is an invaluable source of material on the Mormon War.

3. Ibid., pp. 47-51, and Roberts, *CHC*, vol. 4, p. 297.

4. Magraw, *Letter to President James Buchanan, 6 October 1856*, pp. 2-3. (In following references to the letter *The Utah Expedition*, reference will be to House Executive Document No. 71.)

5. The quotations are from Bancroft, *History of Utah*, pp. 490-91.

6. Furniss, *The Mormon Conflict, 1850–1859*, "Journal History of the Church," pp. 54-55.

7. The other two alleged murders were those of Almon Babbitt and John Gunnison.

8. Drummond, W. W. *Letter to Attorney General Jeremiah S. Black*, pp. 212-14.

9. Bolton, *Letter to Attorney General Jeremiah S. Black*, pp. 214-15.

10. "The Notorious Judge Drummond," in the *Millennial Star*, vol. 19 (1857), pp. 328-33.

11. Furniss, pp. 66-67.

12. George W. Lay to W. S. Harney, House Executive Document No. 71, pp. 7-9.

13. Roberts, *CHC*, vol. 4, pp. 220-21.

14. Stewart Van Vliet to Captain Pleasanton, House Executive Document No. 71, pp. 24-26.

15. Edmund B. Alexander to Officers of the United States Army commanding forces en route to Utah, or Governor Cumming, House Executive Document No. 71, pp. 38-40

16. These tents were conical, open at the top so smoke from the center of the floor could easily rise and escape.

17. Kane later explained his reason for traveling incognito; after hearing the terrible reports about Mormon behavior that reached him in the East, he wished to see how he, as an unknown visitor, would be received by Mormons who did not know him. He was gratified to find that he was well received.

18. Roberts, *CHC*, vol. 4, p. 349, "History of Brigham Young, Ms," entry for 15 August 1858.

19. Browne, A. G., Jr., "The Utah Expedition," *Atlantic Monthly*, April 1859.

20. Brigham Young's remarks were printed in pamphlet form in Salt Lake in 1858, as *A Series of Instructions and remarks by President Brigham Young at a Special Council, Tabernacle, March 21, 1858*. Original copies are in the Libraries of the University of Utah and Yale University.

21. For an account of these explorations, see Stott's *Search for Sanctuary*.

22. Roberts, *CHC*, vol. 4, p. 424; from the original minutes of the meeting.

23. See Roberts, *CHC*, vol. 4, pp. 429-32.

24. House Executive Document No. 71, pp. 167-68.

13

Aftermath

The miserable howling and demonic yells of the midnight brawlers, maddened by the intoxicating draught, contrasts strangely with the peace which has ever before reigned in Deseret.

General Johnston established the camp of the federal troops in Cedar Valley, a few miles to the west of Lake Utah, about 35 miles south of Salt Lake City. It became known as Camp Floyd, thus honoring the name of the secretary of war, a designation not without irony in view of Secretary Floyd's later failures and disgrace. (The name was later changed to Camp Crittenden.)[1] The camp was inhabited by some 4,000 troops, the largest such assemblage of military in the republic to date, in time of peace. There was in the area an additional population of about 3,000 non-Mormon employees, suppliers, hangers-on, camp followers, entrepreneurs, prostitutes, gamblers, and sellers of spirits.

The buildings of the camp were constructed mostly of adobe, much of it provided by Mormons living in the nearby settlement of Cedar Fort. The large quantities of lumber required came from the mountains north of Salt Lake City, again supplied by Mormons. The influx of this mixed population into Zion was certain to cause problems, and it did, but it also brought economic prosperity. According to Campbell, the Big Cottonwood Lumber Company, which was church-supported, netted close to $200,000 from sales of lumber used in the construction of the camp.[2]

There was, of course, the other side of the coin. Though Camp Floyd was at some distance from Salt Lake, the city inevitably felt the impact of its presence. The chief clerk of the territorial legislature, John L. Smith, wrote to Thomas Stenhouse of the "miserable howling and demonic yells of the midnight brawlers," maddened by drink.[3] A community beguilingly designated Frog Town (now, Fairfield) became established a few miles southeast of the camp and soon acquired a reputation for all manner of evil. Here, after all, was a very large body of men who had been without women for a long time, and nature took its course. Attempts were made upon Mormon women, which presented difficulties. But there were many Indian squaws and girls in the vicinity; and the problem was less here, because the braves used the money so obtained to buy whiskey. The Utah Expedition, mounted to bring law and order to the territory, did bring a degree of federal control, but clearly it brought disorder as well.

Let us examine, now, the roster of the eight federal appointees sent here to do the job.

Governor Alfred Cumming. As we have seen, a man well disposed toward the Saints, for the most part accepted by them, set down in a difficult situation, and determined to make a good job of it. He came in advance of the army, without military escort, and was as well received as could be hoped for.

Chief Justice Delany R. Eckles. Brigham Young took note of Judge Eckles in an entry in his manuscript history. "The ermine must sit *gravefully* on the soldiers [shoulders?] of a chief justice who employed the influence of [his] high position in performing services as a pimp, to provide gratification of lust to army lieutenants, and that by the seduction of wives and mothers."[4]

Associate Justice Charles E. Sinclair. Brigham's manuscript history gives us a glimpse of his honor:

> Judge Sinclair . . . got so drunk that he had to be led out of the house, by two of his friends, to *spew;* he was so drunk he could not stand; his friends laid him on the snow, and put snow on his head and face; in this situation he laid and spewed until his stomach was emptied, he was then led back to the house; they had to go through a small gate, which would only admit of one person at a time; consequently his honor had to stand by his own merit; but his *understanding* . . . refused to perform their office, and his honor pitched upon his head, into the snow.[5]

Associate Justice John Cradlebaugh was assigned to the southern judicial district and convened his first court in Provo on 8 March 1859.

Two days earlier he had asked Assistant Adjutant General F. J. Porter to provide federal troops to guard prisoners who would appear before him, as there was no jail in Provo. This request was granted, to the dismay of Governor Cumming and the outrage of the Mormons. The troops camped near the courthouse, creating a situation not conducive to thoughtful judicial procedure. Cradlebaugh impaneled a grand jury in an attempt to determine responsibility for the Mountain Meadows Massacre, but he found their deliberations unsatisfactory and dismissed them.

On 20 March, while Cradlebaugh's court was in session, Governor Cumming traveled to Provo and asked the commanding officer to withdraw the troops. The request was ignored. Word was sent by express to Washington. When the U.S. Attorney General Jeremiah S. Black learned of this situation he was much displeased at this clear misuse of the army. Black, after conferring with President Buchanan, wrote to Cradlebaugh stating firmly that only the governor of the Territory was empowered to requisition all or part of the army. The guarding of prisoners was the responsibility of the marshal, not the judge. The marshal had made no indication that he needed troops. Cradlebaugh had exceeded his authority, as had the general who honored the request of the judiciary, when, in fact, his responsibility was to the executive, to the governor: ". . . the disregard of these principles and rules of action has been, in many ways, extremely unfortunate."[6]

The judge didn't last long in the Territory; he was reassigned to Carson Valley, which shortly became part of the Territory of Nevada. From there Cradlebaugh was elected representative to the Congress, where he delivered anti-Mormon homilies.

Secretary of State for the Territory of Utah John Hartnett was no friend to the Mormons. Brigham and Hartnett antagonized each other, and their relationship was hostile. Hartnett was alleged to have said that he hoped a row would break out between the Mormons and the army.

Superintendent of Indian Affairs Dr. Jacob Forney did not get along well with the Indians. Chief Arapeen, brother of and successor to Chief Walker of the Utahs, said that Forney's heart was small and dark as night, that his speech was like bawling, and went in one ear and out the other.[7] Judge Cradlebaugh accused him of filing false vouchers. Forney was eventually dismissed from the Indian Service.

United States Attorney Alexander Wilson had more trouble with Judge Cradlebaugh than he did with the Mormons. He objected to Cradlebaugh's handling of the Mountain Meadow Massacre inquiry in Provo. He also opposed Cradlebaugh's absurd contention that his court could not take judicial cognizance of President Buchanan's pardon proclamation. He returned to the States early because of his wife's health.

Territorial Marshal Peter K. Dotson, a Virginian, went to Utah in 1851. Brigham Young had employed him for a time as manager of a distillery, after which he had been mail and express agent. He was appointed U.S. marshal in 1855, went to Washington in 1857, and returned to the valley with the army. He served as marshal until 1 August 1859, when he resigned. No doubt his departure from the service was hastened by difficulties with Brigham, which were occasioned circuitously by criminal acts perpetrated by a group of greedy entrepreneurs at Camp Floyd.

This group, which included Myron Brewer and J. M. Wallace, conceived the plan of counterfeiting the camp's quartermaster's drafts, drawn upon the assistant treasurer of the United States, at St. Louis, to their own financial gain. They enlisted the services of a Mormon engraver, David McKenzie, who had engraved plates for Brigham Young, to duplicate the plate used by the quartermaster. The assignment was completed successfully and skillfully, but the execution of the plan was inept and the scheme was soon exposed. The principal miscreant, Brewer, was arrested, and forthwith confessed and turned state's evidence, naming the engraver and also implicating someone in Brigham's office, alleging that he was the source of the paper upon which counterfeit notes had been printed. In consequence, the engraver was arrested.

Dotson visited the engraver's atelier and impounded his tools and equipment. He found the plates intended for Deseret currency and appropriated those as well, thus exceeding his authority. When the plates were eventually returned to Brigham, they were damaged, and Brigham sued Dotson for illegal seizure and damage. After a lengthy trial Brigham was awarded damages of $2,600, forcing Dotson to sell his Salt Lake house. As noted above, Dotson resigned his position in August 1859.

McKenzie was tried, found guilty, and sentenced to two years in the penitentiary.

What was it like, then, in the Territory of Utah in the interim between the end of the Mormon War and the beginning of the Civil War, one of whose consequences was the closing of Camp Floyd (by then Camp Crittenden) and the departure of the Utah Expedition? Camp Floyd was established in 1858, and Camp Crittenden was abandoned in 1861. Historian Roberts's title for the chapter concerned principally with this interim is "A Chapter of Horrors." There is no question but that the federal troops had been hoping for a time of Mormon-bashing and that the absence of overt military conflict with them was disappointing. As for the Mormons, they were glad to return to their homes, but for the most part they had no use for the army and wanted the troops out of there. Let us see how things were between these two bodies through the eyes of one of the army officers.

Captain Jesse A. Gove, officer of the Tenth Infantry, was a native of Concord, New Hampshire. He wrote many letters to his wife, as well as to the *New York Herald* and other Eastern newspapers. He was, somewhat to his surprise, favorably impressed by Salt Lake City— the emptied city. Writing from camp on 2 July he described his first traverse of the city. "We found the city evacuated, all had gone to Provo except a few men whom they left to burn the city if ordered. The city is 50 per cent better in structure and situation than I expected to find. It is beautifully laid out and watered at every street." He had not so favorable an opinion of the Mormons. "The people are at Provo. They are impudent and rebellious still. They say they will accept the pardon, but that the President is a fool; that they will not obey anyone but Brigham Young. They don't want the army and won't have it. Such is the result of the pardon, a miserable policy which the government ought to be damned for."

Six days later the army had not yet found the site for Camp Floyd but they had had some experience with the Saints.

The people are like all fanatics, just such credulous people as the Mil-
lerites . . . under the most perfect control of the priests and bishops.
Contrary to what we expected, the men seem as much attached to Brigham
Young and the church as was pretended from representatives made before

we entered the valley. We expected to find many disaffected men and women, but they hold no intercourse with us only in the way of trade in vegetables and fowls, and are as tenacious as ever in the beliefs of their doctrines. The women are under the most positive bondage; there can be no doubt of it. They look and appear dejected, and would undoubtedly live differently if they could.

A few days later he wrote of "the utmost coldness between the gentiles and Mormons." On 29 July, on a few days' leave from camp, he wrote from a Salt Lake hotel: "We have been here six days, and a more non-intercourse visit among a people I never knew. The Mormons are still isolated. . . . We cannot ever mix, as clannishness is the only safe mode of maintaining their organization."⁸ Gove wrote that he and Captain Cumming, the governor's nephew, had been entertained at the home of Governor and Mrs. Cumming, where they had met some of the church leaders, together with their wives. "But," complained Gove, "they do not, any of them, invite us to call."

Gove also wanted to see Brigham Young, but that wouldn't happen either. Brigham had gone into a kind of seclusion; he appeared at no public meetings, and he was not to be seen on the streets unless accompanied by a substantial armed bodyguard. The doors to his home and office were guarded day and night, and armed guards were present within at night. Nor was this altogether without cause, for at this time at least one attempt was set in motion to arrest him—on a trumped-up charge of complicity in the attempted forgeries at Camp Floyd. The officers charged with making the arrest attempted to enlist the support of Governor Cumming. The governor was outraged, as he later reported.

"I listened to them, sir, as gravely as I could," continued Cumming, "and examined their papers." They rubbed their hands and were jubilant; "they had got the dead-wood on Brigham Young." I was indignant, sir, and told them, "By God, gentlemen, you can't do it! When you have a right to take Brigham Young, gentlemen, you shall have him without creeping through walls. You shall enter by his door with heads erect, as becomes representatives of the your government. But till that time, gentlemen, you can't touch Brigham Young while I live, by God!"⁹

Though social intercourse between Mormon and Gentile was at a minimum, a considerable financial exchange shortly developed. At first Brigham had spoken of having no traffic with the intruders, but it soon became apparent to everyone that the federal incursion into the territory could be something of a gold mine. There was a community of 7,000 or more within 35 miles of the city, and possibility for profit was surely there. In addition, the church treasury was at low ebb.

The Mormons sold a variety of things to the camp: salt, eggs, vegetables, pies, buttermilk, dried fruit, dried fish, and meat. Individual entrepreneurs, with or without the blessing of the church, sold a whiskey known as Valley Tan. The camp bought from the farmers hay, straw, and grain. Mormons made adobe bricks for the camp's construction, and sold the quartermaster much lumber as well. The real bonanza fell to the Saints, however, when the army had to return to the States because of the Civil War. On 16 July 1861 a massive auction was held at the camp, and about $4 million worth of government stores were sold for about $100,000, or two and a half cents on the dollar. Of these sales, about 40 percent were to Brigham Young.[10]

This sale leads us, deviously and briefly, to the Salt Lake Theater. This theater, completed in 1862, was modeled after the Drury Lane Theater in London. It seated an audience of 3,000. It was elegantly constructed, and was far and away the grandest theater west of the Mississippi. Many of the finest artists of the day performed upon its stage. The point here is that the nails used in its construction were made from iron left behind by the Utah Expedition.[11]

The Utah Expedition brought a measure of financial gain to the Mormons, but it also brought a time of anxiety and violence. In the interim between the arrival of Governor Cumming and the departure of the army a large population of Gentiles was introduced into what had until then been a relatively closed society of Mormons, and that meant trouble. The problem lay partly with the army personnel, but more so with those who had come with it. Hundreds of troops were not soldiers in any real sense; they were teamsters who had been stranded, together with the army, at Camp Scott. Many of them had been enlisted, since there was not much else to be done with them. They were discharged from Camp Floyd at intervals, and the Saints noted these mass discharges with much dread.

Most of these men were discharged with government warrants, but without transportation or rations. Naturally they drifted into Salt Lake

City, to whose streets they brought violence and danger. This was mostly
Gentiles fighting Gentiles. And it wasn't just the teamsters, there were
also the whiskey sellers, prostitutes, adventurers, and gamblers. An entry
in *Brigham Young's History* in January 1859 put it this way:

> A large portion of the officers were men of intemperate and grossly licentious
> habits, and the soldiery were largely enlisted from the dregs of the foreign
> emigration. There were several hundred men who had been discharged
> by the government after their arrival in Utah, and had no means of
> subsistence except by stealing. They had gambled away and otherwise
> squandered their earnings, and were therefore ready to rob, or commit
> any other crime to obtain subsistence.[12]

Though many of the troubles in this interim period did not involve
Mormons, there were also some serious incidents between Saint and
Gentile. We briefly note here one example, the Spencer-Pike affair.

Howard Spencer was the son of one of the owners of a ranch
in Rush Valley, part of which had been possessed (reserved) by General
Johnston for the army's need for pasture and hay. The ranch was on
or near the limits of the reserved property. In March 1859 Spencer
and a co-worker, Alfred Cliff, went to the ranch to round up their
stock, planning to stay in Daniel Spencer's house overnight. They met
a group of soldiers who told them they could not, that the house was
on a government reserve. A struggle followed, in which Sergeant Ralph
Pike fractured Spencer's skull with his gun barrel. Spencer fell to the
ground unconscious.

An army surgeon was summoned from Camp Floyd. He found
a part of Spencer's skull overlapping another, did some sawing, and
made such repair as he could. His procedure was successful, and Spencer
made a slow recovery. Brigham's *History* reports that Spencer had a
letter from General Johnston giving him permission to occupy the
premises, which General Johnston denied. Sergeant Pike's report was
that Spencer had attacked him with a pitchfork. Spencer said he was
using the pitchfork to fend off Pike's attack. Pike was later indicted
by grand jury for assault and battery, was arrested and brought to Salt
Lake City on 11 August. On Main Street he was met by Spencer, who
asked him if his name was Pike. Answered in the affirmative, Spencer
shot him and escaped. Three days later Pike died.

The next day soldiers from Camp Floyd went to nearby Cedar

Fort, set fire to a haystack, and fired some 60 rounds at Mormons trying to put the fire out. Nearby buildings burned to the ground, but no one was hurt. The Mormons made a loud complaint to General Johnston. He said he would post a guard at Cedar Fort, but admitted he had a problem controlling the soldiers as long as Spencer, who had murdered one of their comrades-in-arms in cold blood, was at large. Spencer never did come to trial. I have been unable to find later references to him.[13]

During this interim period curiosity brought a number of eminent visitors to Salt Lake City. One who later wrote of his impressions at considerable length was Horace Greeley, distinguished editor and founder of the *New York Tribune*. He began a ten-day stay in the city in July 1859. Another visitor was Richard Francis Burton, British explorer and linguist. He arrived in Salt Lake in August 1860 and was in the area almost a month. Greeley published his views of the Mormons in his *Overland Journey from New York to San Francisco*. Burton's opinions appeared in *The City of the Saints*. Brigham Roberts found Greeley's account disappointing and superficial, although he granted that the great editor

INTERVIEW BETWEEN BRIGHAM YOUNG AND HON. HORACE GREELEY AT SALT LAKE CITY.
Harper's Weekly, 3 September 1859

intended no injustice and tried to be fair. Roberts had a more tolerant view of Captain Burton's book. It was, wrote Roberts, more pretentious than Greeley's, and it did not present a thorough analysis, but it was the fairest and best book written by a non-Mormon. That was Roberts, writing in 1930.[14] We shall now inquire briefly into the accounts of these two formidable and intelligent observers.

Greeley had a two-hour conversation with Brigham Young in the presence of other church people, including Heber C. Kimball and Daniel H. Wells. (See illustration.) His questions were primarily about Mormon theology. Example: Am I to regard Mormonism as a new religion, or as simply a new development of Christianity? Brigham responded to the effect that there could be no true Christian church unless its priesthood was directly commissioned by, and had immediate access to, the Son of God. Thus all other churches are beyond salvation? Yes.

In response to other questions Greeley learned that the church believed in a personal devil and in eternal punishment, that baptism by immersion was essential, that infant baptism was not practiced, that polygamy was the divine will. Each Mormon man determined for himself to what extent he could act in accordance with that duty. As for slavery, though Brigham didn't like it himself, it was also a divine institution and should so remain until the curse on Ham was removed from his descendants. Did that mean that when Utah achieved statehood it would be a slave state? No, said Brigham, slave labor would not work in Utah. Greeley learned that no officer of the church was paid for his services; with the single exception of Brigham, all others had work outside the church. Brigham had never been paid anything by the church. He estimated his personal worth at about a quarter of a million dollars. He knew, he said, how to acquire property and how to take care of it.

And what of the Danites? Brigham heard of them only through scandalous Gentile lies. Finally, how was it that the Mormons were the objects of almost universal aversion and hatred? Nothing new in that, said Brigham, that goes back to the crucifixion of Christ. God's ministers have been so treated in all ages.

Greeley's report about Brigham's mein during the interview is at least as interesting as the content.

> He spoke readily, not always with grammatical accuracy, but with no appearance of hesitation or reserve, and with no apparent desire to conceal

anything, nor did he repel any of my questions as impertinent. He was very plainly dressed in thin summer clothing, and with no air of sanctimony or fanaticism. In appearance, he is a portly, frank, good-natured, rather thick-set man of fifty-five, seeming to enjoy life, and to be in no particular hurry to get to heaven. His associates are plain men . . . and looking as little like crafty hypocrites or swindlers as any body of men I ever met. The absence of cant or snuffle from their manner was marked and general. . . .[15]

Greeley attended two services on one Sunday in the Tabernacle, and didn't think much of what he heard. He heard Orson Pratt in the morning and John Taylor in the afternoon. He found that neither had prepared his discourse, they simply delivered a hodgepodge of rambling, dogmatic, and ill-digested homilies. The assumption in each case was that the Saints were God's chosen people, and the rest of mankind was floundering in heathen darkness. "I am not edified by this sort of preaching," Greeley wrote. "I do not think good men delight in this assumption of an exclusive patent for the grace of God."[16]

And here, of course, Greeley gave at least part of the answer to the question he had earlier asked Brigham: why so many Gentiles viewed the Mormons with such aversion. Because they were the only ones with the right answer, the right knowledge, the right church, the only ones with the key to salvation. Greeley found this a "gross and wooden perversion of the magnificent imagery whereby the Bible foreshadows a great spiritual transformation." He noted that he had been told that Heber Kimball did indeed pray for his enemies—he prayed that they might all go to Hell. "Neither from the pulpit nor elsewhere have I heard from a Mormon one spontaneous, hearty recognition of the essential brotherhood of the human race—one generous prayer for the enlightenment and salvation of all mankind.[17]

Historian Roberts's disappointment with Greeley's account is understandable.

As for the governmental situation that Greeley observed, he considered the federal judiciary, the federal army, and the federal executive to be shams. Brigham Young had the territory in his breeches' pocket; the church was (as Greeley saw it) the only power. Greeley proposed a solution to the difficulty. Reappoint Brigham as governor, he suggested, and "let the Mormons have the territory to themselves—it is worth very little to others, but reduce the area by cutting off Carson Valley on the one side, and making a Rocky Mountain territory on the other, and then let them go on their way rejoicing."[18]

Greeley didn't foresee that great mineral wealth would later be found in the valley. The Territory later *was* reduced, both to the east and the west, as he had proposed.

Richard Francis Burton spent more time in the valley than did Greeley, and he gave a much more *detailed,* though not necessarily a better, account. As already noted, Roberts considered Burton's book the fairest written by a Gentile. After all, Burton's report was that he found the Mormons to be peaceful, industrious, and law-abiding. And he was clearly sensitive to the persecutions that had followed them. Burton's book is indeed written in what may be called pretentious prose. Burton was a linguist, and his account of the Mormons suffers from an overdisplay of that preoccupation. He likes to use such words as *boustrophedon* and *titubantly,* for example, which will disenchant some readers, or at least send them to the dictionary.[19]

Burton makes no pretense of being able to penetrate into the soul of Mormonism, but he does report at great length about what he asked, learned, and saw during his visit. He met with Brigham, of course, and it is interesting to compare his report with Greeley's.

His manner is at once affable and impressive, simple and courteous; his want of pretension contrasts favorably with certain pseudo-prophets that I have seen. . . . He shows no signs of dogmatism, bigotry, or fanaticism, and never once entered—with me at least—upon the subject of religion. He impresses a stranger with a certain sense of power. . . . His temper is even and placid; his manner is cold—in fact, like his face somewhat bloodless. . . . Where occasion requires, he can use all the weapons of ridicule to direful effect, and "speak a bit of his mind" in a style which no one forgets.[20]

Brigham didn't speak to Burton of religion, because Burton, from a sense of delicacy, didn't ask him any direct questions about it. He had a considerable interest in the religion, however, and heard a number of sermons and discourses in the Tabernacle. Burton wrote first of hearing Brigham address the multitude. When he rose, all fell silent. Brigham expectorated into a hidden spittoon, took a sip of water, and began. The beginning of his talk was hesitant, uncertain, barely audible. But as he built up steam "the orator warmed, his voice rose high and sonorous, and a fluency so remarkable succeeded falter and hesitation that . . . the latter seemed almost to have been a work of art." Burton found Brigham's manner pleasing, his words spoken rather than preached. Then he echoes Greeley's observation. ". . . If it had a fault it was rather rambling and unconnected."21 After hearing so much about Brigham's practical good sense, Burton admits that, with respect to this discourse, he was "somewhat disappointed."

Finally, one of Burton's observations about life in Salt Lake City in 1860 is indeed surprising. He dined one evening with Governor and Mrs. Cumming, after which a number of guests, including Mr. and Mrs. T. B. H. Stenhouse, dropped by for conversation. The evening concluded, Burton wrote: "Long after dark I walked home alone. There were no lamps in any but Main Street, yet the city is as safe as at St. James's Square, London. There are perhaps not more than twenty-five or thirty constables or policemen in the whole place. . . ."22 This report is entirely at variance with innumerable other reports by Mormon and Gentile alike, including the epigraph to this chapter, which is from a letter from a Mormon to Stenhouse after the army had arrived and before Stenhouse had returned to Salt Lake.

The interim between the end of the Utah War and the beginning of the Civil War ended with the departure of the Utah Expedition from Fort Crittenden, a leave-taking celebrated with a degree of bitter joy by a *Millennial Star* editorialist. In celebrating the departure of the army from the valley, that writer assumed that the purpose of the expedition had been to destroy the Mormon religion. Nothing to date, he wrote, had so clearly shown the utter futility of trying "to injure or retard the progress of the Church and the kingdom of God." That a bloody battle with the Mormons had been on the minds of a part of the military can in no way be denied, but the expedition had not been dispatched to the Great Basin to destroy the Mormon church.

The editorial writer maintained that many, all over the world, had been joyful in their belief that the army would destroy the church and had treated the Mormons even worse than usual in consequence of that. "Some, indeed, went so far as to think that life itself was a boon too good for such as they to enjoy." And, he pointed out, when the army left, selling off at very low prices all of its surplus except munitions, they destroyed the weaponry and ammunition rather than leaving it for the Mormons to protect themselves from the Indians. That rationale—

to protect Utah citizens and emigrants from Indian attack—had been offered as one of the reasons for the army's presence.

"Thus has ended the great expedition against the Latter-day Saints in Utah, which had become world-renowned, in consequence of the extravagant hopes that were indulged in by its originators respecting its success. It should be known hereafter in history as 'Buchanan's Folly.' "[23]

Notes

1. John Jordan Crittenden was a distinguished American statesman, U.S. senator, attorney general in three administrations, and governor of Kentucky. He finished his last senate term in 1861. He labored diligently toward conciliation between the free and slave states, but his plans, which included solving the issue by amendments to the Constitution, failed. His two sons fought on opposing sides in the Civil War.

2. Campbell, *Establishing Zion,* p. 274.

3. This chapter's epigraph is from Smith's letter to Stenhouse, cited in Roberts, *CHC,* vol. 4, p. 462.

4. *HBYM-B,* p. 249.

5. Ibid., p. 269.

6. Black's letter is in United States Senate, 36th Congress, 1st Session, Executive Document No. 32, pp. 2-4.

7. Ibid., pp. 262, 270.

8. See Hammond, *The Utah Expedition, 1857-58,* pp. 188-89. Many visitors to present-day Salt Lake City are impressed, as was Gove, by the rivulets of clear water running down the gutters of the broad streets. Gove served in the Civil War as a colonel in the 22nd Massachusetts Volunteers. He was killed in the battle of Gaines's Mill, 27 June 1862.

9. See Stenhouse, *The Rocky Mountain Saints,* p. 411, for a report of conversation with Governor Cumming.

10. Bancroft, *History of Utah,* pp. 575-76.

11. Campbell, *Establishing Zion,* pp. 283-84.

12. *HBYM-B,* pp. 271-72.

13. Ibid., pp. 279-80, 282-83, 294-95, and Roberts, *CHC,* vol. 4, pp. 503-05.

14. Roberts, *CHC,* vol. 4, pp. 523-31.

15. Greeley details his conversation with Brigham in *Overland Journey,* chap. 21, pp. 209-18.

16. Ibid., pp. 220-21.

17. Ibid., p. 223.

18. Ibid., pp. 228-29.

19. *Boustrophedon:* descriptive of writing that is written, and read, from left to right, then right to left, so continuing, emulating the course of the plow in furrowing. *Titubantly:* stammeringly, staggeringly, unsteadily.

20. Burton, *The City of the Saints,* pp. 238-39.

21. Ibid., 261.

22. Ibid., 224.

23. *Millennial Star* 23 (1861), pp. 612-13.

14

The Civil War

The government of the United States is dead, thank God, dead. It is not worth the head of a pin.

We are not here as aliens from our government, but we are tried and firm supporters of the Constitution, and every constitutional right.

Mormon reaction to the outbreak of the Civil War was complex; it involved the conflicting interests of theology and of politics. From the theological point of view, many Mormons took the beginning of the war as a sign that the millennium was at hand; the United States would self-destruct, drawing other nations down as well; all would perish, save those in the Kingdom; the Second Coming was just around the corner. Such was the thought of some Mormons, including Heber C. Kimball, who made the statement in the first epigraph above. At the same time the Mormons were trying to gain statehood. How could they be accused of disloyalty when they were trying to get into the Union, the same Union that others were trying to secede from?

Part of the basis for the theological argument lay in a revelation received by Joseph Smith on Christmas Day in 1832.

Verily . . . the wars that will shortly come to pass, beginning at the rebellion of South Carolina . . . will eventually terminate in the death and misery of many souls. . . . The Southern States shall be divided against the Northern States, and the Southern States will call on other nations, even the nation of Great Britain . . . and they shall also call upon other nations in order to defend themselves against other nations; and then war shall be poured out upon all nations.[1]

As the Civil War approached, Utah again mounted a vigorous effort to join the Union as a state. As early as 16 December 1860, four days before the secession of South Carolina, the Utah delegate to Congress, William H. Hooper, wrote to George Q. Cannon: "I consider we can redress our grievances better in the Union than out of it; at least we'll give our worthy 'Uncle' an opportunity of engrafting us into his family; and if he doesn't want us, we must then carve out our own future."[2] Hooper noted that many House members had told him they would gladly give up the Gulf states in exchange for Utah. At the same time at least two delegates from southern states were seeking support from Utah, pointing out to Hooper what a boost would be given to their cause if Utah joined in the rebellion. Hooper's response was that their problems with the government would be solved within the government, or they would endure them.

Abraham Lincoln was inaugurated as President on 4 March 1861. Five weeks and four days later, on 12 April, at 4:30 A.M., Brigadier General Pierre Gustave Toutant Beauregard ordered the firing on Fort Sumter. The Civil War had officially begun.

The United States Army was now out of Utah, but the cloud of distrust continued between the Territory and the federal government. Another attitude of the Mormons toward the Civil War appeared, namely, aloofness and detachment. On 4 July 1861 John Taylor said:

> In regard to the present strife, it is a warfare among brothers. We have neither inaugurated it, nor assisted in its inauguration. . . . We know no north, no south, no east, no west; we abide strictly and positively by the Constitution, and cannot by the intrigues or sophism of either party, be cajoled into any other attitude.[3]

Lincoln's first appointment as governor of Utah, John W. Dawson, was a disaster. Dawson arrived in the Territory on 7 December 1861 and addressed the legislature a few days later. He immediately antagonized the community with accusations of disloyalty. During the rest of the month he was said to have made indecent proposals to at least one respectable woman and to have been guilty of other questionable behavior, to such extent that he secluded himself in his quarters, where he was reported to be either sick or insane. He resigned and fled the Territory on the last day of the year. His brief appearance in our narrative ends with his arrival at the mail station at Mountain Dell. Here he was set upon by eight men, beaten, and robbed. He survived and continued his journey. From the mail station at Bear River he wrote to the *Deseret News* of the attack and named the eight men. Three attempted to flee to California, and all three were shot and killed. The others were remanded for trial.[4]

Utah still yearned to join the Union, though some of the Mormons might see it as being in process of dismemberment. This need culminated in the convening, in Salt Lake on 20-23 January 1862, of a constitutional convention. Another constitution for the State of Deseret was adopted, with Brigham Young as governor. Heber C. Kimball was named lieutenant governor and John M. Bernhisel delegate to Congress. A memorial to Congress was also adopted, this to accompany the constitution to Washington.

On 14 April, Brigham Young, having called the Deseret legislature to meet, delivered an address proclaiming the right to statehood. The second epigraph at the head of this chapter is from that address. The legislature optimistically named George Q. Cannon and William H. Hooper as senators from the State of Deseret, and a contingent of Mormons went to Washington in search of statehood. The Deseret constitution and the accompanying memorial were presented to the House and Senate on the 9th and 10th of June respectively, delegate Bernhisel acting in the House, the vice-president and Senator Latham from California presenting in the Senate.

Senator Latham moved that Cannon and Hooper be admitted to the floor of the Senate, but the motion was set aside and nothing came of it. The constitution and the memorial were given to the Committee on Territories, and nothing came of that either until 22 December. On that date the committee reported favorably with respect to Utah, Nevada, Nebraska, and Colorado. Nevada became a state in 1864, Nebraska in 1867, and Colorado in 1876. Utah would remain a territory until 1896.

Back in the Territory the church was coming to grips with its own version of the Civil War, and this brings us to the paranoid psychosis of Joseph Morris. Morris, a Welshman, had joined the church in 1849 and had emigrated to the valley. By 1859 he was expressing in long letters to Brigham Young the claim that he, Morris, was now the prophet, that he was the true holder of the keys to the kingdom in the dispensation of the fullness of times. Not only was he an incarnation of Moses, he was also the seventh angel written of by John in Revelation 20. Accounts differ with respect to whether Brigham deigned to respond to these outpourings.

Morris was based in South Weber, a small community on the Weber River at the mouth of Weber Canyon, between Salt Lake City and Ogden. Here he began to collect followers, including the bishop of his ward, Richard Cook. This was getting serious, and on 11 February 1861 John Taylor and Wilford Woodruff went to South Weber to hold a public meeting and evaluate the situation. Bishop Cook declared that he believed in the new prophet, and that Brigham Young had failed in his leadership of the church. Fifteen other church members agreed with their bishop. These apostates were excommunicated forthwith, but with surprising gentleness. Referring to those disfellowshipped John Taylor said, "Treat those well who cannot believe as you do, they have expressed themselves very candidly, you can afford to treat them well."[5]

Less than a month after this meeting Morris announced the formation of his new church, the Church of Jesus Christ of Saints of the Most High. On 6 April the first baptisms were performed and the church began with six members—as had Joseph Smith's some three decades earlier. The six grew rapidly to several hundred and eventually to about a thousand. They settled into a communistic group, centered about a part of South Weber known as Kington Fort.

Morris's appointed date for the Second Coming came and passed several times and some members became disaffected. When they tried to reclaim their property, Morris, Cook, and others held them imprisoned in Kington Fort. An affidavit setting forth this unlawful imprisonment was put before Chief Justice Kinney, and on 22 May 1862 he executed a writ of habeas corpus, requiring that the held men be brought before him. The writ was ignored. The judge issued a second writ on 11 June and dispatched it to Kington Fort in the hands of Robert T. Burton and Theodore McKean, the deputies of Marshal Lawrence, who was out of the territory at the time. Burton and McKean went forth accompanied by some 250 armed militia.

The troops reached Kington Fort on 13 June and sent in a message that said, in effect, surrender in 30 minutes or else. The result was a three-day siege in which Morris and others, including two posse members, were killed. The Morrisites would later go on trial.

Independence Day 1862 was approaching, and the Saints made a particular effort to celebrate the occasion, thus providing further evidence of their patriotism. On 28 June the City Council of Salt Lake City published a document, *Preamble and Resolutions,* outlining their plan. The preamble is worth quoting in full, in view of the political atmosphere at the time.

> While we lament the deplorable condition of our once happy country, the independence of which was purchased by the best blood of our sires, we hail with pleasure the approaching anniversary of the birthday of the Nation, and in view of perpetuating our free and liberal institutions which have for so long a time inspired the patriotism of every true American citizen, and the strangers of other climes, who have sought an asylum under the protecting aegis of our glorius Constitution, therefore. . . .[6]

The following resolutions detailed the logistics of the fete. Three days after the celebration Stephen S. Harding, Dawson's successor as governor, arrived. Curiously enough, Harding had known Joseph Smith in New York in 1830, and had been present when the first title page of the Book of Mormon came from the press in Palmyra. He had kept the page and later, in 1847, had given it to the church. On Pioneer Day, 24 July, a day that the Mormons celebrated that year with great enthusiasm, the governor addressed a huge gathering in the Bowery. He made a good impression. He came, he said, as a messenger of peace and good will. He declared that he had no religious prejudices to overcome. Applause. The good impression was, however, to be short-lived.

Nor were the Mormons to be free for long of a federal military presence. The atmosphere of distrust that began with the Utah Expedition would continue for a long time. A measure of that distrust is seen in the army's destruction of all the munitions it couldn't take with it when it abandoned Fort Crittenden. Further indication of continuing federal unease with respect to the Mormons was the decision of Secretary of War Edwin M. Stanton to send *another* detachment of troops to Salt Lake, ostensibly to guard the Overland Mail and Telegraph routes passing through the valley, in spite of the fact that the Mormons were entirely willing to perform that function; the mail and telegraph were important to them also. The new detachment of troops came from California, about 700 volunteers under the command of Colonel Patrick Edward Connor, a man much prejudiced against the Mormons.

Connor first entered the city—alone, without military escort—on 9 September 1862. After studying the topography of the city, he decided to make camp on elevated ground, between Red Butte and Emigration canyons, two and one-half miles east of Temple Square, a location from which he could command the city. Writing on 14 September Connor expressed his views of the city's population in a letter to his commanding general in San Francisco. The Mormons, he wrote, were traitors, murderers, fanatics, and whores. "The people publicly rejoice at the reverse to our arms and thank God that the American government is gone as they term it, while their prophet and bishops preach treason from the pulpit."[7] He described the proposed location of his camp, noting that it would be much more efficient than the Fort Crittenden site. He also reported that Governor Harding was most anxious that the troops be camped near the city.

On 20 October Connor led five companies of infantry and two of cavalry into the city, and immediately got off to a poor start. A rumor had reached him that the entrance of the army into the city would be resisted, so the troops marched in with bayonets fixed and rifles loaded, brass band blaring, a display that, naturally enough, enraged the Mormons. There had been no intent to oppose the movement of the detachment into the city.

The march stopped briefly, as a courtesy, at Governor Harding's house. The governor addressed the troops with words of welcome and of warning. He was glad to meet them, he said, and told them their mission was one of peace and security not just with respect to the government but to every individual in the Territory. If they performed their duty properly, they would have his support. "But," he added, "if on the contrary you . . . should run wild in the riot of the camp—should break over the bounds of propriety, and disregard that discipline that is the only possible safety for yourselves, then shall I not be with you."[8] He finished by saying that in the line of duty he was with them to the death.

Connor called for three rousing cheers for country and flag, and three more for the governor. The march then continued to the chosen site, bands playing, bayonets at the ready. From this site cannon could be directed toward Temple Square and Brigham Young's house and office. The site became at that moment Camp Douglas, a government military reservation, now called Fort Douglas.

The presence of 750 or so troops on elevated terrain, looking down on the city, could not be said to comprise a serious military threat. As one reporter to the Eastern press put it, the Nauvoo Legion could have used them up before breakfast.[9] But they were an affront and an irritant, and there was plenty of hostility between camp and city. A measure of the distrust with which the Mormons viewed the army is seen in the episode of the colonel's promotion. There was trouble with the Indians to the north, particularly the Shoshones and Blackfeet, who were attacking and killing emigrants and miners. On 29 January 1863 Colonel Connor, who was said to hate Indians, marched his troops to Bear River to join them in battle, which he did to such effect that it became a massacre. Probably as many as 300 Indians were killed, including women and children.

For this public service the colonel was promoted to brigadier general. When the word reached Camp Douglas, on 29 March, the troops struck up the band to serenade General Connor and fired celebratory cannon, this between 10:00 and 11:00 P.M. At the sounds of firing, the alarmed citizenry swiftly dressed, seized weapons, and assembled in large number at Brigham's house prepared for battle. The sound of band music was pacific (who mounts a surprise attack accompanied by fanfare?), cooler heads prevailed, and it was much ado about very little. But the incident reveals the tension then present between the army and the civilian population.

Though Governor Harding's Pioneer Day address to the Mormons had been friendly and had been greeted with much applause, in the light of subsequent events one must wonder how much of his thinking Harding was, in that speech, revealing. As early as August he was writing to Secretary Seward that, in his view, the Mormons were not ready for statehood. Were the Saints loyal to the government of the United States. In his opinion, he wrote, they were not. He described what he was hearing in the Tabernacle:

> . . . Brigham Young and other preachers are constantly inculcating in the minds of the crowded audiences who sit beneath their teachings every Sabbath that the United States is of no consequence, that it lies in ruins, and that the prophecy of Joseph Smith is being fulfilled to the letter. According to the prophecy, the United States as a nation is to be destroyed. That the Gentiles . . . will continue to fight with each other until they perish and then the Saints are to step in and quietly enjoy the posses-

sion of the land and also of what is left of the ruined cities and desolated places.[10]

This is more than a little curious, considering that the Mormons, months before, had put their case for joining the Union before the Congress. What did they really think? It is not easy to say. These were the early days of the war and things looked dark. Was application for statehood something like an insurance policy in case the nation did survive? Who can say? In any case, Harding's views, here expressed, are at variance with those set forth in his earlier address.

The situation began to worsen when, on 2 December 1862, Harding issued a proclamation declaring the following 1 January to be a day of Thanksgiving and Praise to Almighty God. The granaries of the Mormons were full to overflowing, and no scourge had fallen upon them "while in other and fairer portions of the land the Demon of Civil War has driven his blood-stained chariot over desolated fields and deserted cities . . ."[11] The governor requested a general observance of that day.

Later that month Harding addressed the legislature in what was perceived as an insulting manner. Their territorial laws must be drastically changed, he said. He reminded them that the Morrill Act was now law, and that they were in danger if they heeded the words of their authorities telling them the law was unconstitutional. Moral anomalies, he told the legislators, couldn't continue to exist side by side. Either the general society would have to subordinate itself to Mormon doctrine, or the Mormons would have to behave like Gentiles; the conflict between the two could not continue. He also accused the Saints of lack of loyalty. According to Stenhouse, the manner of the speech was worse than the matter.

The assemblage listened in stony silence. The legislature did not order the remarks printed, and the *Deseret News* took no note of it. Word reached Washington that the governor's address had been suppressed. The Congress printed it and sent Harding a thousand copies. The committee on territories went into session, and delivered a negative report on the Utah legislature. The first of January came, and the day of thanksgiving was not observed.

The governor and his constituency were now truly estranged, but there was worse to come. The two appointed associate justices for the

Territory at this time were Charles B. Waite and Thomas J. Drake. Judge Waite had a brainstorm and brought Waite and the governor into a scheme that would emasculate the courts of the Territory in which most of the work was done, the county probate courts. They sent to Washington proposed amendments to the organic act of 1850 that had created the Territory. Its principal provision would drastically curtail the functions of the probate courts, whose responsibilities would be limited to probating wills, writing letters of administration, and appointing guardians. They sent their proposed act to Washington on 3 February 1863, recommending its passage by Congress. It was introduced to the Senate by O. H. Browning of Illinois.

Naturally, delegate Bernhisel learned of this and communicated with the folks back home with all dispatch. The Mormons were scandalized by this attempt to strip them of all judiciary power, and on 3 March mounted a mass meeting of protest, in consequence of which the governor and the two judges were asked to resign (they didn't), and President Lincoln was petitioned to withdraw Governor Harding and the two judges. The petition claimed that Harding and the two associate justices were "strenuously endeavoring to create mischief and stir up strife between the people of the Territory of Utah and the troops now in Camp Douglas . . . and, of far graver import . . . between the people of the aforesaid Territory and the Government of the United States."[12] The president was asked to remove the offenders forthwith.

On 19 March, not quite two weeks after the mass meeting of protest, the trial of the Morrisites began in the court of Chief Justice Kinney. Sixty-six men were found guilty of resisting the posse, and were fined $100 each. Ten others were tried for the deaths of the two slain members of the posse, and seven of these were found guilty of second-degree murder. They received sentences ranging from 10 to 15 years. Governor Harding now generated more animosity by pardoning all seven. His "To all whom these presents shall come, greeting" doesn't go far to specify why the pardons were granted, mentioning only "divers good causes."[13] He also pardoned the 66 men who had been fined. The grand jury of the third district court lost no time in declaring its outrage.

We . . . present his "Excellency" Stephen S. Harding . . . as we would an unsafe bridge over a dangerous stream—jeopardizing the lives of all who pass over it, or, as we would a pestiferous cesspool in our district, breeding disease and death.

Believing him to be an officer dangerous to the peace and prosperity of this Territory . . . treating nearly all the Legislative acts with contumely; and last of all, as the crowning triumph of his inglorious career, turning loose upon the community a large number of convicted criminals.[14]

Lincoln didn't fire the judges, but in May he relieved the governor of his duties. He appointed James Duane Doty to succeed, and Harding left the Territory in June. Doty had been superintendent of Indian Affairs in the Territory for two years, was no narrow partisan to any faction, and was respected by Mormon and Gentile alike. He was a good candidate to carry out Lincoln's three-word policy toward the Mormons—leave them alone. As a sop to the Gentiles, Lincoln also withdrew chief Justice Kinney and Secretary Frank Fuller, who were thought, by some, to be too friendly with the Mormons.

Conditions improved under Governor Doty, but tension and distrust remained between army and city. General Connor had his own solution to the "Mormon problem," which brings us to a brief historical introduction to mining in the Territory. As early as 1848, ore thought to contain silver had been found by Sanford and Thomas Bingham in a canyon in the Oquirrh range a short distance southeast of Salt Lake City, which became known as Bingham canyon. (This location is very near what would later become the Kennecott open-pit copper mine, the largest such in the world.) Fearing the possibility of a gold or silver rush into the Territory, Brigham had asked the brothers to keep their discovery secret, and they had done so.

On 17 September 1863, however, galena bearing silver was again discovered in the same canyon, by both a group of Mormons who were logging, and by a group of officers and wives on a picnic from Camp Douglas. One of the Mormons, George Ogilvie, took a sample to General Connor, who had it assayed. Connor encouraged Ogilvie to locate the vein, and together they staked a claim and founded the Jordan Silver Mining Company. The wife of a camp surgeon, Mrs. Robert Reed, made a separate discovery and filed a claim on 18 September; and yet another claim, the Vedette, was filed the same day. A large surrounding area was promptly and formally organized as the West Mountain Quartz Mining District.[15]

Back, then, to Connor's solution. His plan was to publicize the presence in the territory of precious ores. This would, he thought, bring in a flood of Gentile miners and prospectors who, when their numbers were sufficient, could counterbalance Mormon domination and, through the ballot box, assume political control. He used his troops, when other duties permitted, as prospectors, to contribute to the discovery of locations of other valuable deposits. And in November 1863 he began, at Camp Douglas, to publish an anti-Mormon paper, *The Union Vedette.* Connor stated his case bluntly in a letter published in the first issue:

> The general commanding the district has the strongest evidence that the mountains and canyons in the Territory of Utah abound in rich veins of gold, silver, copper and other minerals, and for the purpose of opening up the country to a new, hardy, and industrious population, deems it important that prospecting for minerals should not only be untrammelled and unrestricted, but fostered by every proper means.[16]

The letter went on to state that all prospecting parties coming to the valley would have adequate and sufficient military protection. In succeeding issues of the *Vedette* Connor sternly warned the Mormons against threatening or using any violence against newly arrived miners and prospectors.

General Connor further enraged the Mormons in July 1864 when he appointed Captain Charles H. Hempstead as provost marshal for Salt Lake City, and stationed him and his provost guard on South Temple, opposite the entrance to the Tabernacle.[17] Rumor spread that there would be an attempt to arrest Brigham Young. Brigham was visiting the southern settlements at the time, and when he heard of the stationing of the guard he returned to the city, accompanied by an armed guard of 500 men. Vigorous complaint was made to Connor's superiors in California. Major General Irving McDowell ordered Connor to remove the station. He was there, McDowell indicated, to guard the mail and telegraph routes, not to govern the city.

As the end of the Civil War neared and Union victory became ever more certain, Mormon attitudes changed, particularly with respect to the arrival of the millennium. The United States was not going to fall apart, bringing other nations down with it. As Wilford Woodruff admitted, "The end is not yet." Abraham Lincoln easily won reelection in 1864 and the Gentiles and Mormons rejoiced together. The atmosphere in the valley was changing, at least for a time, into something more friendly. As the day of Lincoln's inauguration, 4 March 1865, approached, the mayor of the city, Abraham O. Smoot, issued a call for celebration. "Resolved, by the City Council of Great Salt Lake City, that we cheerfully join in the public celebration and rejoicings of that day throughout the United States, and that we cordially invite the citizens, and organizations, military and civil, of the Territory, county and city, to unite on that occasion."[18]

A parade a mile long marched through the city, and the marchers included both the Nauvoo Legion and the United States Army. Bands played martial airs, orations were delivered, and cannon were fired in loud salute. The city council entertained the army officers at a banquet. To cap the day, the Nauvoo Legion escorted the army back to Camp Douglas. In the next issue of the *Vedette* the day was hailed as a significant occasion. The article noted that the demonstrations had been so altogether different from those of previous experience that the day merited special notice as an important event in the history of Utah.

Less than two months later city and camp united again, this time in mourning the death of Lincoln. The Civil War interim ended. In the months and years ahead the church would confront many challenges and problems.

Notes

1. *Doctrine and Covenants,* Section 87. The revelation mentions South Carolina, which later was the first state to secede from the nation. At the time the revelation was received, however, President Andrew Jackson was having a great deal of trouble with South Carolina over a tariff bill that had been passed by Congress. When South Carolina determined to nullify the act, Jackson said he would hang every man in the state, but the conflict was eventually solved by compromise. For some reason this revelation, received in 1832, was not published until 1851. When the Civil War started, the Mormons saw that as a fulfillment of prophecy. See Campbell, *Establishing Zion,* pp. 289–90.

2. Roberts, *CHC,* vol. 5, p. 2.

3. Roberts, *CHC,* vol. 5, p. 11; *Deseret News,* 10 July 1861.

4. Roberts, *CHC,* vol. 5, pp. 13–14. Roberts does not give the results of any ensuing trial.

5. Ibid., p. 42.

6. Tullidge, *History of Salt Lake City,* p. 268.

7. Campbell, *Establishing Zion,* pp. 293–94.
8. The governor's remarks are given in full in Tullidge, pp. 282–83.
9. Ibid., p. 317.
10. Campbell, p. 291.
11. Tullidge, pp. 271–72.
12. Ibid., p. 311.
13. See Tullidge, p. 319. Of the seven names mentioned in the pardon, four are Scandinavian.
14. Ibid., p. 322.
15. This brief history is based on Campbell, pp. 305–07.
16. Ibid., pp. 325–26.
17. The provost guard, a cavalry company of 76 men, was headquartered in a house belonging to the church, thus adding insult to injury. The house had been rented to Captain Stover as a military storehouse. General Connor ordered Stover and his stores back to the camp, and the guard took over the house.
18. Tullidge, pp. 331–34.

15

Zion Threatened

To their developed intellects now, Mormonism seemed a crude jargon of sense and nonsense, honesty and fraud, devotion and cant, hopeless poverty to the many, overflowing wealth to the favoured few—a religion as unlike their conceptions of the teachings of Christ, as darkness is to light.

Of the problems facing the church in the post-Civil War years, we shall begin with that posed by several Mormon intellectuals and relative sophisticates, men (and at least one woman) more in tune with the outside, contemporary world of ideas and thinking than their brothers and sisters. These were church members who liked to think for themselves and who became increasingly uneasy about accepting the absolute authority imposed upon them by their church. Two of these men were Elias L. T. Harrison and William Godbe, both British converts.

Elias Harrison was an architect by profession, but his real interest appears to have been in writing. Together with his friend, Edward W. Tullidge, he had begun to publish a small magazine, *Peep O'Day*, which had expired by virtue of the limited market in the valley for a literary magazine. Later, with the financial backing and help of William Godbe, he had tried again with *Utah Magazine*, of which he was the editor. He was active in church affairs, and was president of a Quorum of Seventies. Godbe was a successful merchant, member of the city council, and one of the ten wealthiest men in Salt Lake.

As we observe them now, Godbe is traveling to New York to purchase goods for his stores. Harrison is with him for vacation and rest, and to get away for a few weeks from their magazine, which is having a hard time.

As the two men traveled across the plains they had plenty of time for reflection and conversation. They were troubled men, and what troubled them were their thoughts about their religious affiliation. They found that the text of the Book of Mormon strained their credulity as to its historicity. With respect to Doctrine and Covenants, many of Joseph's revelations seemed to them more like Joseph Smith than divine inspiration; the revelations teemed with contradictions, which suggested human rather than celestial origin.[1] As for their thoughts about their leader, Brigham, they were downright unkind. He was, they thought, "a hopeless case; many of his measures were utterly devoid of even commercial sense, and far less were they clothed with divine wisdom—in all his ways he was destitute of the magnanimity of a great soul, and was intensely selfish."[2] The men realized they were on the verge of apostasy, and they arrived in New York in a state of considerable anguish. They didn't *want* to leave the valley, their friends. But how could they continue in Brigham's church?

In their hotel room that night the two men prayed for help and guidance. A voice came to these troubled men in desperate need. This initial communication is not detailed in any source known to this writer, but the men were calmed and eased. The next morning Godbe went out to conduct his business, while Harrison stayed in the room preparing a series of questions to put to the entity that had addressed them the night before. Godbe returned later in the day. That evening they spent two hours asking questions and receiving answers. They remained in New York for three weeks, and a very curious three weeks it was.

Godbe went about his business during the day, while Harrison spent his time in the hotel room writing down questions to ask. For two hours or so each night they held what can be loosely described as a seance. In Stenhouse's account there was no medium (other than themselves), no Ouija board, no table rapping, just spirits they could communicate with. A band of spirits came to them and conversed with them "as friends would speak to friends. . . . One by one the questions prepared by Mr. Harrison were read, and Mr. Godbe and Mr. Harrison, with pencil and paper, took down the answers as they heard them given by the spirits. This is their statement, and they firmly believe it."[3]

The student of psychiatry and abnormal psychology will have a hard time making rational sense of this, though the believer in parapsychological phenomena, or in spiritualism, might find it less mystifying. The concept of *folie à deux* comes to mind but it must be noted that in Stenhouse's account the answers were heard by *both* participants. Simultaneous auditory hallucination is impossible. The skeptic will raise the possibility of hoax. Stenhouse, who knew both well, states that they were men of unimpeachable veracity. The questions asked were related primarily to their problems with the church, but other subjects, such as Darwinism were not excluded, since they were in contact, as they reported, with many "distinguished historical persons." Campbell suggests that Godbe and Harrison were participating in seances with a then renowned medium, Charles Foster.[4] This seems a reasonable assumption, though no documentation is provided.

When Godbe and Harrison returned to Salt Lake they reported— to a small circle of friends only—what they had learned. The first to be informed were Edward W. Tullidge and Eli B. Kelsey. Tullidge was a member of a Seventies Quorum and was copublisher of the *Utah Magazine*. Kelsey was also president of a Seventies Quorum. These four determined to use their magazine to mount an indirect attack on Brigham, who, they thought, was setting up a dynasty of his own, following the example of King David, considering the people to be his "heritage." What they had been told in New York was that they must work to preserve what was true in Mormonism, to reject what was false.

They considered Brigham to have departed from the true church, as founded by Joseph, and they launched their indirect and insidious attacks in the hope that other Mormons would see the light as they did. They informed a small inner circle of their experience in New York and of their intention to undermine Brigham's authority. Among those gathered into the new movement were Thomas Stenhouse and his wife. At the time Stenhouse was editor of the pro-Mormon *Salt Lake Telegram*.

An example of what the *Utah Magazine* attacked: Mormon doctrine was millenarian. The Millennium hadn't been brought by the Civil War, true enough, but it was on its way. Brigham frequently preached about the coming disintegration of the world (except for those saved, of course). Kelsey wrote an article demonstrating the *growth* of the world. Tullidge wrote of Great Characters in world history, that Brigham would seem less in comparison. The magazine attracted the attention of many, including the hierarchy of the church. As time went on the assaults became more direct. Here is Elias Harrison:

> There is one fatal error which possesses the minds of some . . . that God Almighty *intended the priesthood to do our thinking.* . . . Our own opin-

ion is that, when we invite men to use free speech and free thought to get into the Church, we should not call upon them, or ourselves, to kick down the ladder by which they and we ascended to Mormonism. They should be called upon to think on as before, no matter who has or has not thought in the same direction. . . . Think freely, and think for ever and, above all, never fear that the "Ark" of everlasting truth can ever be "steadied" by mortal hand or shaken.[5]

This was dangerous writing, not exactly a subtle undermining. In an article on mining, "The True Development of the Territory," they put the Godbeites' fat in Brigham's fire. This article, published in October 1869, five months after the completion of the transcontinental railroad, suggested that the brightest future of the territory lay in the development of its mineral resources. This was a direct attack upon Brigham and the priesthood, who discouraged all interest in mining because such development would attract Gentiles to the territory and they didn't want that. "I want to make a wall so thick and so high around the territory," Brigham had proclaimed in the Tabernacle, "that it would be impossible for the Gentiles to get over or through it."[6]

Brigham was furious when this article was brought to his attention, and that afternoon, in the School of the Prophets, he called for Harrison, Godbe, Stenhouse, Tullidge, and three others. Since they were not present, a message was sent forthwith to each:

Dear Brother: I hereby inform you that a motion was made, seconded, and carried by a unanimous vote of the School of the Prophets today, that you be *disfellowshipped* from the Church until you appear in the School and give satisfactory reasons for your irregular attendance there.[7]

The accused did not yield to Brigham's wrath. They appeared before the high council with dignity and resolve saying:

We claim the right of respectfully but freely discussing all measures upon which we are called to act. And if we are cut off from this church for asserting this right, while our standing is dear to us, we will suffer it to be taken from us sooner than resign the liberties of thought and speech to which the gospel entitles us. . . .[8]

The men were excommunicated. A few days later, in the *Deseret News* of 3 November 1869, the First Presidency published a notice warning the Saints against the teachings of the *Utah Magazine,* and declaring, in addition, that it wasn't a publication fit for perusal.

The Godbeites established their own church, the Church of Zion, and held their first meeting on 19 December. The new movement gathered some adherents, but probably no more than 200. One convert, Amasa Lyman, was notable; he had been an apostle who was excommunicated in 1870. He had a great interest in spiritualism, and traveled from town to town holding seances.

In the long run, the impact of the Godbeites on the church was not of any real significance. The attitude of the church toward the authority of the priesthood was (and is) entirely unaltered. Witness the remarks of Elder Bruce R. McConkie at a church conference, 7 October 1984:

> On every issue it behooves us to determine what the Lord would have us do and what counsel he has given through the appointed officers of his kingdom on earth. No true Latter-day Saint will ever take a stand that is in opposition to what the Lord has revealed to those who direct the affairs of his earthly kingdom. No Latter-day Saint who is true and faithful in all things will ever pursue a course, or espouse a cause, or publish an article or book that weakens or destroys the faith.[9]

The Godbeite movement did not present a serious threat to the Mormon establishment, but there were other causes for concern, including the completion of the transcontinental railroad. The famous golden spike was driven at Promontory Summit on 10 May 1869, and travelers could now ride from coast to coast on the train. The tracks passed through Ogden, not Salt Lake City, but the distance between the cities was only about 35 miles. Inevitably more Gentiles would come to the valley, and Brigham viewed this as a threat.

The real threat to Zion in the years following the Civil War, however, was from the Congress of the United States. The attack was preceded by a visit to Salt Lake City by Schuyler Colfax, who was, at that time, speaker of the House of Representatives. He would later be vice-president in the administration of President Grant.

Colfax visited the valley in June 1865 in the company of William Bross, lieutenant governor of Illinois and editor of the *Chicago Tribune;* Samuel Bowles, editor of the *Springfield* (Massachusetts) *Republican;* and Albert D. Richardson of the *New York Tribune.* Colfax and company were received as guests of the city and were given a very friendly welcome. On the second day of their visit Colfax addressed a large gathering from the balcony of their hotel. It was a friendly and complimentary speech, which the audience punctuated with cheers and with laughter. In a serious vein he commended the Mormons for what they had achieved. He wanted, he said, to bind the Atlantic and Pacific states together with bands of iron, that the Union might be more compact and homogeneous. All that was required from the Mormons was allegiance to the Constitution, obedience to the laws, and devotion to the Union. The audience cheered. The remarks of his three traveling companions were equally well received.

On a different occasion Colfax and Brigham had a lengthy and friendly discussion. Colfax offered his solution to the problem of statehood for Utah: a new revelation abolishing polygamy. To this Brigham made a surprising response, saying he would welcome such a revelation. Polygamy was not in the Book of Mormon, and it wasn't an essential practice in the church; it was a privilege and a duty. At the same time, he said, the practice did have biblical authority.[10] Both Brigham and Colfax addressed a very large crowd in the Bowery on Sunday. According to Bowles's report, Brigham's sermon was unprofessional and unsatisfactory, in sharp contrast to Colfax's eloquently delivered eulogy on the "life and principles of Abraham Lincoln." Bowles's farewell to the city is not without interest:

> But adieu to Salt Lake and many-wives-and-much-children-dom; its strawberries and roses; its rare hospitality; its white crowned peaks; its wide spread valley, its river of scriptural name; its lake of briniest taste. I have met much to admire, many to respect, worshipped deep before its nature—found only one thing to condemn. I shall want to come again when the railroad can bring me and that blot is gone.[11]

About two weeks after this visit another important traveler, James M. Ashley of Ohio, came to the valley. Ashley was a man of some importance to the Mormons, as he was chairman of the House committee on territories. He gave to John Taylor and George A. Smith a gloomy report. He said there was more feeling against the church than ever before, that another army would come, that the remainder of Sherman's troops would commit appalling atrocities in Utah as they had in Georgia.[12]

According to Tullidge, sentiment against the Mormons began to intensify in consequence of speeches made by Colfax after his return to Washington. The crusade against the Mormons, wrote Tullidge,

> . . . began immediately on the return of the Colfax party from their tour of investigation of the Great West, first in the agitation of the public mind by the speeches and expositions of Speaker Colfax relative to the Pacific States and Territories, in which polygamic Utah came in constantly for a sharp and special treatment.[13]

As already noted (p. 157) an antibigamy, or antipolygamy, bill had been signed by Lincoln in 1862, but it had generally been thought to be unenforceable. The first of a number of new attacks on the Mormons by Congress was launched in June 1866 with the introduction, by Senator Benjamin Wade of Ohio, of a bill whose thrust was to strip the Mormons of all forms of self-government. The Nauvoo Legion, then functioning as a territorial militia, would be put under the (federally appointed) governor, who would also appoint and commission all of the militia's officers. The church would lose its tax-exempt status on all property valued in excess of $20,000. A full report of all church financial operations and transactions would have to be provided annually, under oath. All jurors would be selected by the U.S. marshal. Church officials could not solemnize marriages. All of which is to say that the Wade bill was drastic and far-reaching, but it failed to pass.[14]

In December 1967 Senator Aaron H. Cragin of New Hampshire introduced a bill that was even more drastic, but it died in committee in the 1867–68 session.

In January 1869 Representative James M. Ashley of Ohio introduced a bill offered as a solution to "the Mormon problem." His solution was to divide the Territory of Utah between the State of Nevada and the Territories of Colorado, Montana, and Wyoming, leaving only a strip left in the middle as the territory of Utah—too small ever to become a state. He addressed the House in support of his bill on 14 January.

> In my judgment this bill will make the best disposition which can be made of the Mormon question, by reducing the territorial area of that prospective state, thus giving the Mormon community notice that no state government will ever be organized there by our consent; and that so soon as the pop-

ulation in the adjacent organized states and territories shall be able to take care of this population, which, voting as a unit, has persistently for fifteen years defied the government of the United States and for eight years flagrantly disobeyed its laws, the control of affairs there shall be given to the "Gentile" population.[15]

Ashley went on to ask for passage of the bill. Representative Washburne of Illinois rose to say that in view of the fact that this bill seemed to call for the dismemberment of the Territory of Utah, in all fairness they ought to defer consideration until the delegate from that territory was present—he being, that day, absent because of sickness. Ashley would have none of that at first, but in the end he agreed to postponement.

The delegate from Utah, William H. Hooper, responded in the House on 25 February. His presentation was thoughtful, gentlemanly, and a credit to the Mormon cause. One can but agree with Roberts when he says that Hooper's address should take its place among the important documents in the history of Utah. Hooper began by noting that he would, when it was in order to do so, offer an amendment to Ashley's bill that would strike out all of its provisions that related to the Territory of Utah. He then launched into a comprehensive history of the Mormons, beginning with a description of the valley.

"This colony," he said, "planted some twenty years ago in a savage wilderness, remote from other civilized association, divided from either ocean by vast spaces of desert, was, like the kindred colonies of Massachusetts, of Maryland, and of the Carolinas, the offspring of religious persecution." If, as proposed by Ashley, the Mormon settlements were partitioned out among the neighboring territories and states, that action would be followed by calamitous civil strife. He quoted then, at length, from Thomas Kane's famous address to the Philadelphia Historical Society, in which Kane had described the devastation of the exodus from Nauvoo.

Hooper spoke of the heroic march of the Mormon Battalion, and of their commendation by their commanding officer, Colonel P. St. George Cooke. He took note of Stansbury's report: "In their dealings with the crowds of emigrants that passed through their city the Mormons were fair and upright, taking no advantage . . ." He quoted observations by John Gunnison, and named other outsiders who had given favorable reports on what they had seen of the Mormons: Richard

Burton, Charles Dickens, Horace Greeley. Did the people of the rest of the country fear to share boundaries with the people here described? Could the Congress attempt to expatriate an entire people? Hooper recalled past religious contests, noting the destruction of 100,000 French Protestants. "Can such a thing, in this age of enlightenment, occur in free and tolerant America?" Surely not. Hooper had a different proposal.

> Abandoning all appeal to the cowardly, who are seldom generous, I turn to the courageous, who are strong in the conviction of their own moral power, and tell them that if Mormonism is a fatal heresy they owe it to its own deluded disciples to neglect none of the legitimate means of argument and practice for their conversion. If Mormonism is an error there is no community on the face of the globe and no class of people so vitally interested in its refutation as the majority of the people of Utah, who are its victims. Rather than curtail the proportions of the Territory and cut off its settlements from contact with the railroad you should seek to enlarge its area, encourage its population by all classes of good citizens, giving the amplest protection of law by substituting for its present organization a more ample, complete, and sovereign form of government, leaving the issue with God and the inevitable forces of nature.

"Let us have peace," concluded Hooper. "Let us . . . teach the whole world of men how good and 'how pleasant it is for brethren to dwell together in unity.' "[16] It was an able and impressive performance. Ashley's bill did not become law.

Senator Cragin reintroduced his bill in December 1869. It has no less than 29 sections, which contained everything the Mormons had objected to in the Wade bill, plus some new ideas of his own, including abolition of trial by jury in cases arising from the antibigamy act of 1862. Such cases, in the gospel according to Senator Cragin, could be prosecuted without indictment. Two months later, on 8 February 1870, Representative Shelby M. Cullom of Vermont introduced in the House a similar bill, somewhat gentler in its provisions but still considered vicious by the Mormons. The bill went to the committee on territories. It was reported back to the House on 16 and 17 February, was again read, and was published.

The Cullom bill, with 34 sections, makes for difficult reading. Cullom explained it section by section to his colleagues, and spoke of what he was trying to crush out: the bold and defiant institution of polygamy, a practice that, he said,

. . . has gone hand in hand with murder, idolatry, and every secret abomination. Misery, wretchedness, and woe have always marked its path. Instead of being a holy principle, receiving the sanction of Heaven, it is an institution founded in the lustful and unbridled passions of men, devised by Satan himself to destroy purity and authorize whoredom.[17]

The feeling of Congress toward the Mormons was indeed hostile at this time, but the Saints were not altogether without defenders. During discussion of the Cullom bill, on 23 February, Representative Thomas Fitch of Nevada spoke in opposition to the measure. He made it clear that he didn't support the practice of polygamy, but noted that the Mormons were a population that chose to govern themselves in their own way, and that, with the one odious exception, were making a success of it. "We might make diligent search to find a community more peaceful, industrious, or thrifty than these Mormons." Besides, he said, the passage of this act would be seen by the Mormons as a declaration of war, and one of their responses would be to tear up three or four hundred miles of the newly completed railroad![18]

After Fitch's remarks, Representative Sargent of California spoke to the same effect about the threat to the railroad, and made the additional point that he didn't think the Cullom act was necessary. He'd been in Utah recently, and based upon what he had heard, talking with Mormons and Gentiles, he felt that polygamy would fall by the wayside of itself if left alone. He had been told that among the Mormon women there was a growing distaste for polygamy. "It was said that the daughters of Brigham Young themselves refused to marry Mormons, and sought every opportunity to cultivate the acquaintance of Gentile young men there, and preferred them in marriage, however much it might be against the opinion of their father."[19]

Still, the Cullom bill was passed by the House on 25 March. When this news reached Salt Lake the citizens assembled in mass meeting on 31 March, and a memorial was sent to the House and Senate. The Mormons set forth the reasons why the Cullom bill should not become law. Their practice of polygamy was justified, they said, in that it was "a principle revealed by God, underlying our every hope of eternal salvation and happiness in heaven."[20] The memorial quoted Joseph Smith's revelation that established the practice, and noted that the Cullom bill would put them in the position either of rejecting God's command or disobeying the government they wished to honor and respect. The Cullom bill was, in their view, in direct violation of the First Amendment to the Constitution: Congress shall make no law respecting an establishment of religion or prohibiting the free exercise thereof. Many other provisions of the bill were also in violation of other parts of the Constitution.

> We beseech of you, gentlemen, do not, by the passage of harsh and despotic measures, drive an inoffensive, God-fearing and loyal people to desperation. We have suffered, God knows how much, in years past for our religion. We fled to the mountain wilds to escape the ruthless hand of persecution; and shall it be said now that our government, which ought to foster and protect us, designs to repeat, in the most aggravated form, the miseries we have been called upon to pass through before?[21]

The Cullom bill, after its passage by the House, was sent over to the Senate, which withdrew Cragin's bill in favor of Cullom's. Debate on the Senate floor was lively. Here is Cragin, on 16 May, speaking on behalf of the Cullom bill:

He began by quoting the platform in the Republican convention of 1856 deploring the "twin relics of barbarism, polygamy and slavery." Well, slavery had been dealt with; now it was time to take on polygamy. The remonstrating memorial of the Mormons had referred to Joseph's revelation establishing polygamy, and so now did Cragin. "Was there ever such arrant, wicked humbuggery passed off upon deluded mortals?" He quoted an apostate, John Hyde. "The Mormon polygamist has no home. Some have their wives lotted off by pairs in small disconnected houses, like a row of out-houses. Some have long low houses, and, taking a new wife, build a new room on to them, so that their rooms look like rows of stalls in a cow-barn!"

Cragin spoke at length of the Mountain Meadows Massacre. "This is but one picture," he said. "I might give many more if I thought the Senate would bear with me. This ought to be enough to induce every Senator to vote for the bill under consideration." But there was more, much more. Hyperbole aplenty, malice aforethought, emotion surging. Finally, he reached his peroration: "When miners and other emigrants, not Mormons, shall flock to that Territory and make it their home the loathsome and festering monster of polygamous Mormonism will perish and be buried out of sight."[22] The hour was late. It was immediately moved that "the Senate do now adjourn."

When the Cullom bill was voted upon it failed to pass. One more bullet had been dodged by the Mormons. The question arises, why? With anti-Mormon sentiment running high throughout most of the land, why were these bills defeated? Well, the Civil War was over, and the nation had something else to focus on other than polygamy, namely, the completion of the transcontinental railroad. Congressmen from California and Nevada, who presumably knew the Mormons better than did most of their colleagues, had presented their view that if war was declared, which was how passage of virulent anti-Mormon legislation would be seen in the valley, the Mormons would destroy some of that precious track, postponing the dream for an unknown number of years. Heavy commercial interests were at stake here, and no doubt Congress felt this pressure. So the bills failed and the railroad was completed. It would soon be bringing change to the valley, and many people. Among the earliest visitors would be Vice-President Colfax.

Notes

The best source for the history of the New Movement, as the Godbeite questioning is sometimes called, is that of Stenhouse, a participant, in *The Rocky Mountain Saints.* It is also discussed at length in Roberts, *A Comprehensive History of the Church (CHC)* and, in less detail, in Bancroft, *History of Utah.*

1. Many church members had had such doubts earlier on. From the days of the beginning of the church, one of the prime motivations of its intense missionary efforts was to replace members who had left because of loss of faith.
2. This harsh opinion is cited by Stenhouse, *The Rocky Mountain Saints,* p. 630.
3. Ibid., p. 631.
4. Campbell, *Establishing Zion,* pp. 322–24.
5. Stenhouse, p. 637.
6. Bancroft, *History of Utah,* p. 647.
7. Stenhouse, p. 639.
8. Bancroft, p. 649.
9. Naifeh and Smith, *The Mormon Murders,* p. 148.
10. Tullidge, *History of Salt Lake City,* p. 353.
11. Tullidge, p. 356.
12. Roberts, *CHC,* vol. 5. pp. 180–81.
13. Tullidge, p. 358.
14. Campbell, p. 325, and Roberts, *CHC,* vol. 5, pp. 225–26.
15. *Congressional Globe,* 40th Cong., 3rd Sess., pp. 363–64.
16. Ibid., Appendix, pp. 242–48. All quoted material in the paragraphs relating to Hooper's remarks are taken from Hooper's speech, which is given in full.

17. The complete text of Cullom's bill and his remarks are in *The Comgressional Globe,* 41st Cong. 2nd Sess., pp. 1367–73.
18. Ibid., pp. 1517–18.
19. Ibid., pp. 1519–20.
20. U.S. Congress., *Memorial Adopted by Citizens of Salt Lake City, Utah Territory.* 41st Cong., 2nd Sess., Senate Misc. Document No. 12, Serial 1408, p. 1.
21. Ibid., p. 5.
22. Ibid., pp. 3573–82.

16

End of an Era

I want to make a wall so thick and so high around the territory that it would
be impossible for the Gentiles to get over or through it.

As a matter of fact there was no dread of the advent of the railroad either
by the church leaders or by the body of the Latter-day Saints.

The rails of the Central Pacific and the Union Pacific were joined on
10 May 1869 on Promontory Summit, about 85 miles northwest of
Ogden. The last tie was of elegantly polished California laurel. The
last rail was ceremoniously affixed thereto with three spikes of precious
metal. Nevada provided a silver spike, offered with these words: "To
the iron of the east and gold of the west Nevada adds her link of silver
to span the continent and wed the oceans." Arizona contributed a spike
of gold, silver, and iron. "Ribbed with iron, clad in silver, and crowned
with gold. Arizona presents her offering to the enterprise that has banded
the continent and directed the pathway to commerce." The spike from
California was of gold.

These three spikes were driven in with ceremony, the prominent
visiting dignitaries each given an opportunity to tap the silver sledge
hammer upon one. Many, unaccustomed to such labor, missed the spike
altogether, to the great amusement of the onlookers. The last to be
driven was the famous one of California gold—made of 23 twenty-
dollar gold pieces. It was engraved: "The Pacific Railway, first ground
broke Jan. 8, 1863, and completed May 10th, 1869. May God continue
the unity of our country as this railroad unites the two great oceans
of the world." This final spike was driven home by the chief engineer
of the Union Pacific, Major General Grenville M. Dodge.[1] The spike
was so wired into the telegraph line that each blow sent a signal to
every receiving station along the line, from the Atlantic to the Pacific.

The completion of the Union Pacific Rail Road at Promontory Point, Utah, at 3:05 P.M., New York time, 10 May 1869. (From a photograph by A. J. Russell.)

After the spike was driven a telegraph message was sent to President Grant informing him that the transcontinental railroad was completed.

Two locomotives, one from each railroad, faced each other from opposite sides of the last tie. The locomotives approached each other until they touched. Champagne bottles were smashed upon both. Speeches were made, and wine flowed freely. Dignitaries gathered in the private car of Leland Stanford, president of the Central Pacific. Many bottles were uncorked, many speeches made on that great day.[2] (The ceremonial spikes were prudently soon removed before someone could steal them. According to Dodge these were later manufactured into miniature spikes as mementos.)[3]

The higher dignitaries from Utah, in whose territory the joining was accomplished, were unaccountably and conspicuously absent. No spike, no governor of the territory; above all, no Brigham Young.

Agitation in the United States for the construction of a railroad to the Pacific antedated the emigration of the Mormons into the Great Basin by a number of years, going back as far as the opening of China to trade with the West, which began in the 1830s. As early as 1852 the Utah territorial legislature had placed before Congress a memorial that petitioned for the construction of a railroad to run from either the Mississippi or the Missouri River to the Pacific. Abraham Lincoln had railroads (as well as slavery) on his mind when he visited Council Bluffs (Grenville Dodge's home town) in 1859. During this visit he conferred with Dodge, soliciting his advice with respect to the best route for a railroad to the West. "From this town out the Platte Valley," Dodge said, with no hesitation at all. He knew the terrain well.[4] Others early on had also suggested that the road should begin by traveling along the Platte, thence over South Pass, through Salt Lake City, turning west south of the lake to follow the Humboldt River.[5] Still others had suggested many alternative routes.

During the Civil War years Congress passed a number of acts granting subsidies to finance the construction of the railroad. The two companies involved were the Union Pacific, founded in 1862, and the Central Pacific, founded a year earlier. The subsidies ranged between $16,000 to $48,000 per mile depending upon terrain. In addition, the companies were given land—some 25 million acres of it. As proclaimed on the golden spike, first ground was broken early in 1863.

There can be no question but that, though the Mormons generally favored the building of the railroad, the attitude of Mormon leaders, especially Brigham Young, was profoundly ambivalent. For many reasons they both wanted and feared this new development. On the positive side, the railroad would facilitate the gathering of the Saints; they could be transported across the plains in less time and at smaller cost, and this was seen a large plus. Further, the valley was short of money; and the building of the railroad, and the attending economic developments after its completion, would no doubt bring a cash flow to the valley.

But there was a strong undercurrent of fear in the Mormon community, fear of what the Pacific railroad would bring. Though the road spanning the continent would unite the United States and its territories, both economically and culturally, as never before, the Mormons didn't want *that* kind of union, and they would fight against it. One obvious immediate fear was of the influx of five or six thousand Irish, German, or men of other nationalities coming to build the road. They weren't worried about the workmen as such, as much as they were about what they were sure to bring with them—"bummers, gamblers, saloon and hurdy-gurdy keepers, border ruffians, and desperadoes generally, who prey upon the laborers. . . ."[6] (That particular threat was largely taken care of by raising a Mormon labor force to do the work, as will be seen shortly.)

But there were deeper fears. The *Deseret `News* issued a warning on 21 May 1968: "The railroad is going to make a great change in affairs here, and our people should moderate their expectations and prepare themselves for the alteration which appears inevitable."[7] The ideal of Brigham and of the hierarchy was that the kingdom would be self-sufficient and homogeneous. The railroad would be bringing Gentiles and commerce from the East and from the West. This threatened to alter the essential character of their society by dilution, if nothing else. Apart from social—let alone theological—concerns, was the threat of economic change. The Mormons were in the process of setting up their own industries, in wool, cotton, wagon and furniture manufacture, and the like. Would cheaper goods from the East threaten these industries? Probably. And if so, wouldn't that lead to local unemployment? Again, most likely.

The largest economic threat, however, was the mineral richness of the Great Basin. As we have seen, General Connor and his California volunteers had discovered valuable mineral deposits aplenty, and had tried to spread the word about them, while the Mormons downplayed their worth. Also, Connor and many of his men, Gentiles all, had staked claims. Much of the mineral wealth was already owned by Gentiles! We have seen also that the Godbeites had set forth the view that the real development of the territory lay in its mineral wealth. Now the railroad was coming, and its presence would make it profitable to develop and exploit these resources; a Great Basin equivalent of the California gold rush was exactly what Brigham couldn't countenance. Defensive measures must be taken.

In 1867 Brigham established a new School of the Prophets. This was not a school in any ordinary sense of the word but rather an organization of almost a thousand ranking members of the Salt Lake priesthood. It took its name from a somewhat similar organization founded by Joseph Smith in 1833, but this one was confronted with problems far different from those of its forerunner. Theological concerns apart, the school was something like an economic task force or planning board. Arrington suggests that the principal reason for its establishment was to deal with the economic problems posed by the approach of the transcontinental railroad. Membership was by card only, and proceedings were confidential. It will be remembered that the ex-communication of the Godbeites was instituted by the School of the Prophets. It was a powerful group, its influence extending throughout the territory, in which were established many branches of the school. Its total membership was about 5,000.

Among the problems attracting the school's attention was that presented by the possibility of an influx of Gentile construction workers and accompanying camp followers. The school sponsored a contract, drawn in Brigham's name, with the Union Pacific Company to construct the grade for the road from the head of Echo Canyon to the mouth of Weber Canyon; the contract was later extended to cover the distance to the shores of the Great Salt Lake.

The school also established a variety of cooperative enterprises, designed to obviate Mormon unemployment by putting the Saints to work manufacturing and selling. The rails were to be used for the importation of raw materials, not finished products. To convert the kingdom into an industrial empire the Mormons would have to build a network of Mormon railroads, connecting all of Zion with the transcontinental line. The school was also instrumental in protecting the land rights of Mormons whose farms and homes were threatened by the government's grant to the Union Pacific of land along the right-of-way.[8]

The final route of the railroad, when both companies had completed their surveys, bypassed Salt Lake City. This was a serious blow to Brigham. If there *was* to be a transcontinental railway then he wanted, indeed did his best to demand, that it pass through Salt Lake City. His view was that the major east-west junction should be at Ogden, the road running thence southward to Salt Lake City, continuing to the south of the lake, then turning westward from there. To facilitate the selection of Ogden as the junction city, which it logically was in any case, Brigham and other church leaders put together a land package of some 133 acres on the west side of Ogden. Some of this land they obtained by donation from dutiful church members, other parts of it were bought for as little as $50 per acre. This parcel they then offered to the astounded railroad companies, jointly, as a gift, provided only that they would use it for their switching yards, depots, and shops. The offer was accepted with the greatest alacrity, and Ogden became a railroad junction.[9]

Although Ogden seemed to most the obvious choice for the junction city, there was, briefly, some competition for that designation. Spearheaded by a group of ambitious businessmen from the West Coast, a group of Gentiles determined to found a city on the railroad line, about 20 miles north of Ogden. This city they named Corinne. Its townsite was laid out in February 1869—the only Gentile settlement in the Territory. It was distinctive both in that its population was Gentile and in the way in which the city was laid out. This was such that the streets ran parallel with the railroad, rather than square with the compass, as was generally the case with the Mormon settlements. From the beginning, Corinne was meant to be a city, not a town, and in time, the capital of the Territory as well as the intermountain junction of the two railroads. Such was the magnitude of the dreams of the city's founders.

It didn't turn out that way, but while the construction of the line was passing through, and for some time after, it was a bustling community. To say the least, however, the Gentile city of Corinne was not gentle. It became, in fact, notorious, with a kind of frontier wildness not to be found elsewhere in Utah. Twenty-nine saloons operated in it for a time, and prostitution was a flourishing business, the town at one time containing no fewer than 80 "soiled doves" (Mountain English for ladies of the night).

There was more to the town than that, of course. Respectable families lived there, there was a Catholic church, even an opera house. When the railroad got going, many touring stock companies stopped at Corinne and played to packed houses. But the junction was fixed at Ogden, and Corinne declined. It is still on the map—in very small print—just west of Interstate 84.

Brigham and other church leaders did everything they could to pressure the two companies to run the road south from Ogden to Salt Lake, but to no avail. It later transpired that both companies had, independently, determined upon the northern route but had not told Brigham, thus hoping to avoid a work stoppage by the Mormon workers. Chief Engineer Dodge later gave this report:

> We had only one controversy with the Mormons, who had been our friends and had given the full support of the church from the time of our first reconnaissances until the final completion. It was our desire and the demand

of the Mormons that we should build through Salt Lake City, and we bent all our energies to find a feasible line passing through that city and around the south end of Great Salt Lake and across the desert to Humboldt Wells, a controlling point in the line. We found the line so superior on the north of the lake that we had to adopt that route with a view of building a branch to Salt Lake City, but Brigham Young would not have this, and appealed over my head to the board of directors, who referred the questions to the government directors, who fully sustained me. Then Brigham Young gave his allegiance and aid to the Central Pacific, hoping to bring them around the south end of the lake and force us to connect with them there. He even went so far as to deliver in the tabernacle a great sermon denouncing me, and stating a road could not be built or run without the aid of the Mormons. When the Central Pacific engineers made their survey they, too, were forced to adopt a line north of the lake. Then President Young returned to his first love, the Union Pacific, and turned all his forces and aid to that road.[10]

Though Brigham did indeed help materially in the construction of the railroad, he was absent from the ceremonies marking its conclusion, and we must wonder why. (The governor, Charles Durkee, was absent as well, but his failure to attend poses no question. He had been traveling in the East and had returned too late to attend the ceremonies.) On 10 May that year Brigham had been visiting the settlements to the south, and didn't return to Salt Lake until the day after the big event. Still one must think that at least a spike of Utah metal would have been donated to join the others. Historian Roberts, not a writer given to overstatement, referred to the absence of the leaders—and of a spike —as an irretrievable blunder.

One is inevitably drawn to the conclusion that Brigham's non-participation was based, perhaps unconsciously, on his deep-rooted ambivalence toward the railroad, even though he had participated in its construction and had earlier sought to have one built. He wanted the railroad, and he feared it. After all, as in the first epigraph at the head of this chapter, he had said often enough that he'd like to keep *all* Gentiles out. (The second epigraph is from historian Roberts's text.) From the very beginning he had thought of the Great Basin as his self-sufficient kingdom. He had times beyond counting inveighed against commercial and social intercourse with the Gentile world. Arrington suggests that Brigham absented himself because of simple pique at the roads' decision to bypass Salt Lake City.[11]

So, Salt Lake was left isolated about 37 miles from the main line. The Mormons immediately formed the Utah Railroad Company to forge a connecting line with the transcontinental road. This link, which later became part of the Union Pacific, was completed on 10 January 1870, just eight months after the golden spike was driven. On this day the festivities included the driving of another last spike, this one of Utah iron, pounded home by Brigham.[12] There was a nice symbolism here. The Utah Central was a railroad built with Mormon money and labor, a symbol of their independence, but it was built to link with the great new transcontinental road. This augured beyond all doubt the Mormons' integration into the Gentile world, and particularly into its economic life. The economic interaction that had already begun with the use of Mormon labor on the transcontinental railroad continued with the construction of the Utah Railroad between Ogden and Salt Lake City; that connecting link was built using iron from the Union Pacific, iron collected in lieu of wages because of the Union Pacific's cash problems, caused by their haste to complete ahead of the Central Pacific.

The completion of the railroad brought to an end the beast-drawn and the handcart travel period in Mormon history. It brought the probability of economic benefit, while at the same time ending earlier Mormon dreams of self-sufficiency.

The Mormons referred to themselves as a peculiar people, and they feared that the Gentiles brought in by the railroad would alter the ambience of their society. There was, in addition, a considerable body of opinion in the East that the railroad would indeed alter the composition of the population of Zion, even to the extent of solving the "Mormon problem." For example, General William Tecumseh Sherman said in a letter to General Dodge, dated 16 January 1867: "I regard this road of yours as the solution of the Indian affairs and the Mormon question, and, therefore, give you all the aid I possibly can. . . ."[13]

The completion of the transcontinental railroad did not bring immediate prosperity to the Mormons. It brought, instead, financial crisis, because both railroad companies failed to pay their contractors and workers on time or in full. They had run out of funds in their headlong race against each other. The Union Pacific was in particular trouble, extremely short of funds, because of its rather flagrant association with the Credit Mobilier of America. This was the construction company that had built most of the railroad. It had been formed by a number of influential shareholders in the Union Pacific, including Oakes Ames, U.S. Representative from Massachusetts, and Thomas Clark Durant, builder of railroads. The two companies were entwined in Byzantine fashion, dealing with one another in contracts amounting to millions of dollars. These machinations came to light after the completion of the railroad; it was one of the major financial scandals in American history. Millions of dollars found their way into greedy hands, and the Union Pacific couldn't pay the Mormons what they were owed.

This led to what was in large part, for a time, a barter economy in which produce, tithing credits, stocks and bonds in the planned Utah Central Railroad, and other substitutes for cash were the basis of the Mormon economy. Three months after the completion of the railroad the Central Pacific still owed the Mormons about $1 million, and the Union Pacific owed more than that. The latter company arranged to discharge part of its debt with construction materials, iron, and rolling stock; this wasn't cash, but the partial settlement could be put to use by the Mormons in the construction of the Utah Central Railroad.

The financial problems consequent upon the railroad companies' failure to settle their accounts properly with the Mormons weren't the only ones brought by the completion of the railroad. Among other visitors to the valley it brought Schuyler Colfax, now vice-president under Grant, again accompanied by William Bross and Samuel Bowles. We have already seen that Colfax was no friend to the Mormons, and on this second visit he directly challenged the church by asserting his contention that the doctrine of plural marriage was not a *religious* consideration. He expressed disappointment that Brigham hadn't followed his suggestion, proffered on his first visit, to produce a revelation forbidding plural marriage. Colfax entered into strenuous debate with John Taylor, who pointed out that, among civilized nations, marriage has always been considered to be a religious ordinance. Colfax simply denied that their doctrine of plural marriage was religious, said that it was contrary to U.S. law, and admonished the Mormons to obey the law.

The Godbeites conferred with Colfax and took him into their confidence. He was pleased to hear of the revolt against authority within the church, and during a tour of the city with Thomas Stenhouse, Colfax confided *his* thought, which was to do what he could to ensure that the government of the United States mount another military campaign against the Mormons.

"Will Brigham Young fight?" he asked the astonished Stenhouse.

"For God's sake, Mr. Colfax! Keep the United States off." Stenhouse suggested in the strongest terms that the effect of another military action, another Mormon War, would be to drive back into the arms of Brigham Young those Mormons who might now be thinking about rebelling against Young's authority.[14]

Back in Washington, Colfax did what he could, during the first years of Grant's administration, to maintain anti-Mormon feeling in the halls of Congress. His influence soon evaporated entirely, however, as he was brought down in disgrace because of his involvement in the Credit Mobilier scandal.

The completion of the transcontinental railroad did not bring with it a sweeping "Gentilization" of the kingdom. Change, of course, it did bring, and it brings us as well to the end of the period covered by this volume, although we are not prohibited from taking a few fleeting glances ahead.

Brigham Young ruled the church until a quiet death at his home on 29 August 1877. Though his death, probably caused by a ruptured appendix, was quiet, it had been preceded by some upheaval, of which we mention but one instance—his marriage, in 1868, to Ann Eliza Webb, who was 23 or 24 years old. She was a firebrand, found life in the Young household not to her liking, and sued for divorce in 1875. She sought large sums of money from Brigham. A much smaller sum was granted, but Brigham refused to pay. His defense included the fact that since the marriage, being polygamous, had been illegal to begin with, no divorce could arise therefrom. Ann Eliza's attempt at extortion failed. The judge, citing Brigham's refusal to pay anything, sentenced him to 24 hours in the penitentiary, which he served. Ann Eliza traveled far and wide for years, speaking of the evils of Mormonism. (Irving Wallace wrote a novel about her, *The Twenty-Sixth Wife.*)

Brigham's estate was a complicated one to settle, since it involved a considerable intermingling of church and personal properties. Ann Eliza had stated Brigham's worth to be $8 million. Others, friends and associates, thought it might be in the neighborhood of $2 million. To the surprise of many, the amount available to the heirs was but $224,242.[15]

John Taylor became the third president of the church in October 1880, after an apostolic interregnum of a little more than three years. Wilford Woodruff, from 1887 to 1898, was the fourth president of the church. During his reign Utah, the church having abandoned plural marriage, finally achieved statehood.

The church, based now in a state of the U.S., continued to grow and, perhaps, to inch toward the mainstream of American life. Interesting problems, beyond our present scope, lay ahead. How would the church confront racial problems? Should blacks become priests? Bishops? Would the role of women remain subsidiary? Would the church oppose the Equal Rights Amendment? Indeed it would. But growth and prosperity would continue.

Joseph Smith, Jr., founded the church with eight members in a small room in Fayette, New York, on 6 April 1830. As the decade of the 1990s begins, the church is growing faster than any other on earth. By the end of this century there will be, by present projections, more Mormons beyond the United States than within the nation. This writer must wonder how young Joseph might have responded had he, in some way, been shown that night, in Fayette, the future dimensions of the empire he was creating. Would his mind have boggled at such magnitude? Or might his response have been "But of course"?

Notes

1. General Grenville M. Dodge, an engineer of considerable talent, had served the Union well in the Civil War and was much admired by Generals Grant and Sherman. Dodge's contribution had been an impressive ability to repair railroads and bridges after they had been damaged by Confederate action.

2. For further accounts of this historic day, see Perkins, *Trails, Rails, and War,* pp. 238–42.

3. Dodge, *How We Built the Union Pacific Railway,* pp. 24–25.

4. Perkins, pp. 47–53.

5. See Cotterill, "Early Agitation for a Pacific Railroad, 1845–1850," esp. p. 410.

6. Arrington, *Great Basin Kingdom,* p. 246.

7. Ibid., p. 239.

8. For an extended analysis of the activities of the School of the Prophets, see ibid., pp. 245–51.

9. Alexander and Allen, *Mormons and Gentiles,* pp. 71–72.

10. Dodge, pp. 27–28.

11. Arrington, *Great Basin Kingdom,* p. 485, n. 22.

12. Roberts, *CHC,* vol. 5, pp. 249–52.

13. Dodge, p. 14.
14. Roberts, *CHC,* vol. 5, pp. 282–87.
15. Arrington, *American Moses,* p. 425. A lengthy account of the settlement of Brigham's estate is given on pp. 422–30.

Part Two

17

A New Stylometry

Why, Sir, I think every man whatsoever has a peculiar style which may be discovered by a nice examination and comparison with others, but a man must write a great deal to make his style discernible.

Johnson spoke those words to Boswell on 13 April 1778, about two centuries before the computer could be brought in to assist in the laborious processes involved in establishing a scientific foundation upon which to rest the art of literary attribution. The art and science of stylometry was proceeding actively before the computer, under the leadership of W. C. Wake, Andrew Q. Morton, C. B. Williams, and others. The computer's arrival accelerated the advance of the state of the art to a great extent. That advance is continuing.

In my earlier book, *Trouble Enough,* I presented some preliminary stylometric analyses of samples of text from the Book of Mormon, and concluded from these that no evidence of multiple authorship had been found. The results were well received by non-Mormon scholars, but became the target of criticism by Mormon investigators, particularly John Hilton and his colleagues. That my results came under some attack was by no means surprising, in that they challenged the historicity of the Book of Mormon. It is my opinion, as well as that of my mentor in the stylometric art, A. Q. Morton, that the critiques leveled at my results could be refuted, but at a considerable expense of time and effort, which could be better spent pursuing other stylometric inquiries. Accordingly, I shall let the previously reported work stand as it is, and I now present some new (again, preliminary) stylometric analyses of a different and simpler kind, pioneered by A. Q. Morton.

Though the technique to be used here is new, its foundation, the cumulative sum chart, is old. This chart, or graph, almost always referred to as a *cusum chart* (or Qsum), is simply a graphic depiction of the cumulative sum of the differences between each individual observation in a series of observations, and the average of all of the observations. The sequence of observations, from first to last, is displayed on the horizontal, or x axis. The cumulative sum of the difference between each observation and the average of all observations is displayed on the vertical (y) axis.[1]

The cusum chart, for example, of sentence length will start (unless the first sentence is unusually short or long) at a point near a horizontal axis representing zero and it will end precisely on this horizontal axis. If it does not, an error has been made. Between its beginning and end points the curve may assume almost any shape. One advantage of the method to be described is that no computer is required; a small hand-held calculator will suffice, particularly if it is programmable. I provide in the Appendix to this chapter a simple program that works very well with a Hewlett-Packard 41C programmable calculator.

In Figure 1 is an example of a cusum chart. This one is based on the lengths of the first 25 sentences of Jarom, one of the books in the Book of Mormon. As it happens, in this instance these sentences comprise the entire book, as punctuated in the first edition. The text is supposed to be a first-person historical narrative. It is readily apparent that the text is, as are most texts, a mix of short and long sentences. Sentences 17 and 19 are particularly long, separated by a sentence of near average length, as the chart shows clearly. Sentence length alone has been used in many stylometric analyses beginning in the 1970s, but our interest here is in inquiring into whether the contents of the sentence can be of use in literary attribution, that is, in the identification or differentiation of authorship.

It is reasonable to assume, for example, that different writers will differ in their use of nouns, or words of two or three letters (23LW), or words beginning with vowels (1VW). Recent research by Morton and others has shown that these three components may indeed be useful in author differentiation. Many other aspects of utterance may also be studied, such as use of the word *and,* four-letter words, verbs, and so on. Almost any aspect of a text may be studied, provided only that it occurs throughout the text and often enough to provide sufficient data for analysis.

Figure 2 shows the superimposition of the cusum chart of occurrences of words beginning with vowels upon the chart of Figure 1,

FIGURE 1. Jarom—Cusum of sentence lengths

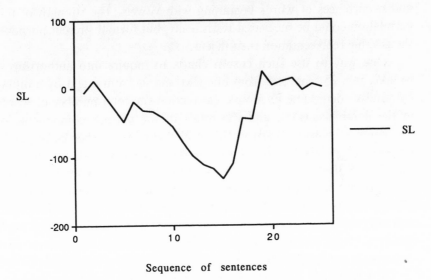

Sequence of sentences

FIGURE 2. Jarom—SL and 1VW

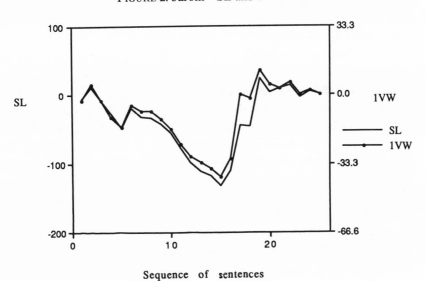

Sequence of sentences

for the same text of Jarom. Sentence lengths are plotted on the left
y-axis, 1VW upon the right y-axis, the numerical values altered in
accordance with the ratio, in the entire text, of the total of all words
to the number of words beginning with vowels. It is apparent that in
this text there is a close linkage, or correlation, between sentence length
and occurrences of words beginning with vowels. The strength of this
correlation could be measured statistically, but for our present purposes
the graphic representation is sufficient.

One way to use such cusum charts to inquire into authorship is
to take, say, 25 sentences from one text and 25 from a text by a different author, determine by simple calculation the total number of words
in the combined texts, and the totals of the various components of
the sentences. Cusum charts of the combined texts are then constructed,
the first 25 points on the chart coming from one text, followed by
the 25 from the other text. Such a chart is shown in Figure 3, in which
the texts of the Books of Abraham and Enos are compared with respect to the use of words beginning with vowels. The Book of Abraham
was purportedly written by the biblical Abraham, translated by Joseph
Smith from an ancient Egyptian papyrus. Enos is a first-person narrative from the Book of Mormon.

It is apparent that there is again a very close correlation between
the total number of words and the number of words beginning with
a vowel. This in itself has no particular significance. Two people with
eyes of an identical shade of brown are still two different people. Different writers may tend to use words beginning with vowels with about
the same frequency, but it is not likely that different writers will use
all the components of sentence structure in the same way.

Figure 4 shows the same two texts—the first 25 sentences of each
—similarly compared, this time with respect to the use of words of
two and three letters. Again the cusum charts are similar. Such charts
could be constructed using either two-letter or three-letter words, but
it is better, in order to make the samples larger, to combine both cate-
gories into a single class.

Again, in Figure 5, are shown cusum charts for texts from the
Books of Ether and Jarom, comparing them with respect to use of
two- and three-letter words. The text from Ether, from the Book of
Mormon, is not the first 25 sentences, but is the first 21 sentences following a lengthy introduction supposedly by the angel Moroni, stating

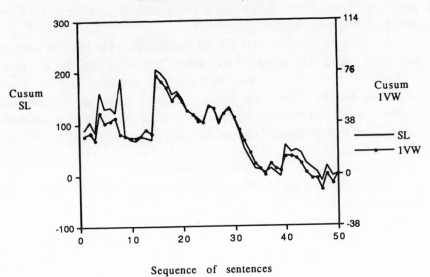

FIGURE 3. Abraham/Enos

Sequence of sentences

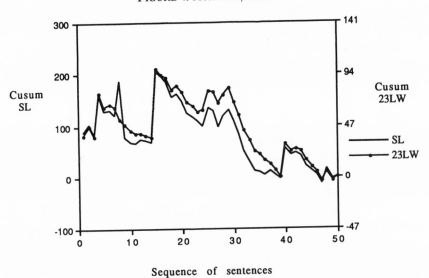

FIGURE 4. Abraham/Enos

Sequence of sentences

that the record to follow was written by Ether. Again we see a close correspondence. There is nothing here to suggest that the texts were written by different authors.

Let us turn, then, to texts known to be written by different writers, this time basing the charts on the writers' use of nouns. We see first, in Figure 6, a comparison between Genesis in the Bible and the Book of Abraham. The authors are different, but the charts are very similar. I show this before the one following, to make the point that all tests do not reveal multiple authorship even when we know that is the case. The additional point is, of course, that when sufficient testing is done, the work of different authors can be differentiated.

An example of such differentiation is shown in Figure 7, in which Enos of the Book of Mormon is compared to Genesis, with respect to use of nouns. These cusum charts are clearly irreconcilable. A different comparison between a text from the Bible and one from the Book of Mormon is shown in Figure 8. The choice of Esther was whimsical, based on the similarity of names. Again the cusum charts are, as expected, substantially dissimilar.

I should not leave this part of the inquiry without noting that all curves based on comparisons of different parts of the Mormon canon are not as similar as those shown in Figures 3, 4, and 5. This is shown in Figure 9, in which Enos and Jarom are compared with respect to occurrence of nouns. The charts are similar at beginning and end, but there is some divergence in the middle. The 1VW and 23LW cusum charts for the same comparison are, on the other hand, quite similar. I emphasize again that the work here presented is intended as a preliminary study only. Clearly more work needs to be done. One advantage of the methods demonstrated here is that anyone can perform such analyses in his or her home, without elaborate equipment. The charts shown in this chapter were printed by a laser printer driven by a Macintosh computer, using the Cricket Graph software program. But such charts may easily be drawn by hand on graph paper. It must be emphasized that the left and right y-axes will always have different scales, and that the ratio of one to the other must precisely reflect the underlying ratios—as, for example, between total number of words and number of words beginning with vowels.

Another method of using cusum charts for author identification is to insert some text from a known author into a text either of a

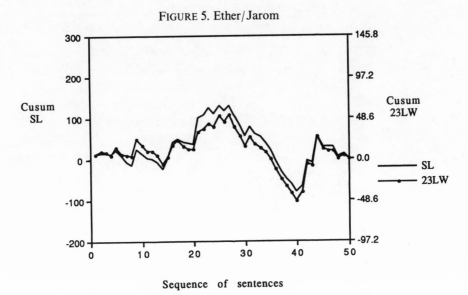

FIGURE 5. Ether/Jarom

Sequence of sentences

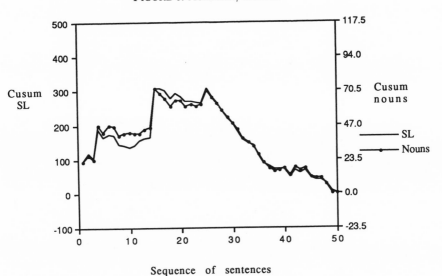

FIGURE 6. Abraham/Genesis

Sequence of sentences

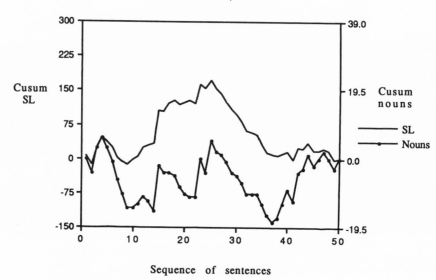

FIGURE 7. Enos/Genesis

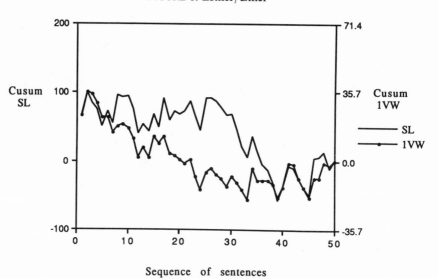

FIGURE 8. Esther/Ether

different known writer or of an unknown writer, and then construct cusum charts from the combined text. The inserted segment can be a rather small one—in fact, for this procedure, the smaller the better. When two large samples are merged together they inevitably affect each other. If the samples are of equal size, they will affect each other·about equally. But if one sample is much smaller than the other, it will affect the larger sample hardly at all. The result is that the change produced will be concentrated at the point of insertion of the smaller sample. An example of this technique is shown in Figure 10.

In these cusum charts the first ten sentences of the King James Joshua have been inserted into 25 sentences of Jarom, from the Book of Mormon. The insertion was made between the 10th and 11th sentences of Jarom. At first glance the figures are not, perhaps, impressive, but it is clear that something happens beginning at sentence 11. The 23LW curve begins to turn toward the SL curve, it crosses it, and continues on below the SL curve, whereas the 23LW curve, to the point of the insertion of the Joshua text, had been above the SL curve.

This is shown more clearly in the computer-enlarged curves of Figure 11, where we have a 14-sentence segment of the two curves—sentences 9 and 10 of Jarom, the ten-sentence insertion of Joshua, and sentences 11 and 12 of Jarom. The effect of the insertion is clearly shown.

Finally, in Figure 12 is shown a similar insertion of a ten-sentence segment of Jarom into the first 25 sentences of Jacob. Both texts are from separate books of the Book of Mormon, and the insertion again follows the first ten sentences of the combined text. The graph shows no effect of the insertion, and thus fails to lend support to the hypothesis that the samples are from different writers, supposedly Jarom and Jacob.

The preceding examples comprise a sufficient introduction to a simpler stylometric methodology with which to inquire into literary attribution. The figures shown reveal no evidence of multiple authorship in a few samples taken from the book of Mormon, said by Joseph Smith to have been written by different writers, a belief held firmly by Mormons. This is not meant to be interpreted, nor would it be proper to so imply, as an indication that the Book of Mormon was written by one author. The examples shown do, however, indicate that examinations that can reveal differences in authorship in cases where different writers are known to have produced the texts fail to reveal

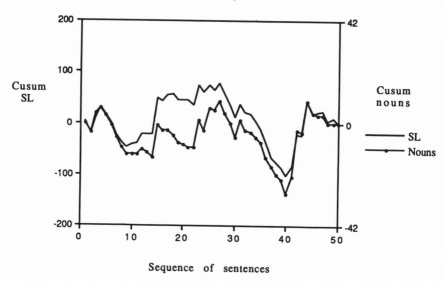

FIGURE 9. Enos/Jarom

Sequence of sentences

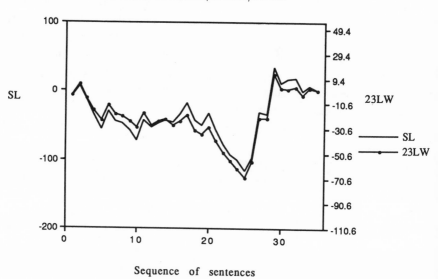

FIGURE 10. Jarom/Joshua/Jarom

Sequence of sentences

FIGURE 11. Jarom/Joshua/Jarom

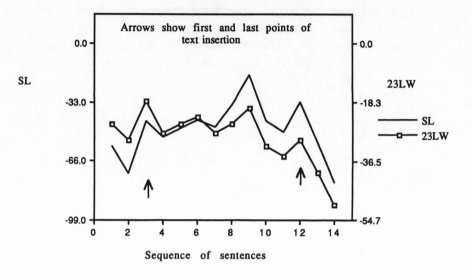

Sequence of sentences

FIGURE 12. Jacob/Jarom/Jacob

Sequence of sentences

such differentiation.

One hundred and thirty years after the publication of the Book of Mormon, questions about its authorship and its historicity continue to arise. It is this writer's hope that work aimed at resolving the major question will continue. As the stylometric art continues to advance, we must be encouraged in the hope that an answer to these questions, acceptable to all, will be found.

Note

1. For a comprehensive exposition of stylometric methodology, see Andrew Q. Morton's *Literary Detection* (1978). A more recent work is *The Cusum Plot* by S. Michaelson and A. Q. Morton (1990).

Appendix

Cusum Program for Hewlett-Packard 41C Programmable Calculator

01 LBL "AQ"
02 CLRG
03 FIX 2
04 STO 01
05 STOP
06 XEQ "QQ"
07 LBL "QQ"
08 RCL 01
09 —
10 ST+ 02
11 RCL 02
12 FIX 0
13 PRX
14 STOP
15 RTN
16 XEQ "QQ"
17 END

The first part of the program clears the storage registers of the calculator and stores the average of the column of observations being worked on in storage register 1. The second part of the program, labeled QQ, computes for each numerical value fed into the calculator its difference from the average of all observations, and cumulates the sum of these differences in storage register 2, at the same time printing them on thermographic tape in the printer being fed by the calculator.

To operate the program the calculated average is entered into the calculator, which is then instructed to execute Program AQ. The first value of the column of data is entered into the calculator, which is then instructed (by pressing a programmed key) to execute Program QQ. This continues until the last figure is reached—whereupon, if no errors have been made, it will print a zero as the last figure.

Step 12 instructs the calculator to print data values to the nearest whole number.

Glossary

APOSTLE. See Quorum of the Twelve.

BLOOD ATONEMENT. The basic concept is that some human acts are so evil that remission of the sin can be occasioned only by the shedding of the evildoer's blood, even unto death. This idea goes back, in the history of human thought, at least as far as the Old Testament, as in this instruction to Noah: "Whoso sheddeth man's blood by man shall his blood be shed" (Gen. 9:6). In the early decades of church history many anti-Mormon writers set forth the view that it was official church policy to (albeit secretly) assassinate those guilty of such crimes as adultery, murder, and apostasy. This view was promulgated by Gentiles to such extent that the church hierarchy considered it necessary, in 1889, to issue a manifesto in disavowal. Dated 12 December 1889, and directed "To Whom It May Concern," the Manifesto made these two principal points: ". . . This church views the shedding of human blood with the utmost abhorrence. . . . We regard the killing of a human being, except in conformity with the civil law, as a capital crime, which should be punished by shedding the blood of the criminal after a public trial before a legally constituted court of the land. . . . We denounce as entirely untrue the allegation which has been made, that our church favors or believes in the killing of persons who leave the church or apostatize from its doctrines."

This official repudiation notwithstanding, it is yet true that the *concept* of blood atonement lingers in memory. As recently as 1987, after the Mark Hofmann pipe-bomb murders, it was reported in the Salt Lake press that Mark's father wished his son to be executed, if he were guilty, this being the only road to his salvation.

CELESTIAL MARRIAGE. Marriage for time lived on earth and for eternity. This ceremony may be performed only in a temple. The contracting parties, either living or dead, are united forever. (The dead participate by proxy.) Such couples are "sealed." Others joined in lesser ceremonies are just married.

COUNCIL OF FIFTY. First established by Joseph Smith in 1844, and continued by his successors, this council is a select group whose activities have always been closely guarded. It was established by Joseph as, so to speak, the legislative arm of the Kingdom of God, one of its first responsibilities having been to study how to deal with the U.S. government in order to secure for the Mormons their constitutional rights. Its basic concern is with temporal matters, and (theoretically) Gentiles may be included in its membership.

FIRST PRESIDENCY. A group composed of the president of the church and his two counselors. All are high priests of the Melchizedic order. The First Presidency is the highest authority in the church. Counselors may also be apostles. The assassination of Joseph Smith left the church without a First Presidency. Church authority was with the Quorum of the Twelve until December 1847, when the apostles chose to establish a new First Presidency under Brigham Young. Brigham selected Heber Kimball and Willard Richards as his counselors.

GENTILE. Anyone who is not a Mormon.

JACK-MORMON. A member of the church who does not respond to church doctrine as earnestly as he might. A Salt Lake relative of this writer may be mentioned as an example. He was a church member, but took pleasure in belonging to a private club in which the Word of Wisdom, particularly with respect to the prohibition of alcohol, was altogether null and void. My relative always referred to himself as a Jack-Mormon.

QUORUM OF SEVENTIES. This quorum is the third-highest body in the church hierarchy. It was first established after the end of Zion's Camp (see *Trouble Enough,* Chapter 8), and all members of the first Quorum of Seventies were chosen from participants in that expedition. This quorum is theoretically equal in authority to the Quorum of the Twelve, which in turn is equal in authority to the First Presidency. Manifestly, this equality of power is for use in an emergency or crisis only. The duty of the Seventies is to act as traveling ministers, "to go into all the earth, whithersoever the apostles shall send them," doing the work of the church, spreading the gospel, managing missions, etc. As the church grew, additional Quorums of Seventies were established. The highest such quorum, the first Quorum of Seventies, is formed by the first council of the first seventy—seven men— together with the presidents of the next sixty-three such quorums.

QUORUM OF THE TWELVE APOSTLES. The second-highest authority in the church. Apostles may also serve as counselors in the First Presidency. The Quorum is often referred to simply as "the Twelve." A principal responsibility of the Twelve during Brigham Young's presidency was to travel the world, preaching the gospel and proseletyzing, and directing the activities of the Seventies (q.v.).

SCHOOL OF THE PROPHETS. An operation initiated by Joseph in 1833 for the purpose of instructing the elders of the church in the content and meaning of Joseph's revelations. Its curriculum later expanded to include the study of Greek and Hebrew. In the first temple built by the church, in Kirtland, Ohio, the top floor contained a number of small rooms intended for use primarily as classrooms for the school. In 1867, after the church moved to the Great Basin, Brigham established another organization using the same name. The school in Salt Lake consisted of more than 900 members, and there were branches in the major settlements. Campbell likened the school's meetings to forums or town meetings in which leading members discussed church and community problems. At times the school functioned as an economic planning board.

SEVENTY. See QUORUM OF THE SEVENTIES.

WORD OF WISDOM. A revelation received by Joseph Smith in 1833. It proscribes the use of alcohol, tobacco, and "hot drinks," interpreted to mean tea and coffee. Other dietary restrictions are also mentioned. The Word was taken casually before the move west, being considered more as advice than commandment. After the move to Utah it was still considered good advice that need not necessarily be followed. After a General Conference in 1851 the Word became much more of a commandment. At present most (but not all) good Mormons take the Word very seriously indeed.

Bibliography

Abbreviations used in Notes:

CHC. A Comprehensive History of the Church, by Brigham H. Roberts. Six volumes and index. Provo: Brigham Young University Press, 1965. For first edition see Flake 7314.

HBYM. History of Brigham Young, Ms. This manuscript history is kept in the church archives, and is not freely available to scholars. Where cited in this book, the reference is always to a citation by another author who had access to the manuscript.

HBYM-B. History of Brigham Young, 1847–1867. This volume consists of abstracts of the manuscript history in the church archives, edited by William L. Knecht and Peter L. Crawley. See bibliographic entry below, under Knecht, ed. The text, compiled in the office of the Church Historian for H. H. Bancroft, is composed of three manuscripts, *Early Records of Utah, Incidents in Utah History,* and *Utah Historical Incidents.* These manuscripts are in the manuscript collections of the Bancroft Library, University of California at Berkeley. This is a most valuable reference, in that the wording of many paragraphs is identical to that of the original manuscript—except for the use of the third person—though the text is not, of course, as complete. Harvard's Widener Library has a copy.

In the Bibliography, "Flake" numbers are references to Chad Flake's *A Mormon Bibliography: 1830–1930.* "Sabin" numbers are references to Joseph Sabin's *Dictionary of Books Relating to America.* "Howes" numbers are references to his *United Statesiana.*

Abbey, Edward. *Desert Solitaire. A Season in the Wilderness.* New York: Simon and Schuster, n.d. (Paperback reprint of McGraw-Hill 1968 edition.)

Alexander, Thomas G., and James B. Allen. *Mormons and Gentiles: A History of Salt Lake City.* Boulder, Colo.: Pruett Publishing Company, 1984.

Andersen, Bernice Gibbs. "The Gentile City of Corinne." *Utah Historical Quarterly* 9, nos. 3 and 4 (July and Oct. 1941), pp. 141–54.

Anonymous. "The Massacre at Mountain Meadows, Utah Territory." *Harper's Weekly* 3, no. 1 (13 Aug. 1859).

Arrington, Leonard J. *Brigham Young: American Moses.* New York: Alfred A. Knopf, 1985.

———. *Great Basin Kingdom.* Cambridge, Mass.: Harvard University Press, 1958.

Bailey, Paul. *Sam Brannan and the California Mormons.* Los Angeles: Westernlore Press, 1953. Special printing and enlarged edition.

Bancroft, Hubert Howe. *History of California.* San Francisco: The History Company, 1884–1890. Flake 283.

———. *History of Utah.* San Francisco: The History Company, 1890. Flake 287.

Bolton, Curtis E. *Letter to Attorney General Jeremiah S. Black*. 35th Cong., 1st Sess., House Executive Document No. 71, pp. 214–15. Part of *The Utah Expedition;* see under U.S. President (Buchanan). Flake 9221.

Brodie, Fawn. *No Man Knows My History,* 2nd ed. New York: Alfred A. Knopf, 1979.

Brooks, Juanita. *The Mountain Meadows Massacre.* Stanford, Calif.: Stanford University Press, 1959.

———, ed. *On the Mormon Frontier. The Diary of Hosea Stout, 1844–1861.* Two vols. Salt Lake City: University of Utah Press and Utah State Historical Society, 1982.

Brown, Benjamin. *Testimonies for the Truth: A Record of Manifestations of the Power of God, Miraculous and Providential* . . . Liverpool: S. W. Richards, 1853. Flake 892, Howes B828.

Browne, A. G., Jr. "The Utah Expedition." *Atlantic Monthly,* April 1859.

Burton, Richard F. *The City of the Saints, and Across the Rocky Mountains to California.* New York: Harper & Brothers, 1862. Flake 1029, Howes Bl033, Sabin 9497.

Campbell, Eugene C. *A History of the Church of Jesus Christ of Latter-day Saints in California, 1846–1946.* University of California, 1952. Unpublished doctoral dissertation.

———. *Establishing Zion: The Mormon Church in the American West, 1847–1869.* Salt Lake City: Signature Books, 1988.

Cannon, George Q. "After Twenty Years." *Juvenile Instructor* 4 (1869), pp. 13–14.

Casey, Kathryn, "An American Harem." *Ladies Home Journal,* February 1990, pp. 116–17, 167–70.

Chittenden, Hiram Martin, and Alfred Talbot Richardson. *Life, Letters and Travels of Father De Smet.* 4 vols. New York: Arno Press & The New York Times, 1969.

Clayton, William. *William Clayton's Journal: A Daily Record of the Original Company of "Mormon" Pioneers from Nauvoo, Illinois to the Valley of the Great Salt Lake.* New York: Arno Press, 1973. Republication of the 1st ed. published in Salt Lake City, 1921. Flake 2427.

———. *The Latter-day Saints' Emigrants' Guide.* Fairfield, Wash.: Ye Galleon Press, 1981. Facsimile edition of the first (1848) edition. Flake 2424.

Cleland, Robert B., and Juanita Brooks, eds. *A Mormon Chronicle: The Diaries of John D. Lee, 1848–1876.* 2 vols. and index. Salt Lake City: University of Utah Press, 1983.

Combs, Barry B. *Westward to Promontory: Building the Union Pacific Across the Plains and Mountains.* New York: Garland Books, 1973.

Congressional Globe. 46 vols. Washington, D.C., 1834–73.

Cotterill, Robert S. "Early Agitation for a Pacific Railroad, 1845–1850." *Mississippi Valley Historical Review* 5, no. 4 (March 1919), pp. 396–414.

Creer, Leland H. *The Founding of Empire.* Salt Lake City: Bookcraft, 1947.

DeVoto, Bernard. *The Year of Decision: 1846.* Boston: Little Brown, 1943.

Dickens, Charles. *The Uncommercial Traveller and Reprinted Pieces, etc.,* in *The Oxford Illustrated Dickens.* London: Oxford University Press, reprinted 1973. See Flake 2830 for first publication.

Dodge, Grenville H. *How We Built the Union Pacific Railway.* 61st Cong., 2nd Sess., Senate Document No. 447.

Drummond, W. W. *Letter to Attorney General Jeremiah S. Black, 30 March 1857.* 35th Cong., 1st Sess., 1858, House Executive Document No. 71. Part of *The Utah Expedition;* see under U.S. President (Buchanan). Flake 9221.

Embry, Jessie L. *Mormon Polygamous Families.* Salt Lake City: University of Utah Press, 1987.

England, Eugene. "On Fidelity, Polygamy, and Celestial Marriage."*Dialogue* 20, no. 4, (Winter 1987), pp. 138–54.

Fales, Susan I., and Chad J. Flake. *Mormons and Mormonism in U.S. Government Documents.* Salt Lake City: University of Utah Press, 1989.

Flake, Chad J. *A Mormon Bibliography: 1830–1930.* Salt Lake City: University of Utah Press, 1978.

Ford, Thomas. *A History of Illinois,* 2 vols. Chicago: Lakeside Press, 1945 and 1946. For first edition, see Flake 3397.

Forsgren, Leona, and Ruby Rasmussen. *The Descendants of Moses Franklin Farnsworth.* Privately printed, n.p., 1972.

Frémont, John Charles. *Report of the Exploring Expedition to the Rocky Mountains in the Year 1842, and to Oregon and North California in the Years 1843–44.* Washington, D.C.: 1845.

Froiseth, Jennie Anderson. *The Women of Mormonism: or, The Story of Polygamy as told by the Victims Themselves.* Detroit: C. G. C. Paine, 1882. Flake 3471.

Furniss, Norman F. *The Mormon Conflict: 1850–1859.* New Haven: Yale University Press, 1960. Also available in reprint, Westport, Conn.: Greenwood Press, 1977.

Garland, A. H. *Letter from the Attorney General, Transmitting, in Response to Senate Resolution of December 10, 1888, a Statement Relative to the Execution of the Law Against Polygamy.* 50th Cong., 2nd Session, 1888, Senate Executive Document No. 21. Flake 9099.

Gove, Jesse A. For his letters, see under Hammond, Otis G., ed.

Greeley, Horace. *An Overland Journey from New York to San Francisco, in the summer of 1859.* New York: C. N. Saxton, Barker and Co., San Francisco: H. H. Bancroft, 1860.

Gunnison, J. W. *The Mormons, or Latter-Day Saints in the Valley of the Great Salt Lake: A History of Their Rise and Progress, Peculiar Doctrines, Present Condition, and Prospects.* Philadelphia: J. B. Lippincott, 1856. Flake 3750. For first edition, see Flake 3746.

Hafen, LeRoy R., and Ann W. Hafen. *Handcarts to Zion: The Story of a Unique Western Migration, 1856–1860.* Glendale, Calif.: Arthur H. Clark Co., 1988.

Hambleton, Madison Daniel. *Journal.* Edited by Howard E. Hardy, unpublished.

Hammond, Otis G. *The Utah Expedition, 1857–58.* Concord, N.H.: New Hampshire Historical Society, 1928. Includes the letters of Captain Jesse A. Gove, written while on the Utah Expedition, together with special correspondence of the *New York Herald.* This is vol. 12 of the New Hampshire Historical Society Collections.

Hansen, Klaus J. *Quest For Empire.* N.p.: Michigan State University Press, 1970.

Hayden, Amos Sutton. *Early History of the Disciples in the Western Reserve, Ohio.* Cincinnati: Chase and Hall, 1875. Flake 3917.

Henrichsen, Kirk. "Pioneer Pottery of Utah and E. C. Henrichsen's Provo Pottery Company." *Utah Historical Quarterly* 56, no. 4 (Fall 1988), pp. 360–95.

Hill, Donna. *Joseph Smith, the First Mormon.* Garden City: Doubleday, 1977.

Hooper, William H. "Extension of Boundaries." *Congressional Globe,* 40th Cong. 2d Sess., app., pp. 242–48.

Ivins, Anthony W. *The Relationship of Mormonism and Freemasonry.* Salt Lake City: Deseret Book Co., 1934.

Ivins, Stanley S. "Notes on Mormon Polygamy." *Western Humanities Review* 10, no. 3 (Summer 1956), pp. 229–39.

Jackson, Richard H. "The Mormon Village: Genesis and Antecedents of the City of Zion Plan." *Brigham Young University Studies* 17, no. 2 (Winter 1977), pp. 223–40.

Kelly, Charles, ed. *The Journals of John D. Lee, 1846–47 and 1859.* Salt Lake City: University of Utah Press, 1984.

Kimball, Stanley B. *Heber C. Kimball: Mormon Patriarch and Pioneer.* Urbana, Ill., and Chicago: University of Illinois Press, 1981.

Knecht, William L., and Peter L. Crawley, eds. *History of Brigham Young, 1847–1867.* Berkeley: MassCal Associates, 1964.

Knight, Hal, and Stanley B. Kimball, *111 Days to Zion.* 2nd. ed. Salt Lake City: Deseret Press, 1984.

Lee, John D. *Mormonism Unveiled.* St. Louis: Bryan, Brand & Co., 1877. Flake 4851.

———. *The Journals of John. D. Lee, 1846–47 and 1859.* See Kelly, Charles.

———. *A Mormon Chronicle. The Diaries of John D. Lee, 1848–1876.* See Cleland, Robert G., and Juanita Brooks.

Lindsey, Robert. *A Gathering of Saints: A True Story of Money, Murder, and Deceit.* New York: Simon and Schuster, 1988.

Linn, William Alexander. *The Story of the Mormons.* New York: Macmillan, 1923. Flake 4945.

Magraw, W. M. F. *Letter to President James Buchanan, 6 October 1856.* 35th Cong., 1st Sess., 1858. House Executive Document No. 71, pp. 2–3. Part of *The Utah Expedition,* see under U.S. President (Buchanan). Flake 9221.

Melville, J. Keith. "Theory and Practice of Church and State During the Brigham Young Era." *Brigham Young University Studies* 3, no. 1 (Autumn 1960), pp. 33–35.

Michaelson, S., and A. Q. Morton. *The Cusum Plot.* A Report of the Department of Computer Science, University of Edinburgh, 1990.

Morgan, Dale. *The Great Salt Lake.* Indianapolis & New York: Bobbs–Merrill, 1947.

———. *The State of Deseret.* Salt Lake City: University of Utah Press and Utah Historical Society, 1987.

Morton, Andrew Q. *Literary Detection.* New York: Charles Scribner's Sons, 1978.

Naifeh, Steven, and Gregory White Smith. *The Mormon Murders.* New York: Weidenfeld and Nicolson, 1988.

Nebeker, John. "Early Justice in Utah." *Utah Historical Quarterly* 3, no. 3 (July 1930), pp. 87–89.

Perkins, Jacob R. *Trails, Rails, and War: The Life of General G. M. Dodge.* Indianapolis: Bobbs–Merrill, 1929. Flake 6311.

Quaife, Milo Milton. *The Kingdom of St. James: A Narrative of the Mormons.* New Haven: Yale University Press, 1930. Flake 6785.

Roberts, B. H. *Studies of the Book of Mormon.* Edited and with an Introduction by Brigham D. Madsen, and with a biographical essay by Sterling M. McMurrin. Urbana, Ill., and Chicago: University of Illinois Press, 1985.

———. *Comprehensive History of the Church of Jesus Christ of Latter-day Saints.* Provo: Brigham Young University Press, 1965. 6 vols. plus index. Earlier edition is Flake 7314.

Sillitoe, Robert. *Salamander: The Story of the Mormon Forgery Murders.* Salt Lake City: Signature Books, 1988.

Smith, Joseph, Jr., et. al. *History of the Church of Jesus Christ of Latter-day Saints.* Salt Lake City: Deseret Book Company, 1976. 7 vols. and index. See Flake 7968.

———. *Doctrine and Covenants.* Salt Lake City: Church of Jesus Christ of Latter-day Saints, 1978. Together with the Book of Mormon and *The Pearl of Great Price.*

Stegner, Wallace. *The Gathering of Zion.* New York: McGraw-Hill, 1964.

Stenhouse, Thomas B. H. *The Rocky Mountain Saints.* New York: D. Appleton, 1873. Flake 8404.

Stenhouse, Mrs. Thomas B. H. *Tell It All: The Story of a Life's Experience in Mormonism.* Hartford: A. D. Washington and Co., 1875. Flake 8392.

Stott, Clifford L. *Search for Sanctuary: Brigham Young and the White Mountain Expedition.* Salt Lake City: University of Utah Press, 1984.

Stout, Hosea. *On the Mormon Frontier. The Diary of Hosea Stout, 1844–1861.* See under Brooks, ed.

Stringham, Guy E. "The Pioneer Roadometer." *Utah Historical Quarterly,* 42, no. 5 (Summer 1974), pp. 258–72.

Talmage, James E. *The House of the Lord.* Salt Lake City: Deseret Book Co., 1969.

Taves, Ernest. *Trouble Enough: Joseph Smith and the Book of Mormon.* Buffalo, N.Y.: Prometheus Books, 1984.

Tullidge, Edward W. *History of Salt Lake City.* Salt Lake City: Star Printing Company, 1886. Flake 9039, Howes T409.

U.S. Attorney General. *Letter from the Attorney General, transmitting, in response to Senate Resolution of December 10, 1888, a statement relative to the execution of the law against polygamy.* Washington, Government Printing Office, 1888. (U.S. 50th Congress, 2nd Session. Senate Executive Document No. 21.) Flake 9099.

U.S. President, 1857–1861 (Buchanan). *The Utah Expedition.* Message from the President of the United States . . . 35th Congress, 1st Session, House Executive Document No. 71. Flake 9221.

Unruh, John D., Jr. *The Plains Across. The Overland Emigrants and the Trans-Mississippi West, 1840–1860.* Urbana: University of Illinois Press, 1979.

Webster, Kimball. *The Gold Seekers of 1849.* Manchester, N.H.: Standard Book Company, 1917. Flake 9666.

Whitmer, David. *An Address to All Believers in Christ.* Richmond, Mo.: 1887. Includes, as Part Second, *To Believers in the Book of Mormon.* Flake 9666. Available in reprint from Pacific Publishing Company, Concord, Calif.

Wright, Norman E. "The Pioneer Odometer." *The Ensign,* August 1981, pp. 30–31.

Young, Kimball. *Isn't One Wife Enough?* New York: Henry Holt and Company, 1954.

Index

Aaronic priesthood, 21
Aiden, William, 179
Alexander, Colonel Edmund, 195-200
Alexander, Thomas, 145n.19
Alger, Fannie (wife of Joseph), 148
Allen, Captain James, and Mormon Battalion, 52
American Fur Company, 60
Anthon, Professor Charles: report on Joseph's translation, 19-20 "Anthon transcript," 35n.3
Arapeen, Chief, 211
Arrington, Leonard, 32n.13, 40, 47n.4, 89, 254, 257
Ashley, Representative James M., and Ashley bill, 242-45
Ashley, William, 67
Astor, John Jacob, 60
Atwood, Millen, 136

Babbitt, Almon W., 105-06, 108-09
Backenstos, Sheriff Jacob, 44
Bancroft, Hubert H., 50, 96, 191
baptism for the dead, 42
Bathgate, Mary, handcart emigrant, 134
Beauregard, General Pierre Gustave, 224
Beeman, Louisa, wife of Joseph, 148
Benson, Ezra T., 55; treatment of forty-niners, 94
Bermingham, Patrick, handcart emigrant, 133-34
Bernhisel, John M., 105, 112; proposed as delegate to Congress, 225; represents Deseret in Washington, 107-08, 111, 231
Bigler, Henry W., and discovery of gold, 87-88; prospects for gold for John Smith, 96
Bingham, Sanford and Thomas, and discovery of ore in the Oquirrhs, 232

Bird, William, 94
Black, Adam, 29
Black, U.S. Attorney General Jeremiah S., 192, 211
Blackburn, Bishop of Provo, 171
Blair, Seth M., U.S. Attorney of Territory of Utah, 112
blood atonement, 35n.3, 168-69, 279
Boggs, Lilburn, governor of Missouri, and extermination order, 29, 184n.6.
Bolton, Curtis E., 192
Book of Mormon, 17, 227; authorship challenged, 22, 276; how published, 22; stylometric study of, 265-76; witnesses cut off from church, 29
Bordeaux, James, 61
Boswell, James, 265
Bowles, Samuel, 241-42, 259
Brandebury, Lemuel H., chief justice of Territory of Utah, 112-15
Brannan, Sam, 45-46, 48n.17; and discovery of gold, 88; travels east to meet Pioneers, 65-66
Brewer, Myron, 212
Bridger, Jim, 67; meets Pioneers at Big Sandy, 64
Brocchus, Perry C., associate justice of Territory of Utah, 112-15
Brodie, Fawn, 34n, 147
Brooklyn (ship), chartered by Brannan, 45-46
Brooks, Juanita, 48n.16, 185n.11
Brooks, Karl, 185n.11
Brown, Bishop Benjamin, comments on effect of gold rush, 89
Brown, James, leader of detachment of Mormon Battalion, 66
Buchanan, President James, 187-88, 191-98, 202-05, 211-12, 222
Buffington, Joseph, chief justice of Terri-

cricket invasion of early crops, 83
Crittenden, John Jordan, 222n.1
Cullom (Shelby N.) Act, 159, 245-48
Cumming, Alfred, governor of Utah, 210-11; accompanies Utah Expedition, 195, 197, 200-06; addresses Mormons in Tabernacle, 203-04; dines with Richard Burton, 221; goes to Salt Lake City with Thomas Kane, 202-06

Dallas, U.S. Vice-President George M., 116
Dame, William H., and Mountain Meadows massacre, 177-82
Danites, 218
Dawson, John W., governor of Utah, 224, 227
Day, Henry R., 112, leaves the territory, 115
Decker, Clara, wife of Brigham, 73, 74n.14
De La Mare, Phillip, 121-23, 126
Deseret Iron Company, 125
Deseret Manufacturing Company, 122-23
Deseret News, 78, 113, 128n.6, n.9, 133, 195, 225, 230, 240, 254
Deseret Pottery, 125
Deseret, State of, 50, 99-110; ceases to exist, 109; constitution of, 102-04; constitution presented to Congress, 108; petition for territorial status, 104-09
De Smet, Pierre-Jean:
  attitude toward Mormons, 74n.11
  describes Great Basin to Brigham Young, 54-55
Deuel, Osmyn and Mary, 73
DeVoto, Avis, 47n.5
DeVoto, Bernard, 38, 45, 47n.5; on President Polk, 53
Dickens, Charles, witnesses Mormon emigration, 119-20, 245
Doctrine and Covenants, on plural marriage, 147
Dodge, Major General Grenville M., 251-53, 256-58, 261n.1
Donner disaster, 65
Dotson, Marshal Peter K., 212-13

Doty, James D., governor of Utah, 232
Douglas, Stephen, A., 45, 108 116
Doyle, Arthur Conan, and view of Mormons, 119-20
Drake, Thomas J., 230
Drummond, Judge W. W., 191-95
Dunklin, Daniel, governor of Missouri, 26
Durkee, Charles, governor of Utah, 257
Dyer, Frank H., U.S. marshal, 161

Eckels, Chief Justice Delany R., 197-210
Edmunds Act, 157-60
Edmunds-Tucker Act, 160
Egan, Howard, 74; murders James Monroe, 115
Eliot, Charles William, president of Harvard, addresses Mormons, 80
Ellsworth, Edmund, captain of handcart company, 132, 134, 144n.7
Embry, Jessie, and study of plural marriage, 158-59
Emigration Canyon, 67
endowment, 39, 41-43
England, Eugene, on plural marriage, 163-64
Evans, Priscilla, handcart emigrant, 135

Fairfield, Utah, 209-10
Fancher, Charles, and Fancher party, 178-83, 197
Farnsworth, Moses, 175, 184n.1
Farnsworth, Philo T., 171, 173n.9
Far West, Missouri, 28-29
Fayette, New York, 23
Ferris, Benjamin G., appointed Secretary of Utah, 117
Fillmore, Millard, U.S. president and vice president, 108, 112, 116-17, 176; appoints Utah Territory officers, 111-12; attitude toward Mormons, 111; signs Compromise of 1850, 109
First Presidency, 77, 83, 96, 101, 162, 280; encourages handcart emigration, 131; relations with Governor Cumming, 203; warns against Utah Magazine, 240-41

Heywood, Joseph L., U.S. marshal of Territory of Utah, 111
Hill, Donna, 34n
Hill Cumorah, 18
Hilton, John, 265
Hinckley, Gordon, 185n.11
History of Salt Lake City, 48n.17
Hofmann, Mark W., forger, 35n.3; 47n.9
Hooper, William H., 224-25, 244-45
Hopkins, Charles, 180
Horne, Joseph, leads group to Salt Lake Valley, 72
Huntington, C. Allen, 145n.18
Huntington Library, 97n.7
Hurt, Garland, Indian agent, 189-90
Hyde, Orson, 37, 105, 108, 117, 123

Independence, Missouri, 25, 196
Independence Rock, 75n.22, 140, 196; reached by Pioneers, 63
Indians (generally), relations of Mormons to, 85-86, 188. *See also* Omaha, Pawnee, Piute, Sioux, Ute
Iowa City, departure point for handcart companies, 132, 135
iron production, 124-25
Ivins, Anthony, W., 47n.13
Ivins, Stanley E., and study of polygamy, 157-58, 165n.17

Jack-Mormon, 280
Jackson, President Andrew, 234n.1
Jackson County, Missouri, persecution of Mormons in, 26-27
Johnston, Colonel Albert S., 200-06, 209, 216-17
Jones, Dan, 33
Jones, Daniel, on rescue mission to handcart companies, 140, 145n.19

Kane, Thomas L., 105, 107-09, 116, 207n.17, 244; accompanies Governor Cumming to Salt Lake City, 202-03; and Jesse Little, 53, 86n.2; relationship with Mormons, 86n.2; during Utah Expedition, 201-04, 206

Kanesville, Iowa, 51, 78; gathering point, 81
Kaysville, Utah, 167-68
Kearney, General Stephen Watts, and Mormon Battalion, 52
Kelsey, Eli B., 239
Kimball, David P., 145n.18
Kimball, Ellen, 74n.14
Kimball, Heber C., 63, 90, 142, 219, 223; at Green River, 66; chief justice of Deseret, 104; counselor to Brigham, 77; comments on approach of U.S. Army, 176; leads first company of Pioneers, 57; lieutenant governor of Deseret, 225
Kimball, Hiram, 136-40, 190
King, William A., constructs new roadometer, 71
Kington Fort, 226
Kinney, Justice John F., 226, 231-32
Kirtland, Ohio, 24, 26, 28
Kirtland Safety Society Bank Co., 28

Lamanites, 85
Latter-day Saints' Emigrants' Guide, 72
Law, William, and *Nauvoo Expositor,* 31
Law of Consecration, 25-26
Lay, George W., 194, 196
Lee, John, handcart emigrant, 133
Lee, John D., 56; and Council of Fifty, 101, 104; and Mormon Battalion funds, 54, 74n.9; and Mountain Meadows massacre, 177-82; plaintiff in trial of Andrew Lytle, 79-80; scavenges after gold rush, 92-93
Lee, William, handcart emigrant, 133
Leonard, Truman, handcart emigrant, 134
Liberty Jail, 30
Lincoln, President Abraham:
appoints James Doty as governor of Utah, 232
appoints John Dawson as governor of Utah, 224
death of, 234
inauguration, 224
petitioned to withdraw Governor

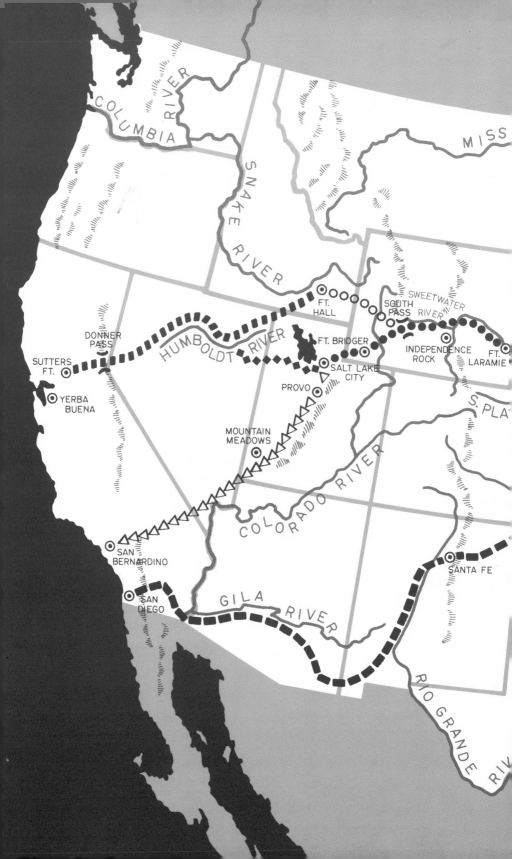